Joseph L. Sooy

Bible Talks with Children

Or, The Scriptures Simplified for the Little Folks

Joseph L. Sooy

Bible Talks with Children
Or, The Scriptures Simplified for the Little Folks

ISBN/EAN: 9783337228415

Printed in Europe, USA, Canada, Australia, Japan

Cover: Foto ©Lupo / pixelio.de

More available books at **www.hansebooks.com**

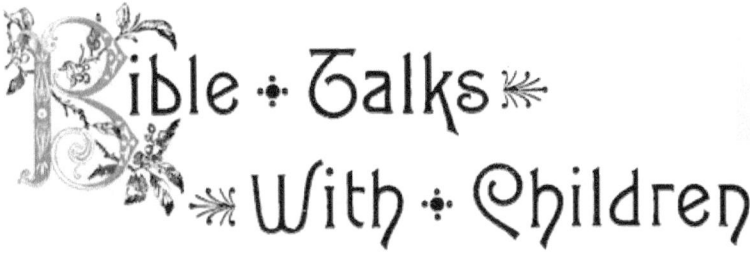

Bible ✠ Talks With ✠ Children

OR

The Scriptures Simplified for the Little Folks,

WITH

LESSONS DRAWN FROM

⁂THE ACTUAL SAYINGS OF CHILDHOOD⁂

By REV. J L. SOOY, A. M.

Illustrated · by · 178 · Full-Page · Engravings.

NEW YORK:
UNION PUBLISHING HOUSE.

Introduction.

This volume is written for the little folks. That the "Talks" contained in it might be adapted to the capacity and comprehension of childhood, a studied *simplicity* of style is adopted. An attempt is made to gather the little ones together and talk *with* them and not *to* them. The lessons drawn from the actual sayings of childhood, which follow most of the "Talks," will be found to be a special feature of the work. In my work with children I have found, that, in order to interest them, we must come down to their simple thoughts and ways of expressing them. And just as children like children for their play-companions, so do they like children's ideas and sayings for their thought-companions.

Two great inspiring facts have been present with me in writing this book. FIRST, *that lasting impressions are those of our earliest years.* How necessary, then, that those impressions should be for the pure and right. The community is inundated with reading matter, journals, magazines, romances, histories, philosophies, etc., and the tendency is to neglect the Holy Word of God, as though its mission were ended, and the mighty themes, of which it speaks, were obsolete. Whatever can be done, should be done to hold childhood to the sublime precepts and teachings that came fresh and living from the pen of inspiration.

SECOND, *beyond all others, this is The Children's Age.* Never before was so much attention and time and study given to the little ones. We hear of children's picnics, children's socials, children's meetings, children's papers, children's day, and so on,

INTRODUCTION.

almost without end. And who dare say, that the increasing growth of the church is not largely due to this? Did not the Master say, "Whoso shall receive one such little child in my name, receiveth me?"

> "'Feed my lambs,' said Christ, our Shepherd;
> Place the food within their reach;
> And it may be that the children
> You have led with trembling hand,
> Will be found among His jewels
> When you reach the better land."

A mother has well said: "The door of millennial glory has a child's hand on the latch."

This volume was not written, therefore, to *please* merely, but for the spiritual good of the children. If *they* are made better by it, then I am well paid. God grant that it may be so, is the prayer of one who loves little children.

J. L. S.

CAMDEN, N. J., August 26, 1889.

Illustrations.

		Page
1.	The Creation of Light,	2
2.	Adam and Eve Expelled from the Garden,	11
3.	Cain and Abel Offering Sacrifice,	13
4.	The Murder of Abel,	15
5.	The Flood,	17
6.	The Dove Leaving the Ark,	19
7.	The Tower of Babel,	21
8.	Abraham Going into the Land of Canaan,	23
9.	Abraham Entertains Three Strangers,	25
10.	Lot Fleeing from Sodom,	27
11.	The Expulsion of Hagar,	31
12.	Hagar and Ishmael in the Wilderness,	33
13.	Trial of Abraham's Faith,	35
14.	The Burial of Sarah,	39
15.	Eliezer and Rebekah,	41
16.	Isaac Welcomes Rebekah,	43
17.	Isaac Blessing Jacob,	45
18.	Jacob's Dream,	49
19.	Jacob Tending the Flocks of Laban,	51
20.	Jacob's Prayer,	53
21.	The Angel Wrestling with Jacob,	55
22.	The Reconciliation of Jacob and Esau,	57
23.	Joseph Sold into Egypt,	59
24.	Joseph Interpreting Pharaoh's Dreams,	61
25.	Joseph Maketh Himself Known to his Brethren,	65
26.	Jacob Going down into Egypt,	69
27.	Moses in the Ark of Bulrushes,	71
28.	Finding of Moses,	73
29.	Moses and Aaron before Pharaoh,	75
30.	The Plague of Murrain,	77
31.	The Plague of Darkness,	79
32.	Death of the First-Born in Egypt,	81
33.	The Drowning of Pharaoh's Army in the Red Sea,	83

ILLUSTRATIONS.

		Page
34.	The Giving of the Law from Mount Sinai,	87
35.	Moses Coming Down from the Mountain,	89
36.	Korah, Dathan and Abiram Swallowed up,	91
37.	Water from the Smitten Rock,	93
38.	The Brazen Serpent,	95
39.	Balaam Stopped by an Angel,	97
40.	The Crossing of the Jordan by the Children of Israel,	101
41.	The Angel Appears to Joshua,	103
42.	The Walls of Jericho Fall Down,	105
43.	Achan Stoned to Death,	107
44.	Joshua Commands the Sun to Stand Still,	109
45.	Sisera Slain by Jael,	111
46.	Deborah's Song of Triumph,	113
47.	Gideon Choosing his Soldiers,	115
48.	Gideon Surprising the Midianites,	117
49.	Jephthah's Daughter Coming out to Meet her Father,	119
50.	Jephthah's Daughter and her Companions,	121
51.	Samson Slaying the Lion,	123
52.	Samson Slaying the Philistines with the Jawbone of an Ass,	125
53.	Samson Carrying off the Gates of Gaza,	129
54.	Samson and Delilah,	131
55.	The Death of Samson,	133
56.	Naomi and her Daughters-in-Law,	135
57.	Boaz and Ruth,	137
58.	The Return of the Ark,	143

		Page
59.	Saul and David,	145
60.	Michal Letting David Down from the Window,	147
61.	David Sparing Saul,	149
62.	The Death of Saul,	151
63.	The Death of Absalom,	153
64.	David Mourning for Absalom,	155
65.	Solomon,	157
66.	The Judgment of Solomon,	159
67.	The Cedars Destined for the Temple,	161
68.	The Queen of Sheba's Visit to Solomon,	165
69.	The Prophet of Bethel,	167
70.	Elijah Raises the Widow's Son,	169
71.	Elijah Confounds the Prophets of Baal,	171
72.	Elijah Nourished by an Angel,	173
73.	Elijah Causes Fire from Heaven to Destroy the Soldiers of Ahaziah,	177
74.	Elijah's Ascent in a Chariot of Fire,	179
75.	The Famine in Samaria,	181
76.	The Angel Destroying the Army of Sennacherib,	185
77.	Cyrus Returning the Vessels for the Temple at Jerusalem,	187
78.	Rebuilding the Temple,	189
79.	Artaxerxes Accords Liberty to the Israelites,	191
80.	Ezra's Prayer,	193
81.	Nehemiah and His Companions View the Ruins of Jerusalem,	195
82.	The Law Read by Ezra,	197

ILLUSTRATIONS.

		Page			Page
83.	Queen Vashti Refusing to Obey the Orders of Ahasuerus,	199	107.	The Wise Men Guided by the Mysterious Star,	255
84.	Triumph of Mordecai,	203	108.	The Flight into Egypt,	257
85.	Esther Confounding Haman,	205	109.	Massacre of the Innocents,	259
86.	Job Informed of His Ruin,	207	110.	Jesus Questioning the Doctors,	261
87.	Job Seated on the Ash-Heap,	209	111.	Preaching of John the Baptist,	263
88.	Isaiah,	213	112.	Baptism of Jesus,	265
89.	Isaiah's Dream of the Destruction of Babylon,	215	113.	Christ Tempted by the Devil,	267
90.	Isaiah's Vision of God's Judgment on Leviathan,	217	114.	Marriage in Cana of Galilee,	269
			115.	Jesus and the Woman of Samaria,	271
91.	Jeremiah Dictating his Prophecies to Baruch,	219	116.	Jesus in the Synagogue,	273
92.	Baruch,	221	117.	Jesus Preaching by the Sea of Galilee,	275
93.	Ezekiel Prophesying,	223	118.	The Miraculous Draught of Fishes,	277
94.	Ezekiel's Vision of the Dry Bones,	225	119.	Jesus Preaching to the Multitude,	279
95.	Daniel,	227	120.	Jesus Healing the Sick,	281
96.	The Three Hebrew Children in the Fiery Furnace,	229	121.	Sermon on the Mount,	283
			122.	Christ Stilling the Tempest,	287
97.	Belshazzar's Feast,	231	123.	The Repentant Magdalene,	289
98.	Daniel in the Lion's Den,	235	124.	Raising of the Daughter of Jairus,	291
99.	Vision of the Prophet Daniel,	237	125.	The Dumb Man Possessed,	293
100.	The Prophet Amos,	239	126.	The Disciples Plucking Corn on the Sabbath,	295
101.	Jonah Cast up by the Whale,	241	127.	Jesus Walking on the Water,	297
102.	Jonah Exhorts the Ninevites to Repentance,	243	128.	The Multitude Fed,	299
103.	Micah Exhorting Israel to Repentance,	245	129.	The Transfiguration,	303
104.	Zechariah's Vision of the Four Chariots,	247	130.	The Lunatic Healed,	305
105.	The Annunciation,	249	131.	The Good Samaritan,	307
106.	The Nativity,	253	132.	Arrival of the Samaritan at the Inn,	309

ILLUSTRATIONS.

		Page			Page
133.	Jesus' Visit to Mary and Martha,	311	156.	Death of Christ,	365
134.	Looking for the Return of the Prodigal Son,	313	157.	The Darkness which Followed the Death of Our Lord,	367
135.	The Father Embracing the Returning Prodigal,	315	158.	Christ Taken Down from the Cross,	369
136.	Lazarus and the Rich Man,	319	159.	The Burial of Jesus,	371
137.	The Pharisee and Publican,	321	160.	The Angel and the Women at the Sepulchre,	373
138.	Little Children Brought to Jesus,	323	161.	Journey to Emmaus,	377
139.	Resurrection of Lazarus,	327	162.	The Ascension,	381
140.	Christ's Entry into Jerusalem,	329	163.	Day of Pentecost,	383
141.	Christ Cleansing the Temple,	331	164.	The Apostles Preaching the Gospel,	385
142.	The Widow's Mite,	333	165.	Peter and John Healing the Lame Man,	387
143.	The Last Supper,	337	166.	Martyrdom of St. Stephen,	389
144.	Prayer of Jesus in the Garden of Olives,	339	167.	Saul's Conversion on the Road to Damascus,	393
145.	The Agony in the Garden,	341	168.	St. Peter at the House of Cornelius,	397
146.	The Betrayal,	343	169.	Deliverance of St. Peter,	399
147.	Peter's Denial,	345	170.	St. Paul in the Synagogue at Thessalonica,	403
148.	The Flagellation,	349	171.	Paul at Ephesus,	405
149.	The Crown of Thorns,	351	172.	Paul Menaced by the Jews,	407
150.	Christ Insulted,	353	173.	Paul's Shipwreck,	409
151.	Christ Presented by Pilate to the People,	355	174.	John on the Isle of Patmos,	413
152.	Christ Fainting Under the Cross,	357	175.	Death on the Pale Horse,	415
153.	Christ's Arrival at Mount Calvary,	359	176.	Babylon in Ruins,	417
154.	The Crucifixion,	361	177.	The Last Judgment,	419
155.	Lifting up the Cross,	363	178.	The New Jerusalem,	423

THE CREATION OF LIGHT.

THE first verse of the first book of the Bible tells us that, "In the beginning God created the heaven and the earth." He *created* them; that means He made them out of nothing. In the frontispiece the artist shows us the creation of light. God just said, "Let there be light; and there was light." When Lottie was a wee bit of a girl she came running in to her mother one day with a handful of roses, and asked, "Ma, how did God make the roses?" But before her mother could reply, she said, "I know; God said, 'Let there be roses,' and there were roses." That is it. Nobody but God can *create* anything. We *make* things; but we must have something to make them out of. But God had nothing; there was no shape, nor form, nor substance, nor anything; but God was. God is eternal; that is, there was always a God. And God spoke and created all things by His wonderful power.

The great work of creation took six days. The first day, He created light; the second day, the deep blue sky; the third day, the seas and dry land, and all plants and herbs, and trees to give us their fruit or their wood; the fourth day, the sun, and moon, and stars; the fifth day, the birds and fishes; the sixth day, beasts, and insects, and creeping things, and last of all, man. And when all was finished, He planted the garden of Eden, and put in it the first man and woman, the best of all that He had made. God gave to the animals beautiful and useful bodies; but to man He gave a soul also, which could never die. God created man, holy and happy. Adam and Eve loved one another and they loved God.

SAYINGS OF CHILDHOOD: I once asked three little girls how we ought to feel toward God, who created us and gave us such a beautiful world to live in; the first said, "We ought to think Him very *nice*"—she meant *good*; the second said, "We ought to be very thankful;" the third said, "We ought to do what He wants us to do." And just think *our* God is everywhere. A little girl once said, "*He is everywhere, without going there.*"

ADAM AND EVE EXPELLED FROM THE GARDEN.

GOD gave Adam and Eve a beautiful home, because He loved them so much. It was called the Garden of Eden. The word Eden in Hebrew means pleasure; so the Garden of Eden might be called the garden of pleasure. It was a very beautiful place. Here grew all kinds of delicious fruit-trees and beautiful flowers; the little birds sang sweetly, and the animals all played together on the green grass.

In the midst of the garden grew two trees; one was the Tree of Life, and the other the Tree of knowledge of good and evil. God told them they must not eat of this Tree of knowledge; He told them plainly that if they did eat of this tree, they would die. And as Adam and Eve had everything that was needful for their use, there was no reason why they should want this fruit. But there came a wicked spirit, called Satan, who is the father of lies, and of all evil. He was envious, when he saw the man and his wife so happy; so he went into the garden, and appeared like a serpent, and spoke to Eve, and tempted her to eat the fruit which God had forbidden. Eve listened to the tempter. She took the fruit and ate, and gave her husband some, and he ate also. God saw all this, and He was very angry. Adam and Eve felt afraid. Why did they fear? Because they knew they had sinned. Sin made them afraid.

One very hot day—so hot that I could not stay in my study—I took my books and found a cool, shady place beside a stream of water. I laid down on the soft grass; soon I noticed the bugs in the grass were all running away from me; the birds jumped from limb to limb and told each other "to look out for him;" the little tadpoles swam to the other side of the stream; a red squirrel came from behind a rock, and, as soon as he saw me, away he scampered. I said to myself, what does all this mean? Surely my hands and face are clean; I cannot be so ugly that everything is afraid of me; what is the matter? Then I thought, *Sin did it.*

In the Garden of Eden, before man sinned, the animals did not fight nor hurt one another; they were not afraid of man; all was love and happiness. But sin came, that

ADAM AND EVE EXPELLED FROM THE GARDEN.

caused all the unhappiness. Because our first parents were disobedient and took the bad spirit for their master instead of the good God, God put them out of the garden, and let them be weak and sickly, and die at last.

The picture shows an angel driving them out. It was a sad day for them and for us. But God pitied Adam and Eve, and us too. He gave them the promise of a future Redeemer who should come into the world, and subdue Satan, and set them and their children free. If we have faith in Jesus, we shall be saved, and live forever.

SAYINGS OF CHILDHOOD:—" Have you anything you did not receive from God ? " asked a teacher of her scholars. "No," they all said but one. He replied, "Yes." "What is that ? " asked the teacher. " Sin," said the boy. But if we repent of our sins and pray for pardon, our Heavenly Father is willing to forgive and to receive us.

CAIN AND ABEL.

OUR last talk told the sad story of how Adam and Eve were driven out of the Garden of Eden. After that they had children. Cain, the eldest son, was very wicked; but Abel loved and prayed to God, and believed in Him.

Our first picture shows Cain and Abel in the act of offering sacrifices to God. Both these sons were brought up to work—and this was right. It is a great sin to be idle. Cain was a tiller of the ground, what we call a farmer; Abel was a shepherd, and took care of sheep. Now, God had commanded them to offer up a sacrifice to Him of the "first fruits;" that is, something of the very best they had. He wanted them to give it with a free heart, and a willing, humble spirit. Abel offered a lamb. He sacrificed the lamb in faith and true obedience. Cain offered a sacrifice too; he brought of the first-fruits of the ground. But he did not confess his sins, nor ask for forgiveness. So God accepted Abel and his sacrifice; but Cain and his sacrifice, God did not accept. He saw that Cain's heart was envious and jealous of his good and gentle brother. Look at the picture, and see how the smoke of Abel's lamb ascends steadily up to heaven, while that of Cain is beaten down to the ground.

CAIN AND ABEL.

When Cain found that the Lord had accepted Abel's offering, and not his own, he became very angry. Satan was in his heart. One day, when Cain and Abel were in the field together, Cain struck Abel and killed him. Our second picture is

"THE MURDER OF ABEL."

Cain thought nobody saw him kill his brother, but God saw him, and asked, " Where is Abel thy brother?" The cowardly, guilty man told a lie, and said, " I know not; am I my brother's keeper?"—as though it were possible to deceive the Almighty. But God had seen Abel die, and He punished Cain, and drove him away, far from his father, and mother, and brothers, and sisters; and he was a vagabond and a wanderer in the earth.

And now, dear children, we have seen who the first murderer was, Cain. But do you suppose he became a murderer all at once? No; he came to it by degrees; just as the acorn grows into the oak. There was a day when Cain had the first feeling of hatred, or anger, towards his brother. That feeling was the beginning. *Heart-murder* is just as bad, in the sight of God, as *hand-murder*. The Bible tells us, that " He who hateth his brother is a murderer."

If we indulge angry and hateful feelings, in our hearts, towards a person, *that* makes us murderers in God's sight. The reason is, that, if we let these feelings stay there, and grow, they will soon make us real murderers.

SAYINGS OF CHILDHOOD.—A little boy seeing two nestling birds pecking at each other, inquired of his elder brother what they were doing. "They are quarreling," was the reply. "No," replied the child, "that cannot be; they are brothers." Dear children, learn to love one another. Learn to "hold in" your temper. The old rule for holding in was, "Think twice before you speak once." Another is, "If you are tempted to be angry, say the Lord's Prayer before you speak." But the best rule of all is to keep close to Jesus.

THE FLOOD.

AS time went on, and men began to multiply, they greatly increased in sin. The world got so wicked, that God saw nothing but evil when He looked down on it. So the Lord determined that He would bring a flood of waters upon the earth to destroy every living thing. How terribly wicked these people must have been, when God saw that nothing else would suffice.

But in the midst of all this wickedness there was one holy man, named Noah. God promised to save him. He commanded Noah to make an ark of gopher wood, and told him how long and how broad it was to be, and how to build it. It was to be a great ship, and yet there have been larger ships built since. You have all heard about that mammoth steamer, the Great Eastern. She is larger than Noah's ark was.

Many years was the ark building; and all that time people laughed at Noah, for his folly, when he told them what God had said. But Noah did as God told him, and when the ark was finished, he stored it with food. And God sent him a pair of all sorts of animals that were in the world, and he put them into the ark. Noah then entered the ark with his three sons, Shem, Ham, and Japheth, his wife, and his sons' wives and "the Lord shut him in."

Then it began to rain. What a fearful storm that was! For forty days and forty nights it rained without stopping, so that even the highest hills were covered; and all flesh died, both man and beast. In the first picture the artist has drawn a high rock which the waters have not yet fully covered. See how the mother lion is trying to save her baby lion. See the people struggling to get on that rock. But even these were all destroyed. But what about Noah? Was he safe? Yes: the ark floated upon the waters. It did not sink, because God kept it up. The storm could not upset it nor the sea get into it, for God took care of it and all that was in it.

Now, dear children, why did God show Noah such grace? I will tell you. It was because God saw that Noah was *righteous*—that means that he tried to be good; and

next, because he believed what God said to him. O, it does always pay to obey our Heavenly Father! Can you tell me, who is our Ark of Salvation? "JESUS." Yes, that is right. Outside of Him all is ruin and death. And to you who are yet outside is the loving message given, "Come thou into the Ark." O, come to-day.

At length, when the rain was over, the ark rested upon a mountain called Ararat; and Noah opened the window. All the ground was covered with water. No green trees or flowers, no living creature to be seen. Then Noah sent out of the ark a raven and a dove. The raven flew about, and did not return to Noah. But the dove was not like the raven; it would not feed upon the dead bodies, and there was no resting-place for it, so it flew back again, and Noah took it into the ark. After a week he sent her forth again; this time she returned with an olive-leaf in her mouth. Noah was very glad to see this leaf, for by it he knew that soon all would be dry and pleasant again.

"THE DOVE LEAVING THE ARK."

After another week he sent out the dove again, but she returned no more.

Then God gave Noah the word to come forth from the ark. Noah's first act, after he came out, was to build an altar unto the Lord, and offer a sacrifice of thanksgiving upon it. God was pleased with his offerings, and made a promise to Noah. The Lord spoke unto Noah, saying, "Behold I establish my covenant with you." Do you know what a *covenant* means? It is an agreement between two persons. So God made an agreement with Noah that he would never destroy the world by a flood again. And God set the rainbow in the clouds as a sign of His promise. Do you know that the rainbow is an emblem of faithfulness? God said, "*I will look upon it, and I will remember my covenant.*"

SAYINGS OF CHILDHOOD :—One little boy's idea of the rainbow was, that it is "the reflection of God's smile." Whenever my little readers look upon the bow, remember God is looking upon it too, and never fear to put your trust in Him. God is very good and kind.

THE TOWER OF BABEL.

WHEN Noah and his family came out of the ark, they went into different places and built cities and houses; and they had many children, and the earth was soon full of people again. These people all spoke the same language. Many of them were very wicked, and the longer time went on the worse they grew. By degrees they forgot God's mercy to their forefathers in saving them from the flood, and they became proud and self-willed. They sought to make themselves great, not to please God; and in their pride, they said, " Let us build us a city, and a tower whose top may reach into heaven; and let us make us a name, lest we be scattered abroad upon the face of the whole earth." They thought if they could build a tower whose top should reach to heaven, they could escape if another flood came upon the earth.

The Lord let them go on for some time in their conceit. They worked hard, piling story above story, until the tower was very high. Then the Lord came down to see the city and the tower, which the children of men builded. God was angry with them, because they forgot Him. So He confounded their speech—that is, made them to speak different languages. They could no longer understand each other; so they had to stop building. This tower was called the Tower of Babel, or confusion, from the confusion of tongues that prevented its being finished. The wicked people were scattered abroad upon the face of the earth.

ABRAHAM GOING INTO THE LAND OF CANAAN.

WE read a great deal about Abraham in the Bible. He was born about 300 years after the flood, and lived in a place called Ur, in the country of the Chaldeans. The people there were very wicked. So God told him that if he would leave his home and go to a land that He would show him, that He would bless him, and make his name great, and that by-and-by the land should be given to his children.

Abraham then had no children; but still he believed God, and did just as God told him. He took with him those that would go of his family—his wife Sarah, and his nephew Lot. He took also all his cattle—great droves of cows, and goats, and sheep, and camels, and asses. In the picture we see the servants driving the flocks. Along the journey they camped out. They pitched their tents wherever the land offered food for the cattle; there they would stay till all the grass was eaten up; then take up their tents, and move to another place. Thus they journeyed till they came into the promised land.

Then the Lord appeared unto Abraham again, and told him to look at the land, for that was the place which his children should have for their own. But, children, don't you think there was a good deal to make Abraham doubt? The country was full of wicked men; Abraham did not own a bit of the land; and he had no child either. Then, as soon as Abraham entered Canaan, "there was a famine." But Abraham had great faith; he was sure that all God says is right and true, and that somehow, though he did not know how, God would do as He had promised.

SAYINGS OF CHILDHOOD:—What is faith? A beautiful answer was given by a little Scotch girl. When her class at school was examined, she replied, "*Wait a wee, and dinna weary!*" A child told me there are 3,600 promises in the Bible. Only think of that, dear children. If you belong to Jesus all these promises belong to you.

ABRAHAM ENTERTAINS THREE STRANGERS.

ONE day, when Abraham was sitting in the door of his tent during the heat of the day, he looked up, and saw three strangers standing near. They were angels sent to Abraham, and bore tidings to make glad his heart. One of these three was the Lord Jesus. The picture which represents the scene is a most beautiful one.

In those early days people were very hospitable. Abraham's kindness would allow no one to pass without offering him rest and refreshment. So he ran to meet them, and bowed himself toward the ground, as was the custom then, and said. "My Lord, if now I have found favor in thy sight, pass not away, I pray thee from thy servant; let a little water, I pray you, be fetched, and wash your feet, and rest yourselves under the tree; and I will fetch a morsel of bread, and comfort ye your hearts; after that ye shall pass on: for therefore are ye come to your servant." So the men sat down, and Abraham ran into his tent to Sarah his wife, and told her to make cakes quickly; then he ran to the field, and took a calf, and killed and dressed it; and he brought the calf, and the cakes, and butter, and milk, and gave them to the men under the tree; and they did eat, and Abraham stood and waited upon them. When the meal was over, the angels asked of Abraham, where was Sarah his wife. And Abraham said, "She is in the tent." Then the Lord, by the mouth of the angels, told Abraham, He would soon give him and Sarah a son. When Sarah, who was still in the tent, heard this, she laughed, and thought it could not be true. The Lord chided Sarah for thus doubting His word, and reminded her that with Him nothing was impossible. After this the angels departed, and Abraham went with them towards Sodom, "to bring them on their way."

LOT FLEEING FROM SODOM.

WE saw in our last talk that Abraham went with the three angels toward Sodom. He only went a short distance to show them the way, as was the custom then. Then two of the angels went on towards Sodom, but the Lord stayed with Abraham and told him that He was angry with those two wicked cities, Sodom and Gomorrah, and was come to destroy them. Abraham thought of Lot right away; his kind heart was touched with fear, lest Lot might be destroyed with the wicked people among whom he dwelt; so he prayed God to save Sodom if fifty righteous people should be found therein. When that prayer was answered, then Abraham begged Him for the sake of forty; then for thirty; then for twenty; until at last God promised that he would spare the cities if there could be found only ten good men therein. Wasn't it good of Abraham thus to plead for Lot? We should all remember our friends in prayer, and ask God to take care of them.

Just think, not even ten righteous men were found! Don't you think they were terribly wicked cities? Lot was the only good man there. All the rest laughed at him because he tried to make them do better. One evening two strangers came into the city where Lot lived. He was sitting at the gate of the city; and when he saw the angels, he arose and bowed respectfully, and brought them to his house, and set supper before them. The wicked Sodomites wanted to harm them; Lot was the only person who would take them in, and shelter them from the wicked people in the street.

After Lot took the angels into his house, they told him to gather together all the members of his family, and to take them all with him out of the city, for the Lord was going to destroy it. Lot had a wife and two daughters at home—he told them; then he went out and spoke to his married daughters, but their husbands would not believe Lot's warning, and he was obliged to leave them behind.

LOT FLEEING FROM SODOM.

In the morning, the angels took hold of Lot, and his wife, and daughters, and led them almost by force, away from their home, telling them, "Escape for thy life to the mountain, stay not, look not behind thee." They were frightened, and begged not to have to go so far as the wild mountains. Might they not go to the little city near at hand? Their wish was granted, and for Lot's sake, this city was spared. Its name was Zoar. In the picture, the artist shows us the city in flames. The walls are crumbling in the terrible heat. Great clouds of smoke roll upward and fill the sky. See how anxious Lot is! His face is lifted to heaven in prayer, while with his arms he urges his daughters on. In this dreadful judgment Lot's wife was disobedient to the commands of the angels: "She looked back from behind her." She did not like to leave Sodom. Perhaps she thought of her married daughters in the city, or wanted to save her goods, or more likely did not quite believe that God was going to burn the place; and so she stood and looked, and the fiery rain fell upon her, "and she became a pillar of salt."

In the morning, Abraham rose very early, and went to look toward Sodom; "and lo, the smoke of the country went up as the smoke of a furnace." But God had remembered Abraham's prayer for Lot, and kept him safely.

Here we see what an evil thing it is to sin against God. This was a terrible fire; but, dear children, "the earth and all the works that are in it" will by-and-by be burned up, on account of the wickedness which is in the world. God spares it for awhile, but its end shall come. Pray, then, to God, that He would save you in that hour, as He saved Lot from burning Sodom, "the Lord being *merciful* unto him."

SAYINGS OF CHILDHOOD:—Sin will certainly be punished. A gentleman making free with the Bible, said, in the presence of others: "I am seventy years of age, and have never seen such a place as hell after all that has been said about it." His little grandson, about seven years of age, who had been listening to the conversation, said: "*Grandpa, have you ever been dead yet?*" But, if we are righteous, as Lot was, we need have no fear. Two little friends slept in bedrooms next to each other. One night a storm came up. After repeating their prayers, and while being put to bed, they expressed great fear of the lightning, which flashed very brightly. They were told not to mind it, it would not hurt them if they were good. And now being left with the doors open, one was heard to call to the other: "Nelly, do you suppose the lightning will strike us if we say our prayers twice?" You see, she thought it was the *saying* of the prayers that moves God. But, let us remember it is the heart God looks at. A child six years old said: "When we kneel down in the school-room to pray, it seems as if my heart talked." That is what I want you to learn—*the heart element in prayer*. I think Abraham must have prayed with *all* his heart, when he asked God to save Lot. Words are nothing, if the heart prays not. And, on the other hand, you can pray and not speak a word. "I said in my heart," and "My heart crieth out," is the language of the Psalmist.

THE EXPULSION OF HAGAR.

 ESIDES Sarah, his first wife, Abraham had another wife, named Hagar, who was an Egyptian woman. Several of the patriarchs, or good men of that period of the world, had more wives than one; God permitted this in that dark age; but it was not according to His rule in the beginning of the world, and Christ, when he came, forbade it. Now Hagar had a son named Ishmael, and Sarah had a son named Isaac. Ishmael was now almost grown up, and he behaved very unkindly to his little brother Isaac, mocking and teasing him when they were playing together. Sarah, with all the tenderness of a mother, could not bear that her boy should be treated in this way; and so she begged Abraham to send away Hagar and her son Ishmael. Now Abraham loved both his boys; and he was grieved that they should quarrel, and that Sarah should ask him to punish Hagar and Ishmael so severely. But God commanded Abraham to do this. Remember, children, God saw Ishmael teasing his little brother Isaac. It displeased God. "God," says Matthew Henry, "takes notice what children do in their play, and will reckon with them if they say or do amiss, though their parents do not."

And so Abraham rose, in the morning, and called Hagar, and gave her a bottle of water, and bread, and her son Ishmael, and sent them both away. Doré the artist, has made the picture look like early morning. It is twilight—or just before the sun fully appears.

SAYINGS OF CHILDHOOD:—A little neighbor asks; "Does God always hear the naughty words we speak in our play?" Yes; and He can read the *thoughts* that arise in your hearts, when you feel naughty towards your little companions. Are you not sorry to grieve your Heavenly Father? O, do go to Him and tell Him how sorry you are, and ask Him not only to forgive, but to take it all away; ask Him earnestly.

HAGAR AND ISHMAEL IN THE WILDERNESS.

HAGAR and Ishmael went into the wilderness of Beersheba. They wandered about in that wild country; the water in the bottle was soon gone, and there being no prospect of getting more, she expected nothing less than the death of her child. It was very hot, and Ishmael fainted, and his mother cast him under a bush; and she went a "good way off," for she said, "Let me not see the death of the child." And she lifted up her voice and wept.

Our picture shows the stricken mother in agonizing prayer; Ishmael lies on the ground, ready to die. And the poor boy cried aloud; "and God heard the voice of the lad, and the angel of God called to Hagar out of heaven, and said unto her, what aileth thee, Hagar? fear not; for God hath heard the voice of the lad where he is. Arise, lift up the lad, and hold him in thine hand; for I will make him a great nation. And God opened her eyes, and she saw a well of water; and she went, and filled the bottle with water, and gave the lad drink." And God was with Ishmael, and made him well, and he grew up and lived in the wilderness, and became an archer, or hunter.

SAYINGS OF CHILDHOOD.—A dear boy wants to know " if God opened a well for Hagar and Ishmael just then, or was there one there all the time, and she did not see it?" Well, children, I think God *created* it then and there. But, no matter which is true; God can take care of us wherever we are. If even our friends forsake us, let us never forget to trust in Him. A little fellow eight years old, who was without a relative in the world, was asked by a lady, if he did not have any fears as to whether he would get along in life. The child looked into her face and gravely replied: "Don't you suppose God can take care of a little boy just as well as He can of a man." Certainly, noble little fellow. God is as careful of the smallest child, as He is of the oldest or the greatest man. Only trust Him, and obey Him!

TRIAL OF ABRAHAM'S FAITH.

AFTER Hagar and Ishmael were gone away, God spake to Abraham, and said, "Take now thy son, thine only son, Isaac, whom thou lovest, and get thee into the land of Moriah; and offer him there, for a burnt-offering, upon one of the mountains which I will tell thee of." Don't you think, dear children, that was a strange command from God? But God didn't want to make Abraham unhappy. No, He only wished to try Abraham's faith, to see if Abraham would be obedient, and if he loved God more than his dear child.

Abraham knew that God would not order him to do anything wrong, and so this good man obeyed without a murmur. "Abraham rose up early in the morning, and saddled his ass, and took two of his young men with him, and Isaac his son, and clave the wood for the burnt-offering, and rose up and went unto the place of which God had told him." The journey took three days. I sometimes wish that Moses had given us some of the conversation between Abraham and Isaac during that never-to-be-forgotten journey. And now they came near the spot and saw the mountain afar off, where Isaac was to be offered. Leaving the ass and the two young men behind, the father and his son went towards the mountain. In the picture you see the aged patriarch toiling up the mountain, and before him Isaac, carrying the wood with which the sacrifice is to be burnt.

Now Isaac had been taught by his good father to sacrifice to God, as was the custom in those days; and, on the way, he began to wonder where the sacrifice was, and very innocently said: "My father behold the fire and the wood; but where is the lamb for a burnt-offering?" For Isaac did not yet know that he was to be the lamb. Oh, how this must have touched Abraham's heart! Isaac had been a good boy, and it was no wonder, then, if he dearly loved him. But he could not make up his mind to tell him,

TRIAL OF ABRAHAM'S FAITH.

and he only said,—still, perhaps, hoping that God would spare him in the end,—" My son, God will provide himself a lamb for a burnt-offering; so they went both of them together."

But Isaac soon knew he was to be the lamb, for his father built an altar, and put the wood upon it, and bound Isaac, and laid him upon the altar, and took the knife to slay his son. And Isaac did not complain or struggle. He was ready, like his father, to do the will of God. He was about twenty years old. It does not appear that he tried one moment to resist his good old father, who was one hundred and twenty years of age. Oh, how God loves such obedient hearts!

But just as Abraham had the knife ready to slay his son, the angel of the Lord called unto him out of heaven, and said, "Abraham, Abraham, lay not thine hand upon the lad, neither do thou anything unto him; for now I know that thou fearest God, seeing thou hast not withheld thy son, thine only son, from Me."

The trial was over. God had proved Abraham, and his faith had not failed. Then Abraham looked, and saw a ram caught in a bush by the horns, and he offered the ram for a burnt-offering, instead of Isaac. And the angel called again to Abraham, and said, "Because thou hast done this thing, blessing, I will bless thee, and multiplying, I will multiply thee, and all the nations shall be blessed in thy seed." Dear children, I love to read this beautiful story. Don't you? It always reminds me of the love of God, in giving His only Son for a sacrifice for us. The Lord Jesus Christ was the seed of Abraham, who came to save sinners, and to be a blessing to all people. "God so loved the world, that He gave His only begotten Son, that whosoever believeth in Him should not perish, but have everlasting life."

SAYINGS OF CHILDHOOD:—I asked a little boy, was it not wrong for Abraham to take a knife to slay Isaac? Would'nt it have been murder? His answer was, "No; for God could'nt tell him to do what was not right." That is a good answer. God not only *would* not, but *could* not, tell him to do wrong. All that God does is good and right. When He sends us pain, or sickness, or sorrow, He does it wisely, for good, not for evil; we cannot know why, but God knows; let us ask Him to make us obedient to His will as Abraham and Isaac were. You know we are taught to pray that God's "will may be done on earth, as it is in heaven." This means that *we* should obey God as the angels do in heaven. A Sunday-school teacher once asked his class, *how* the angels obey God. Different answers were given; but the best was that of a little boy, who said, "They obey *without asking any questions*." That was a splendid answer.

TRIAL OF ABRAHAM'S FAITH.

One good way to learn to obey God, is to obey our parents. I have sometimes heard a father call to his son, "John, here, I want you to go on an errand." John is making some bobtails for his kite. Instead of minding, at once, what his father tells him, he keeps on with what he is doing, and says, "Won't it do by-and-by, when I get through with fixing my kite?" Now that is not the way in which the angels obey. They do *everything* that God tells them to do; and they do it *at once*, without stopping to ask questions. God has a right to expect this kind of obedience from us. He expects us to do everything that He commands. He never does wrong Himself; and never commands others to do wrong.

THE BURIAL OF SARAH.

YOU remember, my dear children, that Sarah was Abraham's wife. They had lived together many years. But at last, when she was 127 years old, Sarah died in Hebron, and Abraham and Isaac wept for her. Now in all that country Abraham did not own a foot of land, for he was a stranger there.

So he went to the prince to whom Hebron belonged, and begged to buy a field with trees in it, and a rock where there was a deep cave that was called Machpelah. The prince offered to give it to him; but Abraham would not take it as a gift. He agreed for a price, and paid the money for the burying-place. It was not in money like ours now; but in lumps of silver weighed out in balances, and each lump with a mark stamped on it—four hundred of them.

Abraham laid the body of Sarah in the cave of the field of Machpelah. It was usual in those times and in that country to bury people in caves, which were like little chambers cut out of the side of some hill. Abraham was buried there afterwards himself, and so was Isaac, and Isaac's son after him, in the cave of Machpelah. That cave has been kept sacred ever since. There is a building over it now, and no stranger is allowed to go into it; but deep down there is a golden grating, and far within lie these holy men and women of old. Abraham was very much grieved to lose his dear wife, with whom he had lived happily so many years. In the picture we see the good old man led tenderly away after the funeral is over, but still turning back with eager and sorrowful gaze toward the sepulchre.

Dear children, it is very sad to see our dear friends die, and to see their bodies put into the coffin, and laid in the grave; but if they loved God, and we too love Him, as Abraham and Sarah did, we shall meet them again in heaven. This thought comforted Abraham.

SAYINGS OF CHILDHOOD.—A father died, and as they bore him out of the house in his coffin, a little girl asked her mother, "When will they bring papa back?" The mother explained that her papa had gone to heaven; but, if good, they would go to live with him. The child exclaimed: "Hadn't we better be packing up and getting ready?" Little ones, are you ready?

ELIEZER AND REBEKAH.

ABRAHAM was now one hundred and forty years old. Like a kind father, he wanted to see his son happy and doing well in life, and so he wished to see Isaac married. It is true there were young women who lived in Canaan who might have been found, but they did not love and worship God; and Abraham wished to get a pious wife for his son, and not an idolator. Now Abraham had a good and faithful servant named Eliezer, who had lived with him, and Sarah, and Isaac, many years. Abraham called Eliezer, and said, "Go now to Mesopotamia, where I used to live, and find, there a wife for my son Isaac, and bring her here." Eliezer gave his solemn word that he would go; and he took ten of his master's camels with provisions and presents, and journeyed many days.

One evening, when he had come into the neighborhood where Abraham had told him to go, he was tired and weary, and sat down beside a well. He did not know the people who lived there, nor whom to choose for a wife for Isaac; but he prayed to God to send out to him the damsel whom He would appoint to be Isaac's wife. Scarcely had he ended his prayer, when Rebekah, who was a relative of Abraham came out to draw water. She was very sweet and pleasant-looking, and she was also kind-hearted, for she not only gave water to the tired stranger, but also to the camels. The first picture shows the first meeting between Eliezer and Rebekah. You must not wonder, children, at Rebekah going to draw the water, for it was quite usual then, and in that country, for persons of the first rank to be so employed. Industry is no disgrace to any rank, but idleness always is.

Eliezer had asked God to show him, by this very sign, the wife whom he was to take for Isaac, and now he felt quite sure that this was the right person; so he made himself known to Rebekah, and presented her with bracelets and ear-rings. Then Rebekah,

ELIEZER AND REBEKAH.

having learned who he was, ran and told her mother. Soon her brother Laban learned the news; and he ran out to the stranger, and took him to the house of Bethuel, his father, where he was welcomed and provided for. Then Eliezer told all about what he had come for, and asked if Rebekah might go to Hebron, and marry Isaac; and they were willing she should go, for they believed it was God's will.

Then Rebekah said good-bye to her father and mother, and brothers and sisters, and went with her nurse and her maids, upon camels, with Eliezer, to Hebron. Now it happened that Isaac was walking in the field on the evening of their arrival; and seeing them coming, he went towards them. And Rebekah asked Eliezer who he was; and, as is the custom of that country, she put a veil on her face as a token of modesty on meeting Isaac; for nothing in a woman or little girl is so lovely as modesty of behavior. In our second picture,

ISAAC WELCOMES REBEKAH.

He received her with great joy. And Isaac loved her, and she became his wife; and God blessed them, and twenty years after He gave them two sons, who were named Esau and Jacob. Isaac and Rebekah were very proud of their boys, and loved them dearly.

ISAAC BLESSING JACOB.

GOD gave two sons to Isaac and Rebekah. Their names were Esau and Jacob. When they grew up, they were very unlike: Esau was wild, and high spirited, and fond of hunting in the field; but Jacob was quiet and gentle, and liked to look after the sheep and goats. Now to the elder brother, among the Hebrews, belonged many benefits, among the rest he had honor paid him next to his parents; he had a double portion of the inheritance; and the Messiah, or Jesus Christ was to be born, in time, of his family—a blessing of the greatest price. But Esau did not care enough about all these blessings; he did not seem to get anything by them, and he liked what he could get at once, better than what was a great way off.

One day, when he had been hunting, he came home very hot, and tired, and hungry. Jacob was cooking pottage, or soup, in his tent, and, as the children say, "Esau's mouth watered" for some of the savory mess; and he asked Jacob to give him this soup, for he was very hungry. Jacob asked him to give him his birthright in exchange; and Esau, who was wild and hasty, agreed to do so, almost without a second thought. And so Jacob seizing the opportunity, made his bargain, and tricked poor Esau.

Jacob was a better man than Esau. But it was not right of him to trick Esau, and take away his birthright, when he was hungry, and asked for bread. This is a blot in Jacob's character; and it afterwards led to another, as one bad thing generally does. Esau, however, deserved to lose his birthright, for he did not seem to set much value upon it, when he sold it for a paltry meal of soup. It is very sad, and very wicked, to care more for our bodies than our souls, as Esau did; to think more about what we shall eat and drink, than about what we must do to be saved.

ISAAC BLESSING JACOB.

A time was to come when Esau would be sorry for what he had done. His father was old and blind, and must now soon die; he called Esau, and told him to get him some venison, and to dress it, and to bring it to him, that he might bless Esau. Esau obeyed, and went out into the fields to hunt. When Rebekah heard Isaac speak to Esau, she was not pleased, because she wished Isaac to bless Jacob, for God had said Jacob should be greater than Esau. So she called her favorite Jacob, and told him to get her two kids, that she might make savory meat for Isaac, and send it by the hand of Jacob, in order that he might get his father's blessing before Esau returned. There was, however, one difficulty, which was, that Esau was rough, and his skin was very hairy, but the skin of Jacob was smooth. In order, therefore, to deceive her husband, Rebekah dressed Jacob in the clothing of Esau; she covered his hands and neck with the skin of the kids, so that if Isaac felt them, he might believe that it was really Esau who knelt before him.

In this way they deceived Isaac, who was nearly blind. Jacob did succeed in getting the blessing. The picture shows us the aged father, seated on one side of his couch, in the act of blessing Jacob. Dear children, this was a very wicked deception on the part of Jacob and his mother. We must obey God more than man, or woman, or father, or mother. Jacob knew it was wicked to try to deceive his blind father, and he ought to have told his mother so respectfully and meekly. He afterwards suffered for his wicked act severely, and his descendants suffered for it too; for the consequences of sin reach far into the future. Rebekah was punished also, for her dear Jacob was obliged to go away, and I do not think she ever saw her favorite child again.

Scarcely had Jacob received Isaac's blessing, when Esau came in with his venison. And when he found what had been done, he cried bitterly and said, "Bless me, even me also, O my father! hast thou not reserved a blessing for me?" But his sorrow and tears were unavailing. It was too late now. Isaac could not take back that which he had already given; but he tried to comfort Esau by the promise of wealth, and many other good things; but it was not the birthright that he had lost.

SAYINGS OF CHILDHOOD:—Some boys were asked if they recollected any instance in Scripture of a bad bargain. To this, one little fellow replied: "Esau made a bad bargain, when he sold his birthright for a mess of pottage." Children, he always makes a bad bargain, who, to gain this world, loses his soul. "I think Jacob did a mean thing," says one boy. So do I. "Why did you not pocket some of those pears?" said one boy to another, "nobody was there to see you." "*Yes there was; I was there to see*

ISAAC BLESSING JACOB.

myself, and I never wish to see myself do a mean thing." Whenever you tell a lie, or deceive, or do a mean thing, as Jacob did, your conscience troubles you. Do you know what your *conscience* is? A Sunday-school teacher one day asked her scholars that question. Several of the children answered, one saying one thing, and another another, until a little timid child spoke out: "It is Jesus whispering in our hearts." That is it; remember, whenever you are tempted to do wrong, that it is Jesus telling you not to.

JACOB'S DREAM.

ESAU was very angry on account of the loss of his birthright. He hated his brother so much, that he thought, "My father will die soon, and then I will slay my brother Jacob." When Rebekah knew that Esau hated Jacob, and wanted to kill him, she was very anxious about her favorite child. Wherefore she now told Jacob to go away from home; and she also persuaded his father to let him go and visit her brother, Laban, whom she had not seen since the day of her marriage; and Isaac blessed Jacob, and bade him choose one of Laban's daughters for a wife.

So Jacob set out on a long journey alone; he had no one to speak to, no place wherein to rest at night. He went on till night came. Then he was in a dismal place. But he said his prayers; then put some stones into a heap for a pillow, and laid d and fell asleep. God gave him a beautiful dream that night. In the engraving we h.. a picture of his dream. He saw a ladder set on the earth, and its top reached to heaven, and holy angels were going up and down upon it. At the top stood the Lord, and He spoke to Jacob and told him that He was going to give his children all the land he saw — North, South, East, and West; and that He would take care of him, and, in time, bring him safe home again. When Jacob awoke, he felt very happy, and said, "Surely the Lord is in this place, and I knew it not ;" and he was afraid also and said, "How dreadful is this place! this is none other than the house of God, and this is the gate of Heaven !"

And as we ought to remember the mercies of God at all times, he set up a stone there as an altar, and poured oil upon it, and called the name of the place *Bethel*, which means "the house of God." Then he made a solemn vow, that if God would take care of him on his way, and give him food and clothes, he would make a gift to God all his life of a tithe, or tenth part of all he had—which meant, that if he had ten lambs he would offer one of them in sacrifice. Children will you make Jacob's resolve ? Good people love to do like Jacob, and give God their tenth.

48

JACOB TENDING THE FLOCKS OF LABAN.

AFTER his wonderful dream at Bethel, Jacob went on, and came to Padanaram. He came to a field, and a well. There he stopped; and there were flocks of sheep resting near it, waiting for water, attended by their shepherds. Jacob very civilly asked the shepherds if they knew Laban. They told him that they did—that he was well, and that Rachel, his daughter, was then coming with her father's sheep to get water for them.

When Jacob saw Rachel, he ran and rolled away the great stone which covered the well, and "watered the flock of Laban, his mother's brother." Jacob was very glad to see Rachel—she was his cousin; he kissed her, and told her who he was; and she ran and told her father. Then Laban went out to meet him, and was glad to see him, and asked him to stay in his house.

Jacob lived many years with Laban, and kept his sheep. In the engraving, Jacob is seen tending the flocks of Laban, which are gathered near a well, from which Rachel is returning with her pitcher. After fourteen years, Jacob married Rachel, whom he loved very much. And God blessed Jacob and gave him many children, and great possessions of sheep, and oxen, and goats, and camels.

JACOB'S PRAYER.

GOD after a time commanded Jacob to go home to the land of Canaan. So, twenty years after he had fled from the face of his angry brother, he gathered together his wives, and their children, and their maids, and his cattle, and all his possessions, and started. As he journeyed toward Canaan, he saw some angels coming to meet him. They were sent by God to comfort Jacob, and to tell him that God was there, to bless and keep him.

Now Jacob had great need of this encouragement, for he had to pass by the way in which he might meet with his brother Esau. He was afraid because he thought Esau might still be angry with him. Then Jacob sent his servants to tell his brother that he had lived many years with Laban, and was now coming home, and that he was very rich, and he very humbly begged Esau to be kind and friendly to him. But when the servants returned they told Jacob that Esau was coming out to meet him, and "four hundred men with him." Then Jacob was very much afraid, for he thought, that perhaps Esau was still angry with him, and was coming to kill him and all his family.

He, therefore, divided the people and flocks into two bands, so that if Esau fell upon one the other might have time to escape. He put his wife and children in the hindmost band, that their lives might be safe. He then thought that he would send presents to his brother to gain his good will; he ordered servants to go, one after another, with droves of cattle of various kinds, five hundred and eighty animals in all, which they were told to tell Esau were sent as presents to him. After this, Jacob sent his wives and children over the river Jabbok, he himself remaining on its north bank, where he spent the night in earnest prayer.

Our first picture gives this night scene—Jacob bowed on his knees by the river and lifting up his hands in prayer. Jacob knew he had no power to help and save himself; only God could save him, so he went and prayed to Him. These are the arguments he

used with God: 1. God's promises to him; 2. God's great goodness to him; 3. His own obedience to God's directions. Dear children, do you use these pleas when you pray? The first and second will apply to you. Will the third? Are you *obedient* to God's will? We have one strong argument in prayer, namely, *for Jesus' sake.*

Like Jacob, when we are sorry and afraid, we should go to God, who alone can protect and help us. You must not think that Jacob prayed for a great many things that long night. He prayed only for what troubled him at that moment. He was afraid of his brother; and he asked God to take care of him. Let us learn to tell God just what we need at the time.

How long do you think Jacob prayed? Yes, *all night*. Suppose Jacob had prayed one hour, and then said: "There is no use praying longer, I don't get any answer?" But Jacob held on. And after the midnight hour, there appeared to him one, who, though in human form, yet possessed more than human power, and wrestled with him. Jacob knew who He was—that He was the Angel of the Covenant—Jehovah—and he asked for a blessing from Him.

The second engraving represents

"THE ANGEL WRESTLING WITH JACOB."

At length this divine wrestler put Jacob's thigh out of joint, and then said, "Let me go: for the day breaketh," but Jacob still clung to him, demanding a blessing. And the Lord blessed Jacob, and gave him the new name of *Israel*, which means a prince with God. From that time the descendants of Jacob are called Israelites. Jacob called the place Peniel, or the face of God; because he had there seen God face to face.

Jacob felt now peaceful and happy, and, when he saw Esau coming, he had no fear. He went to meet him, and, after the custom of the East, he bowed himself to the ground seven times. And he now had no need to fear; for, in answer to Jacob's prayer, God had filled the heart of Esau with brotherly love and tenderness. When he saw Jacob bowing down before him, Esau ran to meet him, and embraced, and fell on his neck, and kissed him. The third engraving gives this scene—

"THE RECONCILIATION OF JACOB AND ESAU."

They both wept, for they thought of their past hatred and unkindness to one another; but now they wished to live in peace and brotherly love.

JACOB'S PRAYER.

Next Jacob's family all came, and bowed themselves also; and then Jacob offered his presents to his brother. Esau refused to take them at first, but Jacob urged him, and so he took them. And after they had talked together, and Esau had seen the wives, and children, and possessions of his brother, they blessed each other and parted. Esau returned to Mount Seir, where he dwelt, and Jacob went to Succoth. This was a happy end to all their anger and disputings.

SAYINGS OF CHILDHOOD.—A little Irish boy, in school, was asked, "What is reconciliation?" He answered, "Second friendship." Esau and Jacob were now reconciled— they were friends again. Jacob's prayer did it! Children don't forget to pray. A Baltimore policeman found a little boy wandering about one of the wharves of the city at ten o'clock at night, and took him to the station-house. The little fellow was fair-haired and rosy-cheeked, and could speak German only. He had lost his hat. A comfortable bed was made for him on one of the settees. He laid down, but remembering himself, he said, in his native tongue, "I have not prayed yet." Then while three reporters and two policemen reverently bowed their heads, the little hands were clasped, and in childish accent, the "Now I lay me down to sleep" was said. Dear little ones, if you should sometimes forget to pray, do as the little girl did, who, after her doll was quietly in bed, went to it and said: "You must get right up for you forgot to say your prayers."

JOSEPH SOLD INTO EGYPT.

NOW appears a new character on the scene. Among the many beautiful histories contained in the Bible, none has a more wonderful charm than the history of Joseph. Tens of thousands of little children have been made better and wiser by hearing the story of "Joseph and his brethren."

Jacob had twelve sons. The best of all his sons was named Joseph. Jacob loved him very much, and gave him a striped coat of many colors. This roused the jealousy and ill will of Joseph's brothers, and they hated Joseph, and were very unkind to him. Some of the brothers did wrong, and Joseph told his father. This made them dislike him still more. Then one night, God sent a wonderful dream to Joseph. He thought he was binding sheaves in the field, and the sheaves of his brothers all bowed to his sheaf. Soon after, he dreamed again that the sun, moon, and eleven stars bowed before him. These dreams, his brothers and father explained as meaning that they were to bow to him, and his brothers only envied and hated him still more, while his father blamed him for telling such dreams, but kept them in his memory, to see what would come to pass.

Now Jacob's sons, though rich, were compelled to work. One day, when Joseph was seventeen years old, ten of the brothers were out tending their father's flocks, and remained so long that Jacob became uneasy, and sent Joseph to see what had become of them. So off he started in his many-colored coat. When he came in sight of his brothers, Satan entered into their hearts, and they began to plan to kill him. But Reuben, a little braver and less cruel than the rest, said, "Let us not kill him, but cast him into this pit." I think Reuben intended to take Joseph out when they went away, and bring him home safely to his father. So when Joseph came to them, his cruel brothers seized him, and tore off his coat of many colors, and threw him into the pit; but the pit was empty, there was no water in it.

JOSEPH SOLD INTO EGYPT.

Reuben, meantime, went away, thinking Joseph was safe; and the rest of the brethren sat down together and ate bread. While these cruel brothers were eating, they looked up, and saw a great many people coming towards them. The people were Ishmaelites, and they had camels, which carried the spices they were going to take to Egypt to sell. When Judah, another brother, who did not want to have him killed, saw the Ishmaelites, he proposed to his brothers to sell Joseph to them, for Judah loved money. And his brethren agreed to this. So Joseph was taken out of the pit and sold for twenty pieces of silver. In the picture you see the Ishmaelites taking Joseph away with them.

Then the brothers killed a kid, and dipped Joseph's beautiful coat in the blood, and carried it home to their father, to make him suppose that a wild beast had torn his dear boy to pieces and devoured him. Jacob believed this and wept, and rent his clothes, and refused to be comforted. Dear children, don't you think these sons must have been very hard-hearted to make their father suffer thus?

JOSEPH INTERPRETING PHARAOH'S DREAMS.

JOSEPH was sold by the Ishmaelites to Potiphar, who was a captain of the guard to Pharaoh, king of that country. He was a good youth and feared God; he was not idle, nor deceitful, nor disrespectful, nor dishonest; he was very careful of his master's things; and God so blessed Joseph, that Potiphar took a great liking to him, and made him head servant over all his house.

But Potiphar's wife was a very wicked woman, and she tried to tempt Joseph to sin; and, when he refused to listen to her, she was angry, as all bad people are when they cannot persuade the good to join them. So she made up a story that Joseph had behaved ill. Potiphar believed the story; he never took the trouble to find out the truth, but cast him into prison for what he had not done. Joseph went to prison; but God was with him there. He can keep His people wherever they are; and He blessed Joseph, and made the keeper of the prison love him, and soon Joseph was put in charge of all the other prisoners.

JOSEPH INTERPRETING PHARAOH'S DREAM.

Dear children, try to deserve to be trusted, wherever you are. God is everywhere; and, as He was present with Joseph, alike in the pit, and in Potiphar's house, and in the prison, He will be present with each of you if you truly seek after Him. If you always recollect that God sees you, you will do the same when no one is with you as if all the world were watching; and that is the way to be true and just in all your dealings. If you are good only when you are looked at, you are not like Joseph, but are only doing service outwardly. Do just the same when your parents are absent as you would when they are present.

While Joseph was in charge of the prisoners, two grand people came in as prisoners. One was Pharaoh's chief butler who supplied him with wine; and the other was his chief baker, who supplied him with bread. And they were placed, by the captain of the guard, under Joseph's care. One morning when Joseph came to see them, he found them looking sad and unhappy, and he asked them, "Why look ye so sad to-day?" They told him they had been dreaming, and were anxious to know what their dreams meant. Now the Egyptians used to think a great deal of dreams; most dreams, however, have no meaning, but these had, and God put it into Joseph's heart to understand them. Then Joseph asked to know their dreams. The chief butler said his was about a vine, and that it had three bunches of grapes, and that he was squeezing the juice into the king's cup as he used to do. Joseph told him that this meant that in three days he should really hand Pharaoh the cup again; and all the reward Joseph asked for his services was that the butler, when free, would kindly tell the king about him, and get him set free. Then the baker told his dream. He said he dreamed that he had three white baskets on his head; and that in the one at the top he had baked meats for the king, but the birds came down and ate them up. Joseph told him that his dream meant that in three days he would be hanged, and that the vultures and ravens would eat his flesh. And the words of Joseph came to pass exactly as he had foretold. The butler was restored his place, and the baker was hanged. But did the butler remember Joseph, and ask the king to take him out of prison? No; when he was happy and safe himself, he thought no more about Joseph.

Two years more passed away, and still poor Joseph was in prison. Then Pharaoh, king of Egypt, had two wonderful dreams. He thought he stood by the river Nile, and saw seven fat kine come out of it, and feed in a meadow. Soon after he saw seven other kine come out, lean and starved; and they ate up the seven fat ones. Then Pharaoh awoke. He went to sleep again, and again he had a dream; and then beheld, in a dream, seven very fine ears of corn growing upon one stalk; and soon after seven thin, empty ears sprang up beside them, and the bad ears devoured the seven good ones; and the king awoke.

Now these two dreams troubled the mind of the king. He called all his wise men, and asked them to interpret them. But they had no heavenly wisdom, and God did not enable them to explain the dreams. But when the butler heard Pharaoh and the wise men talking together about the dreams, he told Pharaoh about Joseph, who had interpreted a dream for him, and recommended him to try what the young man could do. Pharaoh sent at once for Joseph; and when Joseph had washed and shaved and dressed himself neatly, he stood before the king. Then the king told his dreams, and asked Joseph to interpret them. Our picture shows Joseph in the presence of Pharaoh. Joseph knew that all the wisdom he had, God gave to him, so he said to Pharaoh, "It is not in me, God shall give Pharaoh an answer of peace." And God taught Joseph rightly to interpret the dreams. He said, "The seven fat kine, and the seven good ears of corn, are seven years of great fruitfulness; and the seven thin kine, and the seven bad ears, are seven years of famine. Seven years are coming of great plenty in the land of Egypt, and then seven years of famine will begin, when there will be no corn." Joseph then told Pharaoh that he ought to find some wise man, who would lay up one-fifth part of the corn in the plentiful years, and perhaps buy more, and keep in store, till the years of want, so that the people might not starve.

Then the king believed what he said, and he thought that none could be found like Joseph—so full of wisdom; and he appointed him ruler, next to himself, over all the land of Egypt; and he clothed him finely, and put a ring on his finger, and a gold chain round his neck; and he made him to ride in a fine chariot, and the people bowed to him in respect, as we do to great men, when we approach them. And Pharaoh gave him a name of distinction, as our kings make dukes and lords; and he found him a wife to be his companion and comforter. And Joseph set to work to buy the corn that was over and above what the people wanted to eat in the years of plenty, that he might store it up against the years when the corn would not grow.

And God blessed Joseph in all that he did, and made him the father of two sons, whom Joseph named Manasseh and Ephraim (which names mean forgetting and fruitful); for Joseph said, "The Lord hath made me *forget* all my toil, and hath made me *fruitful* in the land of my captivity."

JOSEPH MAKETH HIMSELF KNOWN TO HIS BRETHREN.

THE years of famine at length began to come, as Joseph had said. There was no corn to reap; all was dry and dead; and the poor people cried for food. And Pharaoh said, "Go unto Joseph; and what he saith to you, do." And Joseph opened the store-houses, and sold corn to the Egyptians. The famine was not only in Egypt, but in all the countries round about; it reached Canaan also; and Jacob and his sons had no bread. So when Jacob heard that there was corn in Egypt, he sent his ten eldest sons to buy some; but Benjamin stayed with his father, for after the loss of Joseph, Jacob could not bear his youngest son to leave him; and he would not send him on the long journey, for he said, "Perhaps some mischief might befall him on the way."

The ten brothers went to Egypt, and came and stood before Joseph, and bowed to the ground. Joseph knew them, for they still looked like shepherds; but they did not know him, for he had grown from a youth to a man, and was dressed like an Egyptian lord. Although Joseph remembered his brothers at once, he behaved toward them like a stranger, and spoke harshly to them. He acted as if he thought they were enemies, come to see if Egypt could be conquered when it was so bare of food. They told him who they were; that they were all one man's sons, and one brother they had lost; the other was left with his father, who could not bear to part with him. Joseph acted as though he would not believe this, and said he must keep one of them in prison, while he sent the rest back to fetch their youngest brother, or else he could not believe them.

The brothers were much distressed to hear this. Now their consciences began to trouble them, and they recollected how they had used Joseph; and they talked to one another, and said, "We are verily guilty concerning our brother." Joseph heard them, and could hardly bear it; he turned aside and wept; but still he kept to his plan. "He took from them Simeon, and bound him before their eyes." Then he commanded their

JOSEPH MAKETH HIMSELF KNOWN TO HIS BRETHREN.

sacks to be filled with corn, and the money they had paid for it to be put into the sacks also; and he let them go. When they found this out as they went home they were much afraid; and when they came home and told their father what had happened, and he saw the money, Jacob was more afraid still. He said, "My son shall not go with you. Ye have ye bereaved of my children: Joseph is not, and Simeon is not; and ye will take Benjamin away; all these things are against me." Reuben answered, "Give him to me, I will bring him to thee again." But Jacob would not let him go.

In a short time they had eaten all the corn they had brought from Egypt. Jacob desired them to go down and buy food again in Egypt, for they knew not where else it could be obtained. But they answered, "We must not, we dare not go without Benjamin; for the man solemnly commanded us to bring him." Then, with great difficulty, Judah got his father to intrust Benjamin to his care. Jacob sent presents to Joseph, and he sent back the money found in the sacks, for he knew it did not belong to him—and good people are always honest; and he prayed God to bless them.

They went, and again bowed themselves before Joseph. Only think of Joseph's heart being so full when he saw Benjamin, that he could not stay with him for his tears, and went away into his chamber to weep! It was love and thankfulness that made him weep. Then Joseph washed away his tears and went to them again. Then he ordered a feast to be made, and Joseph sent messes to all his brothers; but Benjamin's mess was five times larger than any of the others; and "they drank and were merry with him." Still Joseph wished to make further trial of the good and evil that was in the hearts of his brethren. He wanted to see if they still were envious of the one their father loved best; so he made his steward hide his cup in Benjamin's sack of corn, and then go after them, and pretend to think they had stolen it. The servant obeyed, and in the morning he sent them all away. Then the servant ran after them, and overtook them, and charged them with having stolen the cup. But they said they had stolen nothing, and that he might search their sacks. The search was made; and lo, the cup was found in Benjamin's sack. They were all shocked; and the steward said Benjamin must go back and be punished. Then the brothers rent their clothes, and went back again to Joseph, and fell down before him. Joseph made believe he was very angry. Then Judah stood up and told him how much their old father loved his youngest son, and he would be sure to die if the lad did not come home safe. And Judah begged to stay and be a slave in Egypt, instead of his brother Benjamin, for he said if mischief befall the lad, his father would die, and that he could not bear to see.

JOSEPH MAKETH HIMSELF KNOWN TO HIS BRETHREN.

Don't you think this was kind and good on the part of Judah? Joseph was touched to the heart; he could no longer refrain from making himself known to his brethren. So he sent away all his servants and officers, and allowed no one else to be present while he made himself known, for he could not keep from weeping; indeed, he sobbed aloud, so that the Egyptians and the house of Pharaoh heard him. Our picture gives the scene. Then Joseph said to his brothers, "I am Joseph, your brother, whom ye sold into Egypt; is my father yet alive?" His brothers could not answer, they were so frightened; but he would not let them be afraid; he spoke very gently to them again, and told them not to grieve for what had gone before, for God had turned it all to good, and made him be the means of saving all their lives, by storing up the corn in Egypt.

Then he fell upon their necks, and kissed them, and wept upon them; and they all talked long and happily together. The Egyptians heard what had happened, and went to tell Pharaoh, saying, "Joseph's brethren are come." And it pleased Pharaoh well, and he sent a present to Jacob, and wagons to bring him and all his family to Egypt. Then Joseph gave clothes, and money, and food, to his brothers, and sent them away, to tell Jacob, their father, that Joseph was still alive, and was a great and powerful man; and they were to fetch old Jacob, their father, and their wives, and their children, and all they had, and come to live with Joseph in Egypt, where he would take care of them. Dear children, let us learn, like Joseph, to return good for evil. "If thine enemy hunger, feed him."

JACOB GOING DOWN INTO EGYPT.

WHEN Joseph's brothers arrived home, they said to their father, "Joseph is yet alive, and he is governor over all the land of Egypt." Then Jacob's heart fainted within him, for he could scarcely believe the good news. But when they told him all the words of Joseph, and when he saw the wagons which Joseph had sent to carry him into Egypt, Jacob's spirit revived again, and he said, "It is enough: Joseph, my son, is yet alive. I will go and see him before I die."

Then Jacob and his sons began their journey to Egypt. The engraving shows the old man riding on his favorite camel, with his children and grand-children following—in all, seventy persons. On the way, at Beersheba, God spoke to Jacob in the night, and promised to be with him in Egypt, and to bring his descendants out from thence, and to make them a great nation. And when Jacob came near to Goshen, he sent Judah forward, to tell Joseph of his arrival.

As soon as Joseph heard the good news, he had his chariot brought out, and he went to meet his father; and he fell upon his neck, and wept there for a good while. Oh! the joy of meeting again, after so many long years. They had much to tell one another; all the wonderful things God had done; all their past sorrows and fears; and all their joy now. They had not forgotten the love of former years. The old man could only exclaim, "Now let me die, since I have seen thy face, because thou art still alive." So Jacob lived all the rest of his life in Egypt, and was happy with his son Joseph.

Dear children, be good to your fathers and mothers. You see Joseph did not neglect his good old father because he was "a plain man," while he himself was become a great man in the land of Egypt.

SAYINGS OF CHILDHOOD:—A little girl had been taught to pray especially for her father. He had been suddenly taken to heaven. Kneeling at her evening devotion, her voice faltered, and as her eyes met her mother's, she sobbed, "O, mother I cannot leave him *all out*. Let me say, thank God I had a dear father once, so I can keep him in my prayers." Let us remember to thank God for dear fathers and mothers. I know not what you may think of Joseph; but of all the characters of sacred history, I love Joseph best, because he is most like Jesus—so pure, and forgiving, and loving.

MOSES IN THE ARK OF BULRUSHES.

ANY years had passed away. Joseph was dead, and all his brothers. A new king was reigning who did not know Joseph; he was very cruel, and made the children of Israel work very hard to make bricks and build towns for him. By so doing, he kept them very poor, for they had no time to labor for themselves, and he tried to wear them out with slavery, that he might lessen their numbers. "But the more he afflicted them, the more they multiplied and grew."

So the wicked king thought upon another plan to destroy them. He ordered, that whenever a little boy was born to the children of Israel, he should be thrown into the river Nile and drowned. Pharaoh was afraid that, in time of war, the Israelites would fight him, and become his masters, instead of his slaves.

There was a woman of the family of Levi, who loved God; and her husband, too, was a good man. The man's name was Amram, and the woman's name was Jochebed. God gave them a beautiful little boy. For three months, the mother hid her child, that he might not be drowned; but when he grew older and larger, she could not hide him any longer. What must be done? The Holy Spirit taught Jochebed what to do. She made for Moses, a little ark, or cradle, of strong rushes; and she put pitch and clay on the outside to keep the water from getting through. Then, early in the morning, while the infant was still sleeping, she took him and laid him in his little cradle, among the high grass and reeds, by the side of the river, leaving his sister Miriam to watch near him. Jochebed knew that God could keep her little boy, if she could not, and she told all her sorrow to Him.

In the first picture, the artist shows the angels hovering over the sleeping darling. The merciful God heard that mother's prayer. Soon Miriam saw some people coming; who were they? They were ladies; one was the cruel king's daughter, and the others were her maids; and they walked along by the river, for the princess was going to bathe.

They did not see Miriam; she was a little way off, but she could see them, and heard all they said. When Pharaoh's daughter saw the ark among the reeds, she sent her maid to fetch it.

In the second picture,

"THE FINDING OF MOSES,"

the moment selected by the artist is when the ark of bulrushes is being drawn to shore by one of the attendants, while the princess stands under the downy plumes of her two fan-bearers, giving directions in regard to the child. When the little cradle was opened, the baby was crying. That made the princess pity him, for she was not cruel, like her father, and she said, "It is one of the Hebrew children."

When Miriam heard the kind lady speak, she went forward, and said to the princess, "Shall I go and call a Hebrew woman to nurse the child for thee?" And Pharaoh's daughter said "Go." How Miriam's little heart throbbed for joy as she ran to her mother. O mother, O mother! the princess has found our baby, and she has sent me to call a nurse, and I have come for you. O mother, do come quickly! And the mother went and Pharaoh's daughter said to her, "Take this child away, and nurse it for me, and I will give thee thy wages." Surely Jochebed felt that her faith in God was richly rewarded. She brought him home, and nursed him, and he grew; and when he was a little older, she brought him to Pharaoh's daughter again. The princess loved the child and she said, "He shall be my son, and I will name him Moses (or, drawn out), because I drew him out of the water."

SAYINGS OF CHILDHOOD:—A kind woman, one cold winter day, tried to open a door in the third story of a wretched house, when she heard a feeble voice say, "Pull the string up high!" She looked up and saw a string, which, on being pulled, lifted a latch, and she opened the door upon two half-naked children all alone and looking very cold and pitiful. "Do you take care of yourselves, little ones?" asked the woman. "God takes care of us," said the oldest. "And what do you eat?" "When Granny comes home, she fetches us something. Granny says God has got enough. Granny calls us 'God's sparrows,' and we say 'Our Father,' and 'Daily bread,' every day. God is our Father." Tears came to the good woman's eyes as they ought to in ours, and those two "little sparrows," perched in that cold upper chamber, may well teach us some sweet lessons of faith and trust. Dear little ones, you are under the care of the God of little Moses. You are not too small for God to see you. Then love and trust Him.

MOSES AND AARON BEFORE PHARAOH.

NOW when Moses was grown up he did not live with the king's daughter any longer. The king had grown angry with him because he cared for his own people, the Israelites, and he had to flee away and keep sheep in the wilderness. And there he saw a great wonder. One day, as he sat beside the desert, keeping his sheep, he was surprised to see a bush not far off sparkling with light, as though it were on fire; but, although it appeared to be in flames, the leaves did not fall off, nor was the bush consumed. And God's voice spoke to him out of the bush, and told him that the troubles of the children of Israel were to come to an end. God would save them from the cruel Egyptians; and Moses himself was to go and lead them out, and bring them to the good land that God had promised that Abraham's children should have for their own. Moses was to go and tell the king of Egypt that it was God's will that they should go.

Moses was afraid at first, but God promised to keep him. He said to Moses, "Aaron thy brother may go with thee; he can speak well; and I will teach you both what you shall do." So Moses and Aaron went together to Pharaoh, and told him that the great God had commanded him to let the Israelites go, that they might serve Him. But the haughty king answered that he did not know the Lord, neither would he let the people go. God now gave Moses and Aaron power to do wonders, and to work miracles before Pharaoh. They went into the presence of the king. In the engraving, the artist shows Moses and Aaron before Pharaoh. You see the king surrounded by his wise men, his guard and perhaps many others looking on; there stand Moses and Aaron, eighty years old, asking that a great army of slaves may go away to worship their God.

Pharaoh wants a sign to convince him that these messengers come from God. Aaron threw down his rod and it became a serpent. But Pharaoh called his wise men, and told them to try to do the same; and they did so with their enchantments. Had they power to work miracles? No; perhaps God suffered their rods to become serpents that he might work a greater miracle, or perhaps they might have learned to tame serpents, so as to make them look like rods in their hands; and then they might have thrown them

down as Aaron did, and thus pretended to work a miracle. But God made Aaron's rod swallow up their rods. What must have been their amazement when they saw that! They had been accustomed to worship serpents, but what need for them to worship *serpents* any more, when this wonderful God of the Israelites could make out of a stick, one capable of swallowing theirs! Think, too, what a feeble, powerless bit of wood that shepherd's rod was; yet when God used it, what a power it became! So, what a feeble thing the hand of a little child is, but as soon as you put it on God's side, so He can use it, what a power it may become!

Still Pharaoh did not care for all this, nor did he obey the command to let Israel go; and then God said, He would punish Pharaoh. He determined to afflict Egypt with great plagues. First, the Lord commanded Moses to stretch out his rod over the river Nile; Moses did so, and all the waters in the river turned into blood; and when Moses held out his rod again it turned back into pure water. But Pharaoh did not mind, and would not let the people go. Then God told Moses again to stretch out his hand over the river; and there came up such numbers of frogs that they covered the land, and crawled over the tables and into the beds, and even into the ovens of the Egyptians. Pharaoh could not bear to have these frogs everywhere, and said, if they would but go away he would let the children of Israel go. Then Moses asked God to take the frogs away, and all the frogs died; but Pharaoh still continued disobedient and would not let the people go,—and God sent a third plague.

He ordered Moses to turn all the dust in the land into lice; and the lice covered the people and the animals. But Pharaoh's heart was hardened and he refused to listen. Then very dreadful swarms of stinging flies came and covered the land. Nothing was to be seen for flies; and Pharaoh, in his terror, made a half promise that he would let the Israelites go a short distance, if the swarms of flies were taken away; but as soon as they were gone, Pharaoh hardened his heart, and would not let them go.

Then the Lord sent a fifth plague, and brought a dreadful disease, called murrain, upon the cattle of Egypt, and the horses, and asses, the camels, and the sheep, and all the animals that were useful to the Egyptians grew sick and died. In the next engraving the artist shows this

"PLAGUE OF MURRAIN,"

the camels falling down dead, and their masters leaving them in despair. But still Pharaoh remained unmoved. Then Moses took ashes out of the furnace, and threw them up toward heaven, at God's command, and they became dust, and brought sore boils

upon men and beasts. The wicked Egyptian magicians suffered so much pain from these boils, that they were not able to stand, or to go to Pharaoh when he sent for them. But still the king would not attend to God's command.

The next day, God sent a terrible storm, thunder and lightning, and rain and hail—such big hailstones as killed the men and cattle that were out in the fields, and lightning that struck them, and wind that broke every tree in the field. No wonder that Pharaoh was frightened and begged that the storm might cease, and said that then he would let the Israelites go. So Moses prayed to God, and it was all still again. But when the rain was over, Pharaoh was again disobedient, and said, " I will not let the people go." Then God said unto Moses—" Stretch forth thine hand over the land of Egypt for the locusts, that they may come upon the land of Egypt and eat every herb of the field that the hail hath left." And locusts came; and they were so many that the land was darkened by them, and they ate everything which the hail had not destroyed. The king again sent for Moses and Aaron, and begged them to pray for him. And they did pray, and God heard them; but when the plague was taken away, wicked Pharaoh again said, " I will not let the people go."

Then God sent a new and very dreadful plague over the land of Egypt; this was a thick darkness, that lasted for three days. There was no light from the sun nor moon nor stars. And the people could not see to move from their places all the time. Our next engraving is a picture of this

" PLAGUE OF DARKNESS."

Pharaoh again called Moses, and said, " You may go; only let your cattle be stayed." But Moses said, " No, we must take all our possessions with us; we will go with our wives, and our little children, our sons, and our daughters, our flocks, and all that we have." Then Pharaoh was angry, and drove Moses away, and told him never to come before him again. Moses said, " Thou hast spoken well; I will see thy face again no more ;" and he went away from the king.

Dear Children, in the next talk we will see how God *compelled* Pharaoh to obey.

SAYINGS OF CHILDHOOD:—A little four-year old boy prayed: " O Lord bless George, and make him a good boy; and don't let him be naughty again, he sticks to it so." How natural it is for us to stick to our naughty ways. That was the way with wicked Pharaoh. He had a chance to obey, and keep off these awful plagues if he would. God sent him message after message; He waited for him, urged him, warned him; but he would not obey. And it was just because he *wouldn't*. Dear children, I want you

shall learn from this the folly of *daring* God. Be sure that God and you are always on the same side—that is, that He is *for* you, instead of *against* you. In the midst of all the plagues God's people were quite safe. None of the plagues came near their dwellings, or in the land of Goshen, where they dwelt. No harm can come to those who trust in Him.

DEATH OF THE FIRST-BORN IN EGYPT.

AFTER the nine sad plagues that had come upon the Egyptians there was still to be one plague more, the last and worst. This was called the death of the first-born, and was tenfold more terrible than any that had preceded it. Moses told his countrymen that the angel of the Lord would pass at midnight over all the houses, and that he would slay the first-born in every Egyptian house. No one would be spared: Pharaoh's oldest son, the young prince, and the very poorest person's son. They had killed the little Israelite babies, and now their babies should be killed.

But did God kill the first-born of the Israelites too? No; He told them what they must do, if they believed His words, and wished to escape. They were to take a lamb, without spot or blemish, and kill it in the evening; and they were to sprinkle the blood of the lamb upon the lintel, and upon the two door-posts; and afterward they were to roast the lamb whole, and eat it. Where the mark of the blood was, the angel would pass over and do no one any hurt; but the people would be blest and set free, because they believed God, and did as He bade them.

The Israelites listened to Moses, and did as he had told them. They ate their lambs, and packed up their goods ready for a journey. And lo! while they were waiting, there came a terrible shout and cry from the Egyptians, for the destroying angel had killed the first-born in every house. Even the first-born of their cattle died too, because the Egyptians used to worship them. In the picture, the artist shows the destroying angel passing through in the night; in his hand is a drawn sword.

But were the believing, obedient Israelites safe? Yes, wherever there was the blood, the little ones were safe. Dear children, The Lord Jesus Christ is like the lamb of the

Israelites. He was slain, as the paschal lamb was, and His blood was shed upon the cross. Why? To save our souls. The blood of the lamb in Egypt was sprinkled upon the doors; the blood of Jesus must be sprinkled upon our hearts.

SAYINGS OF CHILDHOOD:—A little boy on his father's knee said, "Pa, is your soul insured?" "Why do you ask that, my son?" The boy replied: "I heard Uncle George say that you had your house insured, and your life insured; but he did not believe you had thought of your soul, and he was afraid you would lose it." Dear little one, have you got your soul *insured?* Is the blood sprinkled upon it? Now suppose that in one Israelitish house there had lived a little boy who did not want the blood sprinkled on his door! "What is the use?" he says; "God knows where we live, and He can take care of us just as well without that, and it will look so queer, all the Egyptians will be asking us what we do it for!" How foolish that boy would have been! The destroying angel would have killed him too. We must not be ashamed of the blood. Or, suppose in one house, there lived a little girl who wanted to have her dolly dressed. Mamma explains to her about the lamb and the blood on the door, and that it must be attended to at once, but the child insists that it will do just as well to-morrow, the dolly must be dressed first. Don't you see, that to-morrow would have been too late?" Don't put off giving your hearts to Jesus NOW! God says, "Now is the day of salvation," and God requires *exact* obedience. It was not the blood on the door that saved the babies of the Israelites, but it was *obedience to God.*

THE DROWNING OF PHARAOH AND HIS ARMY IN THE RED SEA.

PHARAOH was at last convinced that it was in vain to fight against God. When the destroying angel came to his palace and killed his eldest son, the king was so frightened that he called for Moses and Aaron in the night, and said, "Rise up, and get you forth from among my people, both ye and the children of Israel; and go, serve the Lord as ye have said. Also take your flocks and your herds as you have said, and be gone; and bless me also." And the Egyptians were so anxious to send the Israelites away, that they helped them to pack up, and gave them rich presents to take with

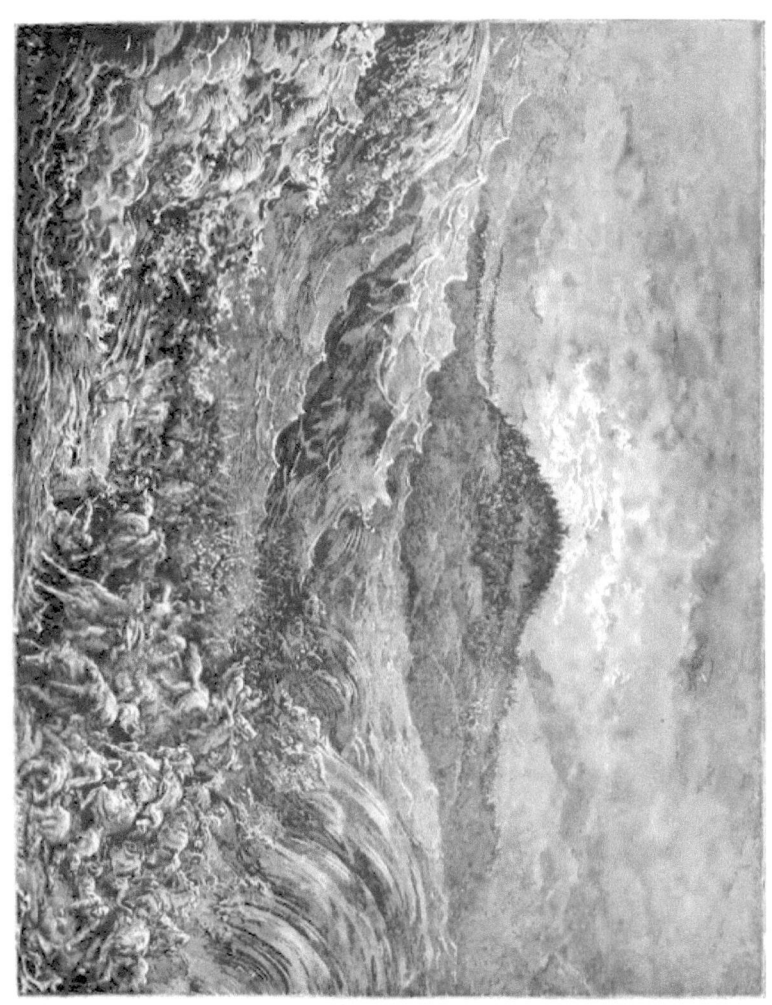

THE DROWNING OF PHARAOH AND HIS ARMY IN THE RED SEA.

them. And now the children of Israel set off to leave Egypt. There were 600,000 men, and many women and children, and very much cattle. They were going through a wild and dreary wilderness, and so God came in a pillar of cloud by day, and of fire by night, to show them the way they should go. Thus they journeyed safe and happy under God's keeping, until they came to a very narrow pass on the borders of the Red Sea; and they encamped there.

But when Pharaoh heard the Israelites were gone, he was sorry he had let them go; and he got all his chariots and horsemen together, and went after the children of Israel to bring them back again. When the Israelites saw him coming, they were sore afraid, and began to blame Moses, and said, "Why hast thou brought us out here to die? It would have been better to stay in Egypt, and serve the Egyptians, than to die in the wilderness." But God spoke to Moses, and told him not to fear. They had only to stand still and see how God would save them. And God Himself showed that He was with them, for the pillar of cloud went behind them, instead of before, and made it dark to the Egyptians, but it gave light by night to the Israelites, so that the Egyptians could not get near them all night.

Then the Lord commanded the people to go on. But where could they go? The great sea was before them; there is no bridge across it; they have no boats. High mountains shut them in, on either side. What are they to do? God says go forward! what, right into the sea? Yes right into the sea. God knew how to find a way for them to escape. He told Moses to stretch his rod over the sea. And then there was a great wonder. The waters of the sea parted, and piled up on each side of them like great walls of glass, or ice; and right in between there was a broad road open for them through the midst of the sea. The Israelites walked through, all of them on dry ground; not one was drowned, for God held back the waters till they were all gone over safely.

Pharaoh and his army followed them, or tried to. They were probably about half way through, when the Lord looked angrily at them through the pillar of cloud. Their chariot wheels dragged so heavily that they said, "The Lord fighteth for them against us." That was just what God said He would do! And then the Lord told Moses to stretch his rod over the sea, and the waters came back again upon the Egyptians, and every one of them was drowned. The artist gives us this picture. You can see the children of Israel all safe on the distant hill; while Pharaoh and his hosts are all being drowned in the sea.

THE DROWNING OF PHARAOH AND HIS ARMY IN THE RED SEA.

In the morning, the Israelites saw their enemies lying dead upon the shore; the Egyptians could hurt them no more now. The children of Israel thanked God, and sang praises to Him; and Miriam and the women danced for joy.

DOINGS OF CHILDHOOD:—Dear children, when God is on our side, we need not fear! There were two little boys. One was crossing a stream of water on a board; the little fellow was afraid till he heard a voice that he knew, say: "Father sees you," then he was afraid no more; he was sure that father would take care of him. The other boy had taken some fruit that he had been forbidden to touch; he heard the same words, knew the voice, but was greatly frightened. What made the difference? It is very plain; the father's voice is always a *comfort* to the child whose conscience is at rest, but a *terror* to the child who is sinning. So the pillar of cloud was a comfort to the Israelites, who loved and obeyed God, but was "darkness" to the Egyptians who did wrong. Some naturalists desired to obtain the wild flowers that grew on the side of a dangerous gorge in the Scotch Highlands. They offered a boy a liberal sum if he would descend by a rope and get them. He looked at the money, thought of the danger, and replied, "*I will if my father will hold the rope.*" With unshrinking nerves, he let his father put the rope about him, lower him into the abyss, and suspend him there while he filled his little basket with the coveted flowers. What a lesson of faith for us, dear children! We need not fear to go where we are held securely by our Heavenly Father's hand. The waters of the Red Sea cannot drown us, and the fires of the furnace cannot burn us if Jesus keep us there!

THE GIVING OF THE LAW FROM MOUNT SINAI.

ALL the children of Israel are now safely out of Egypt. They begin to travel into the wilderness. They have made three days' journey; and, at last a great mountain appears in sight. They move on till they come to it. At the foot of the mountain the procession halts. The people pitch their tents, and rest there. That is Mount Sinai. On the top of that mountain God told Moses that He would come down and meet him, and give him a law, to show the Israelites, and all other people, what he wanted them to do. And God told Moses to set bounds round the bottom of the mountain, so that nobody should come and touch it; and the people were to pray, and wait round it for the holy and awful thing that was to happen. And God told Moses to come up to the top of the mountain, when he should hear a trumpet giving a long, loud sound.

Then there came on the hill-top a dark, black cloud, and the mountain shook and quaked, and there were lightnings, and thunder, and voices, so that all the people trembled. The engraving gives us the scene. It was a fearful thing to see the mountain smoking, and the fire and lightning coming out of the thick darkness. Why was it so fearful? Because the holy, powerful God has come down upon the mountain; God who cannot look upon sin; and who has power to punish all those who disobey Him.

Then the sound of the trumpet was heard. It was an angel's trumpet; the same that shall be heard at the last day, when the graves are opened, and the dead come forth. Moses heard the trumpet. He goes up the mountain. The people all watch him, as he travels up, higher and higher. Now he enters the cloud and they see him no more. Moses is on the top of the mountain talking with God. There God gave him His great law of the Ten Commandments. They were the very same Ten Commandments you read in the Bible. And God means us all to obey the Commandments, just as much as He meant the Israelites to obey them. They are His words, and must be kept.

Afterwards God gave these Ten Commandments to Moses, written upon two tables, or blocks of stone—written with God's own finger. In our second picture we see

"MOSES COMING DOWN FROM THE MOUNTAIN."

where he has been with God a second time. The people are looking at him; his face is

bright and shining; and they fear to come near him. What made Moses' face shine? The bright glory of God which rested upon him while He talked to him in the mountain. When Moses saw that it was painful for the people to look at him, he took a veil, and covered his face, and then spoke to them. He told them all the commands of God, and showed them the new tables. He told them God told him to make a chest to keep the tables of stone in. It was to be made of wood, with gold all over it; and two figures of cherubims were to be one on each side. This chest was to be called the Ark of the Covenant. And it was to be put into a square room, inside a tent, that was to be made with curtains and carried about with the Israelites. It was to be called the Tabernacle. And this was to be a very holy place. And Moses asked them to bring their gold, and silver, and brass, and blue, and purple, and scarlet, and skins of animals, and beautiful stones; these things were to help to make the tabernacle, and all which was to be in it.

The people were glad to bring their riches for the service of God; and many of them were very busy and industrious in the work of God. It is very pleasant, as well as right, to work for God. All have talents; all can do something. Little children, too, can do something. I have no doubt the little Israelitish children helped their mothers to spin the goats' hair, and to carry the wood and stones to help their fathers. Did you ever hear of the little girl who said; "If I can't take a bouquet of a hundred-leaf roses to the teacher I won't take anything at all?" How foolish in her! Another little one brought a spray of red clover, because she had no other flowers, and the teacher was so pleased that she wore them in her belt all day.

SAYINGS OF CHILDHOOD:—A very bright little fellow says, "All the Ten Commandments have *nots* in them. Why don't God tell them *what to do?*" Well, God had to teach the Israelites in somewhat the same way your parents teach you. Your mother and father say to you, "Don't come to the table with dirty hands," "Don't come into the house with mud on your shoes," "Don't speak saucy words." When they have told you these things many times, and they say, "Now be good children;" you know everything they mean; do you not? Now can you tell me how to write the Ten Commandments in *one* word? LOVE. Yes; love God and love our neighbors. If we love God, what will we not do? *Not have any other gods; nor worship any other gods; nor take God's name in vain; nor break the Sabbath day.* If we love everybody what will we not want to do? *Not disobey father or mother; not kill; not commit adultery; not steal; not tell wicked stories about each other; not covet.* Then, to love is to do God's way.

KORAH, DATHAN, AND ABIRAM SWALLOWED UP.

GOD, when he gave the Ten Commandments upon Mount Sinai, chose that Aaron, and his sons, should be His priests. Now a priest was one who offered up sacrifices to God, and burned incense to Him; and when the smoke of the incense went up it was just as our prayers rise up to God in heaven. Once there were some other Levites, named Korah, Dathan, and Abiram, who became jealous of the power given by God to Moses and Aaron; they said they had as much right as Aaron had to be priests, and to offer sacrifices. They persuaded, also, 250 men to come and get censers, and offer incense to the Lord as if they had been priests. Moses fell on his face when he heard this, and asked God to help him; and on the next day, God told all the people to go away from the tabernacle of Korah and his friends.

All the people moved away, and God allowed these three wicked men to put fire into their censers, and to stand at their tent doors, with their wives and children. And Moses told the people that God would now show them which were the priests that He had chosen. As Moses spoke, the ground shook, the earth opened, and swallowed up Korah, and Dathan, and Abiram, and all that they had. All went down alive into the great pit, and the ground closed again and shut them in.

In the engraving the artist gives us a picture of this dreadful scene. Not only did Korah, Dathan, and Abiram perish, but God sent out a dreadful fire, which burnt up the 250 wicked men that offered incense. But although the people were dreadfully frightened at this awful sight, and fled away, still they were not humbled nor sorry for their sins; but they murmured against Moses and Aaron, and accused them of having killed their friends and companions.

SAYINGS OF CHILDHOOD:—I want you to remember, from this talk, that it is a dreadful thing to offend God! A little boy came to his father one day, and said, "O papa, *I have made up with God!*" "Why, my son," said his father, "I hope you had not *fallen out with God*—had you!" "Yes, papa, I had. I was very bad and offended Him, and He was angry with me. But I felt real sorry, and asked Him to forgive me, and He did; and now I am so happy because I've *made up with Him!*" O, children, it is awful to offend the great God who is almighty to save or to destroy forever.

WATER FROM THE SMITTEN ROCK.

SUPPOSE you know that the Israelites were now in a dreary wilderness. All around were great rocks, all parched with the hot sun shining on them. There was no water to drink, and the people got very hot and thirsty; then they began to murmur. They forgot their kind God who so often fed them from heaven, and did not pray to Him. They grew angry, and said, "Is the Lord among us or no?" That was the way they tempted God.

But God bore with them; and He told Moses to take his rod and go to the bare rock, and strike it. And when Moses struck the rock God made a beautiful, clear spring of water come gushing out of it, so that all the people, and all their cattle, and sheep, and camels, could drink and have plenty. The picture shows Moses smiting the rock, and the water flowing down in a clear, fresh stream. How glad everybody seems that there is plenty of water! Don't you think that was good in God? It was God's power that did this miracle; not Moses, nor the rod, but God alone, could bring water out of the rock.

The apostle Paul says, "This rock was Christ." He does not mean Christ himself, but that it resembles Christ—for from Him flows all true happiness, as refreshing to the soul of man as the streams of water were, flowing from the rock, to the Israelites in the wilderness.

DOINGS OF CHILDHOOD:—Learn from this talk not to murmur. I read of a child who murmured about water, just as the Israelites did; not because she had not plenty of it to drink, but she wished God had made it so it could not drown anybody, then she could go on the lake in a boat, and her mother would not be afraid of her drowning.

THE BRAZEN SERPENT.

THE children of Israel seemed never to trust God but just at the moment when they saw His miracles. That was very wicked; for He had promised to take care of them, and they ought to have believed His word. Their sin of murmuring was so great that we read, "The Lord sent fiery serpents among the people, and they bit them, so that many died;" that is He sent serpents, whose bite was like fire, making a similar wound for pain with that which burning coal would make. Where could they flee? The serpents were everywhere. Then the people repented and prayed. And the Lord told Moses, "Make thee a fiery serpent, and set it upon a pole; and it shall come to pass that every-one that is bitten, when he looketh upon it shall live." So Moses made a serpent of brass and set it upon a pole; and it came to pass that if a serpent had bitten any man, when he *looked* upon the brazen serpent, he *lived*.

Dear children, suppose we had been among that vast company in the wilderness; we might have been wandering around, when suddenly we felt the bite of the serpent. Alas! the poison is spreading through our bodies. As we fall, sick and faint, there comes one to us, and says, "Look on that serpent of brass on the pole yonder—look and you shall live!" With great effort we turn our eyes to the object pointed out to us. O joy! we are healed. That is what the artist has brought out in the picture—some are looking and some are not. None lived but those who looked; in other words, obeyed God's commands. If there were any in the camp who thought they would get well without looking at the serpent, they were among those who died.

Now, my little friends, we have all been bitten by sin, and that means death. But, listen! "As Moses lifted up the serpent in the wilderness, even so must the Son of man be lifted up, that whosoever believeth on him should not perish, but have everlasting life." Blessed tidings! If there are any little children who think they can go to heaven without new hearts they are mistaken; God has made only one cure for sin, and the bite of sin is deadly until we "look to Jesus."

BALAAM STOPPED BY AN ANGEL.

FROM the time of Moses, through all the time of the judges and kings of Israel, there were men called prophets. A prophet was a man inspired by God's Spirit to foretell what would happen to others at a time when there was no Bible. Among these prophets there was one whose name was Balaam. This prophet one day saw some men come to his house. They brought him a message that a king named Balak wanted him to come with them and curse the Israelites; and the servants had money with them to tempt Balaam to go. When Balaam saw the money, he wanted to go with them. He knew that it would be very wicked to curse God's people, and he ought to have sent the servants away at once. He should not have dallied with temptation.

Balaam begged the messengers to wait for a night and lodge with him; in the night God came to Balaam, and asked "Who are these men?" Then the prophet told him who they were and why they came; but God told him that he must not go, for what Balak wanted of him was to curse the children of Israel, and God would not have them cursed. So Balaam told the men, in the morning, that God would not let him go; and the messengers went back to their master. But Balak was not to be put off in this way. He fancied that, perhaps, he had not paid respect enough to Balaam. So he sent some princes, higher in rank than the first, and they told Balaam that if he would curse Israel, he should be promoted to great honor. By this time the wicked prophet had had more time to think about it. He weakened under the power of these bribes. Instead of sending them right back, as he should have done, on the strength of what God had said to him before, he showed his strong wish to go by asking Balak's men to tarry over for a night, that he might know what the Lord would say unto him more. This really was an appeal to the Lord to take back his decision, and let him go. And it was in

answer to this petition that God gave him permission to go; but told him that he should not say anything about the Israelites but what God put in his mouth. Balaam knew that God was not pleased with him, but he wanted Balak's rewards; and so, without waiting to be called, he rose early in the morning, and set off with the princes, riding on an ass.

Do you think Balaam was happy? No—he could not be happy; nothing can make us truly happy without God's blessing. When we wish for anything, or wish to go anywhere, we ought to ask ourselves, "Will God be pleased if I do this? Because if not, I cannot have His blessing, and then I cannot be happy." The Bible tells us "God's anger was kindled" because Balaam went. "The Angel of the Lord" came to stand in the way before the disobedient prophet; but Balaam was not thinking of God, and he did not see the angel. But the ass did, and was frightened, and turned out of the road into the field. Balaam was angry at this, and beat the ass to turn it back again. Soon after the ass turned aside again in a very narrow road through some vineyards, with a wall on both sides, and squeezed Balaam's foot against the wall. Balaam beat her again. Presently the road became very narrow; the angel stood before, and there was no room to turn, and the poor ass fell quite down for fear. Now Balaam was very angry, and beat her harder. But it was not the ass that was disobedient; no, it was the prophet who was so wicked and foolish, and the angel was sent to him.

Now God did a wonderful thing. He made the dumb ass to speak. She said, "Am not I thine ass, upon which thou hast ridden for many years past? What have I done? Why hast thou smitten me?" He told her he only wished he had a sword to kill her. The ass asked him if she had ever been like this before. He said, "No." And then God opened Balaam's eyes, and he saw, full before him, God's holy angel with a sword in his hand. This is what the artist has drawn in the picture. Balaam fell down on his face. And now, after the angel had reproved him, he was sorry that he had beaten the ass, and offered to go back again, if the angel wished; but the angel said he must go on now, though he would only be able to speak the words which God put in his mouth.

Then the angel went away, and Balaam went on to Moab. And when Balaam tried to speak curses, God turned them all to blessings; and, instead of saying the children of Israel should come to a terrible end, as Balak wanted him to do, he could only say how happy and well off they should be, with God to take care of them, and be their

King. Only think how angry Balak must have been, when Balaam could not curse, but only blessed. But was Balaam sorry for his disobedience? No, he was frightened, but he was not humbled. His heart was not changed; he was rebellious and covetous still. He went on in his wickedness, and was miserably killed at last.

DOINGS OF CHILDHOOD:—Balaam had a "double-mind." Do you know what that means? Let me tell you. I read of a boy, who started to walk from one town to another. He walked a short distance; then suddenly turned and walked in the other direction; then he changed his mind and walked on again; then turned again and again, and so on. Now what was the trouble with that boy? This was it—he had two minds, apparently wanting to go two ways at the same time. And don't you see? So long as he is constantly changing his mind, he actually gets nowhere. Now that is just what a "double-minded" man is. One will never know where to find him, or be able to judge toward which place he is walking. Such a boy does not know how to say "No" when temptation comes. Dear children, Satan tempts us every day; do we, like Balaam, sway back and forth? Have we a *little* desire to do right, but a *great* desire to get the fun, or the gain, that is promised from doing wrong? A little boy was asked, "Why the Tempter seemed to trouble him so little?" His answer was a good one, "Because I treat him so coolly." It is always the better way, under all circumstances, to treat Satan coolly.

THE CROSSING OF THE JORDAN BY THE CHILDREN OF ISRAEL.

 HE children of Israel were now quite close to the beautiful land God had promised them. They had been wandering about for forty years in the wilderness. Moses had died—the Lord buried him, and no one knows where his grave is. Joshua was now their captain instead of Moses. But before they could go into the promised land they had to get across a river—"a deep river, with rocks on each side, and a stony bottom to it, and the water running very fast indeed." The name of the river was Jordan.

How could they go through? God knew how. He had brought them through the Red Sea, and he could bring them over the river Jordan. God told them what to do. The priests were to take up the Ark, and to go before the people, and to walk right down into the water, without being afraid. So the day following, the priests and the Levites took the Ark and went before the people; and just as soon as their feet dipped into the water, the waters divided, and stood up like a wall; and the priests, with the Ark, went through first, and all the host of the children of Israel followed on dry ground. In the engraving we see them passing over.

When they had all passed over, Joshua called twelve men, one of every tribe, and told them each to take a stone from Jordan, from the place where the priests' feet had stood, and to carry these stones to Gilgal, where they were to leave them. These twelve stones Joshua set up, for a monument in Gilgal, that when, in future time, the Israelites' children should ask, "What are these stones?" their parents might tell them the wonderful story of how God brought His people through the river on dry ground.

SAYINGS OF CHILDHOOD:—"Mary," said a preacher addressing a child convert, "is not the love of God wonderful—is it not wonderful?" She replied, "I do not think it wonderful, because it is *just like Him!*"

AN ANGEL APPEARS TO JOSHUA.

NOW the children of Israel were in the land of Canaan. And no sooner had they come into the land, than there was a strong walled city before them, and its name was Jericho. They must take this city before they could go any further. But how were they going to conquer it? While Joshua was, perhaps, thoughtfully looking around Jericho and contriving how to take it, it came to pass that he lifted up his eyes and looked, and behold, there stood a man over against him, with a drawn sword in his hand. And Joshua went unto him, and said unto him, "Art thou for us, or for our adversaries?" "And he said," Nay, but as a captain of the host of the Lord I am come." Do you know who he was, children? He was the Angel who appeared in the burning bush to Moses. In our first picture you can see him. And Joshua fell on his face to the earth, and worshipped him.

God was showing Joshua that He fought with him. So He told him not to fight with swords, and spears, and battering rams; but that, every day, for a whole week, the priests should take the Ark of the Covenant on their shoulders and walk around the outside of the walls of the city. Seven of the priests were to carry trumpets made of ram's horns, and to blow with them as they passed on before the Ark. The last day, they were to go round the city seven times; and the priests were to blow the trumpets, and the people to shout. The people believed God, and did all He commanded. And when, at last, on the seventh day, Joshua gave the word, "Shout, for the Lord hath given you the city," behold, the walls fell down flat, and the Israelites marched in and took the city.

In the second picture

"THE WALLS OF JERICHO FALL DOWN,"

the artist has given us a very clear idea of this—the walls tumbling down, so that not

THE WALLS OF JERICHO FALL DOWN.

one stone was left upon another. The city was utterly destroyed, and everybody in it; only a woman, named Rahab, and her family, were saved, because she had before shown kindness to some of the children of Israel.

Dear children, the God of Joshua is *our* God. He promised to help the Israelites. He told them that they would not need to fight at all. The battle was His; not theirs. So is our battle with the world. He will not leave us to fight it out alone. Every boy and girl has the Spirit of God to help them if they only want and ask for His aid. He *did* help the children of Israel to take their Jericho; He *will* help us to take our Jericho. I will name some Jerichoes we must take: Anger, Pride, Selfishness, Intemperance, Worldliness and lots of others. We can't take them in our own strength; but, with Jesus for our Leader, the walls of our Jerichoes will fall down flat. The Bible says "Fight the good fight of faith." What is a *good* fight? Did you ever see or hear of one? Well, there is one, and that is a fight against all that is evil. When you try to overcome the bad feelings that you have, that is a "good fight." When you resist temptation and come off the conqueror, that is another good fight. The gospel tells us how to carry on fights like these. We are Christ's little soldiers. It is the good fight of faith that He wants us to fight in. What will He do for those who conquer? Read Rev. 2: 10. Will all of us conquer? All that ask Christ to help them will.

"Oh, do not be discouraged,
For Jesus is your friend,
Oh, do not be discouraged,
For Jesus is your friend,
He will give you grace to conquer,
He will give you grace to conquer,
And keep you to the end."

ACHAN STONED TO DEATH.

GOD told the children of Israel that they must not take any of the spoils of the city of Jericho to themselves, but must set it apart for His service. He commanded them solemnly to mind this order, and told them that if they did not, it would bring a curse upon them, and be a trouble to the whole nation.

But one wicked man named Achan, thinking no eye saw him, disobeyed the command. There he is! Look at him, children! He enters a fine looking house. He finds a wedge of gold, a bag of silver, and a beautiful garment. How tempting they look! He covets them. He says to himself—" How I should like to have these. And why may I not? There is no one here to see. They won't be missed, amid all the spoils of this great city. I'll take them." So he carries them quietly away, and digs a hole in his tent, and buries them there. He thinks no one has seen him. Poor, foolish man! he forgets that "the eyes of the Lord are in every place, beholding the evil and the good." God saw it all, and the Bible tells us how He made it known.

Soon after the taking of Jericho, the Israelites went to take another city called Ai, and, to the surprise of Joshua, their army was defeated, and a number of the soldiers killed, for they had sinned against the Lord. Then Joshua rent his clothes, and fell on the ground, and prayed to God for help and instruction; and God told him that one of his people had sinned, and He commanded him to draw lots to find out the sinner.

Joshua obeyed directly. He called all the tribes, and all the families, and God helped him to find the right man. And Achan was taken. God's eye saw among all the thousands of Israel, and pointed him out to Joshua. Then Joshua took Achan, and all his family, and stoned them to death, and burned the bodies and all the possessions of Achan with fire. In the picture you see the body of Achan covered with the big stones. After they had done this, the Lord suffered the Israelites to take Ai.

SAYINGS OF CHILDHOOD:—Nothing can be hid from the eye of God. A plate of cakes was brought in and laid upon a table. Two children were playing upon the hearth rug before the fire—" Oh, I want one of these cakes," said the little boy, as soon as his mother had gone out. "No, no," said his sister, "you must not touch them." "Mother won't know it," he replied, "she didn't count them." "If she didn't," said the sister, "*perhaps God counted.*"

JOSHUA COMMANDS THE SUN TO STAND STILL.

SOME of the heathen kings, who lived near, united together to fight against Israel. They marched against a royal city called Gibeon, with whose people Joshua had made a league. The Gibeonites were very much frightened when they saw these kings, and their armies, coming to fight them; but they knew where to go for help; they sent to Joshua, and asked him to come and save them from their enemies. So Joshua and his mighty men went up to fight for them. He marched all night to Gibeon, with all his army, and God told him to fear nothing. The kings were soon conquered, and fled from the Israelites; and God not only helped Joshua to kill them with the sword, but He sent down upon them such a dreadful storm of hail, that more men were killed by the hailstones than those that fell in the war.

And in order to show His marvellous power to his people and to their enemies, God did a wonderful thing that day. Joshua and the Israelites were many hours fighting, and they feared darkness would come on, and then they would not know where to find their enemies. But Joshua had great faith in God; so he asked God to work a very wonderful miracle, never seen before nor since. What was it? Joshua said, "Sun, stand thou still in Gibeon; and thou, moon, in the valley of Ajalon." And the sun stood still, and the moon stayed, until all the enemies of Israel were conquered. It was God's power, not Joshua's that made them stand still, and God gave the command in answer to Joshua's prayer.

This wonderful miracle furnishes the picture which the artist gives us. The wide field of battle is seen with the swarming multitudes of the foe; in the foreground we see the host of Israel hurrying on to swell the destruction from the Lord; while a little to the left, Joshua is seen on a little hill, with arm uplifted, commanding the sun to stand still.

The wicked kings went and hid themselves in a cave at Makedah. When Joshua was told that they were hidden there, he caused great stones to be rolled before the mouth of the cave to keep the kings there until the battle was over; then he had them hanged upon five trees, as an example to others, and he destroyed their cities.

SISERA SLAIN BY JAEL.

AND the children of Israel again did evil in the sight of the Lord." God, therefore, punished them again. He sent cruel nations to conquer them, to burn their houses, to steal their children, and drive away their cattle. They were made slaves, and obliged to work to pay heavy taxes to a foreign king, called Jabin, for twenty years. This king was very cruel and very powerful. Sisera, his commander-in-chief, "had nine hundred chariots of iron" to go to battle with. The Israelites felt this, and they repented of their sins and cried to the Lord to forgive and help them. God heard their prayer, and raised up a good woman, named Deborah, and told her to send for a man named Barak, who should lead the Israelites to fight against Sisera.

She sent for Barak, and told him what God had said. But Barak was afraid to go alone, and said, "If thou wilt go with me, I will go;" so Deborah went with him, and ten thousand men, to fight against Sisera. But Deborah told Barak that he should not kill Sisera, but that the Lord would sell the wicked captain into the hand of a woman. Then "the Lord defeated Sisera, and all his chariots, and all his host, with the edge of the sword, before Barak;" so that, in order to get away faster, Sisera came down from his chariot, and ran away on his feet to escape from Barak.

There was a man named Heber who was at peace with Jabin; and Sisera ran to Heber's tent for safety. When Heber's wife, whose name was Jael, saw Sisera coming, she went out to meet him, and said, "Come in, come in, fear not." So Sisera went in and Jael covered him with a mantle; and when he had fallen asleep, for he was very weary with fighting and running so far, she took a large nail of the tent, and crept softly up to his side, and with a hammer drove the nail through his temple into the ground, and killed him.

SISERA SLAIN BY JAEL.

Soon after, Barak came to the door of the tent, and Jael called him in, and showed him his enemy lying dead upon the ground. In the picture we have the story most vividly portrayed. Inside the tent lies Sisera, with the nail in his head, dead. Jael stands in the tent door, which she has drawn aside, so that Barak and his followers, who are seen approaching, may look in upon the fallen chieftain. Thus you see, God delivered Sisera into the hand of a woman; Barak lost all the honor, because he would not do just as he was told, but was afraid without Deborah. He ought to have been ashamed of himself—just as if God could not help him better than Deborah could.

And now the Israelites were resolved to rid the country of the tyrant Jabin. "And the hand of the children of Israel prospered, and prevailed against Jabin, king of Canaan, until they had destroyed Jabin, king of Canaan."

Barak and Deborah felt that it was the Lord, not themselves, nor their soldiers, who had gained the victory over Sisera. Then, according to the custom of the times, they sang a beautiful song of praise to Him. In the next engraving,

"DEBORAH'S SONG OF TRIUMPH,"

the regal figure of Deborah, her glowing countenance and intensity of action, show her exalted mood; and her power over the listening group is shown by their earnestness and deep attention. You may read this song in the fifth chapter of Judges.

SAYINGS OF CHILDHOOD:—Dear little ones, I hope you do not forget to thank God for His mercies to you. The way to show your thankfulness is to do some work, or sing some song of praise, or present some gift as a token of how glad you are. Don't promise, and then not keep it. I heard of a boy who said, "If God will make me well again, I will give my five dollar gold piece to the poor people where the famine is." God made him well and on being reminded of his promise, he said fifty cents was enough for them; he wanted the rest to buy a velocipede! That wasn't a very thankful spirit, was it? I like the spirit of another little boy better, who, when he had laid his head on his soft, clean pillow to sleep all night, said, "Mamma, if Jesus were here I would give him half of my pillow." Don't you think he loved Jesus, and was thankful?

GIDEON CHOOSING HIS SOLDIERS.

THE Israelites had rest from war for forty years. They were prosperous and happy. But sin crept in among them, and brought suffering with it; "and the Lord delivered them into the hand of Midian seven years." And the Israelites were so cruelly treated that they left their towns, and went and hid in caves or hollow places in the rocks. For, when they had sown their land, the Midianites wantonly destroyed the crop, and left no food for man or beast.

Then the Israelites were sorry, and prayed to God to save them. And God had pity on them, and sent His angel to a man named Gideon, to tell him that he was to fight for the Israelites. And Gideon asked for some sign, that he might be sure he was right; the angel told him to take some kid's flesh and unleavened cakes which he had made, and to lay them upon a rock, and to pour out the broth; and when he had done so, the angel of the Lord touched them with the end of his staff, and there rose up fire out of the rock and consumed them. By this miracle Gideon knew that he was indeed called of God to great deeds. So, in the night-time, Gideon took ten men of his servants, and, by the Lord's direction, he cut down the grove, and cast down the altar of Baal, the false god. And when the people saw what Gideon had done by night, they would have put him to death; but Gideon blew a trumpet and called together a great many soldiers, and made them ready to fight.

Before Gideon began to fight, he asked God to promise to save Israel from the Midianites. He asked God for two signs: first, he would put a fleece of wool upon the floor, and if the wool were all wet, and the floor dry, he should believe that God was with him to help him; and the fleece was so wet that he wrung a bowlful of water out of it, while the floor was dry. Still, Gideon did not know what to do, and he asked God for another sign, and that was to be the reverse of this, for the fleece should be dry and the floor wet; "and God did so that night: for it was dry upon the fleece only, and there was dew upon all the ground." Then the brave Gideon knew that he was indeed called of God to deliver Israel.

Soon a large army was gathered together, ready to follow Gideon. But God wished to teach the Israelites that these soldiers had no power to gain the victory, and that He

alone could save them; also, that it was as easy for God to save them with few men as with many. So He told Gideon to say to the soldiers, that if they were afraid, they might return home, and not come to the battle; and twenty-two thousand went away. Still there were too many; so God commanded Gideon, "bring them down unto the water, and I will try them for thee there." So he brought down the ten thousand to the water to drink. And the Lord said unto Gideon, "Every one that lappeth of the water with his tongue, as a dog lappeth, him shalt thou set by himself; likewise every one that boweth down upon his knees to drink." A few of them lapped, putting their hands to their mouths; you can see them in the first picture, in the act of drinking. Gideon counted those who lapped; they were three hundred. Then God said, "By the three hundred men who lapped will I save you; let all the others return home."

Now Gideon had a very, very small army. The Midianites were in great numbers; the Israelites only three hundred. Was he frightened? No; he had no need to fear, for God was with him. At night he took his three hundred men, and gave them each a trumpet, and an earthen pitcher, with a lamp inside the pitcher, so that the light could not be seen. He took a hundred with him, and sent the other two hundred another way, creeping quietly along till they came to the place where the Midianites had set up their tents, and were all lying asleep among the cattle they had stolen. There they lay, and never heard Gideon and the men coming till they were close to the camp, the three parties on three sides. Then, all of a sudden, every one of the Israelites broke his pitcher and let his lamp shine, and blew his trumpet, and shouted,

"THE SWORD OF THE LORD, AND OF GIDEON!"

In our second picture the artist has drawn this scene most vividly. You can see the tents in the darkness, and, on the little hill, the soldiers of Gideon with their lamps. The Midianites were awakened out of their sleep, and terribly frightened. They cried aloud, and tried to flee. They drew their swords, and, unable in the darkness to tell friend from foe, they killed and wounded each other; while those who managed to escape out of the camp were pursued and put to death by the Israelites.

When Gideon had gained all these victories, the Israelites came to him and thanked him, and wanted to make him their king. They said, "Rule thou over us, and thy son, and thy son's son likewise; for thou hast delivered us from the hand of Midian." But Gideon answered, "I will not rule over you, neither shall my son rule over you. The Lord shall rule over you." And for forty years there was peace in the land, until Gideon died.

JEPHTHAH'S DAUGHTER COMING OUT TO MEET HER FATHER.

JEPHTHAH was the name of a man who lived in Gilead; he was very brave and warlike; but his brothers did not love him, and they sent him away. He went to the land of Tob, lying eastward towards the deserts, and there gathered about him a band of outlaws, and " was a mighty man of valor "—so that his fame went back to his native land.

Again Israel returned to false gods. Then God let the Philistines afflict them, and they and the Ammonites troubled them eighteen years. Finally, a large army of the Ammonites marched against Israel, who were greatly frightened, and they cried to the Lord. And the Lord still gracious, heard them yet again. Then they confessed their sins, and trusting in God they gathered an army to meet their enemies. But they had no general. As Jephthah was famed for his valor, the Gileadites now thought of him, and they sent for him to be their leader. Jephthah told them how ill they had used him, but if they would promise to obey his commands, he would come and aid them.

Now the Ammonites were a very wicked people, and God commanded that they should be destroyed, and He promised to give their possessions to the Israelites. Jephthah sent to the Ammonites, and told them this; but they would not attend. Then Jephthah made ready to fight against them. But before he went to the battle, he asked God's help, and made this very rash vow: " If thou wilt give me the victory, then the first thing I meet at the door of my house, when I return in peace, shall be the Lord's; and I will offer it up for a burnt offering."

He soon defeated the children of Ammon; and when the battle was over Jephthah went home again to Mizpeh. Now Jephthah had an only daughter; she was also an only child; she was very dear to him. It was often the custom for women to go out

120 JEPHTHAH'S DAUGHTER COMING OUT TO MEET HER FATHER.

with music and dancing to meet the conqueror on his return. So she waited and looked for him, and when she saw him coming, she ran out to meet him, dancing and singing for joy. In the first picture we see the lovely maiden coming forth with her companions to meet her proud father, little dreaming that by this touching act of filial love she is to become the unhappy victim of her father's rash vow.

When Jephthah saw her he rent his clothes and exclaimed, "Alas, my daughter, thou hast brought me very low, and thou art one of them that trouble me; for I have opened my mouth unto the Lord, and I cannot go back." The poor maiden behaved nobly. She said, with loving resignation, "My father, if thou hast opened thy mouth unto the Lord, do to me according to that which hath proceeded out of thy mouth; forasmuch as the Lord hath taken vengeance for thee of thine enemies, even of the children of Ammon." Jephthah now thought of his foolish vow, and saw how hasty he had been. He must give up his daughter, and never see her again! He had been a mighty conqueror; but he could never be a happy man again.

Jephthah's daughter made one request; she asked that her sacrifice might be delayed. She begged of her father to let her go upon the mountains, and have two months to mourn there with her friends. Her father let her go. Our next engraving is

"JEPHTHAH'S DAUGHTER AND HER COMPANIONS,"

a sweet and mournful picture of this scene on the mountains. Her companions are seated round mourning with her. "At the end of the two months, she returned to her father, who did with her according to his vow." What did he do? I do not know; the Bible does not say. Perhaps he killed her in sacrifice; perhaps he sent her far away, alone, where she could spend all her time in the service of God.

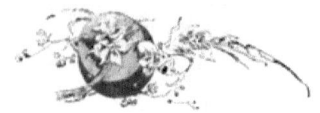

SAMSON SLAYING THE LION.

AFTER Jephthah's death, other judges governed Israel; but the people began again to sin against the Lord, and He gave them up to their enemies the Philistines for forty years. This was a long time to be in sorrow and trouble; but the Israelites deserved punishment. Then the Lord raised them up a mighty deliverer, named Samson, who was the strongest man that ever lived upon earth. His father's name was Manoah. He was a good man, and he and his wife both served God. Samson's birth was foretold by an angel, and his parents were told by an angel, before his birth, of all that they should do unto him. Among other things, the angel told them that they must bring him up as a Nazarite: that is, set him apart for God's service, as he wanted to use him. You remember the Nazarites were people who had made a vow to give themselves to God. They did not drink wine, nor any strong drink; and they never cut their hair nor shaved their heads.

So Samson was born, and grew up. His parents were very careful to attend to all God's commands about him. Samson grew up wonderfully strong. God had given him great strength, because He wanted him to deliver Israel. In one thing he distressed his parents. He desired to marry a beautiful young Philistine, the daughter of their enemies; his parents would much rather have had him choose a wife from among his own people; but Samson was of a different mind, and said unto his father, "Get her for me, for she pleaseth me well." Finding it of no use to argue with him, Manoah and his wife yielded, and went to Timnath to settle the matter.

On the way down, a lion rushed out of the woods, and began to roar against him. Was Samson afraid? No; he was a very bold man, and he ran to the lion, and tore it to pieces, as though it were only a kid, and he had nothing in his hand; it was his great strength alone. But he told not his father and mother.

In the engraving the strength and beauty of the powerful young man are splendidly shown. Samson was yet quite young, and the artist has so pictured him.

SAMSON SLAYING THE PHILISTINES WITH THE JAWBONE OF AN ASS.

SOME time after, Samson passed again along the place where he had slain the lion; and he turned aside to see the dead body of the lion, and he found that a swarm of bees had made their nest in the lion, and had begun to store their honey there. So Samson took the honey, and did eat of it, and he carried some of it home to his father and mother; but he did not tell them where he had found it, for he meant to make a riddle from it, and that would have given them the clue.

Then Samson's father and mother went with him, and he made a feast on the occasion of his marriage, and thirty young men were invited to be at it. Then they passed their time in making riddles, and Samson gave one which he allowed the Philistines seven days to find out; and he would then give them thirty sheets or dresses, in which the Easterns wrap themselves at night, and thirty changes of garments, to wear by day, if they could tell its meaning; but, if they could not, then they were to give him the like. Then he told his riddle, "Out of the eater came forth meat, and out of the strong came forth sweetness." The eater was the strong lion, and the meat was the sweet honey Samson found in it; but no one knew the story of the lion, and they could not guess the riddle. So they puzzled in vain, for three days, to find out the riddle, and when they could not, they went to Samson's wife and frightened her, and told her that they would burn her, and set fire to her father's house, if she did not get Samson to tell her the meaning of his riddle.

So Samson's wife "wept before him" till the seventh day came, and his heart was so touched, that at last he told her the riddle, and she went at once and told the Philistines. Then the Philistines came to Samson, and said, "What is sweeter than honey, and what is stronger than a lion?" But Samson said, "My wife told you, or you could not have guessed my riddle."

SAMSON SLAYING THE PHILISTINES.

Now Samson was obliged to give what he had promised to those who found out the riddle. But how did he get the garments and the sheets? He went out among the Philistines, and slew thirty men, and took their garments, and all that belonged to them, and gave the changes of garments to the young men who had told the riddle. Soon after, Samson's wife was taken away from him and given to one of his companions, and then Samson began to be very angry with the Philistines and determined to punish them. He went and caught three hundred foxes, and tied them two together, tail to tail, with firebrands between them, and he turned them into the corn-fields of the Philistines just at the time of harvest; and all the corn, and vineyards, and olives were burnt. The people to whom the corn belonged were very angry, and when they found out that Samson had done this unto them because his wife had been given to another man, they burned her and her father with fire. Samson determined to be avenged on them for their cruelty, and, though revenge is not proper, yet, in this case, God made his anger to work Israel's deliverance. So Samson fell upon the Philistines, and slew them with great slaughter.

After this, Samson went to live in a rock, which was, perhaps, a fortress, called Etam. The Philistines now went to fight against Judah, and they said they must have Samson, and bind him, and take him prisoner. The people of Judah were frightened, and three thousand of the men of Judah went to the top of the rock Etam, and said to Samson, "Knowest thou not that the Philistine are rulers over us?" "What is this that thou hast done unto us?" And he said unto them, "As they did unto me, so have I done unto them." Then they told him, "We are come to bind thee, that we may deliver thee into the hand of the Philistines." Was not this base of them, because Samson was one of their own countrymen, and the Philistines were all the time oppressors of Israel? Well, the cowards did not like to fall upon him, lest he should smite them, as he had smitten the Philistines, so they entreated him to deliver himself up, and he, not wishing to hurt any of his countrymen, agreed to do so, on condition that they would not kill him when he was in their hands. "And they bound him with two new cords and brought him up from the rock."

So Samson suffered them to bring him bound to Lehi, where the Philistines received their captive with great shouts of joy. Then all in a moment, God gave Samson strength to break the ropes, and he burst them off his arms as though they had been flax that was burnt with fire. Samson had no weapon, but he found the new jawbone of an ass lying near him, and this he made his sword. "He put forth his hand and

SAMSON SLAYING THE PHILISTINES.

took it," and, rushing upon his enemies, he slew a thousand men of the Philistines. In our picture the artist shows Samson standing near the edge of the precipice, slaying the Philistines, and casting them down. Then, as the conquerors of whom you have before read, Samson made a song of triumph, and he sung,

> "With the jawbone of an ass, heaps upon heaps,
> With the jawbone of an ass have I slain a thousand men."

Samson now threw away the jawbone, and, in remembrance of the event, he called the place Ramath-Lehi, which means " the place of the jawbone."

After the slaughter, Samson was thirsty and ready to die, and he prayed to the Lord to help him. It was right of him to go to God in his troubles. We ought always to tell Him when we are in need, and ask Him to give us what is right. God heard Samson's prayer. He made water to spring up like a well, and Samson drank and became strong again. Then he called that spot after a particular name, that God's goodness to him might not be forgotten; the name he gave it was Enhakkore, which signifies *the well of him that cried*, that is, *that cried to God*.

Don't you see, dear children, all this strength which Samson had, came from God? He gave him boldness and courage. "Samson was not so meek, and gentle, and kind, as many people of whom we read in the Bible. He was not like Abraham, nor Moses; sometimes he was revengeful and passionate; but we may hope, that Samson was a true servant of God, and that he trusted in Him for strength to fight against his enemies."

SAMSON CARRYING OFF THE GATES OF GAZA.

NOW, soon afterward, Samson went to Gaza, a city of the Philistines, and he remained there for the night. But the Philistines soon learned that he was come among them, and so they resolved once more to try and catch him. So they "compassed him in," by fastening all the gates of the city; and they put guards to lie in wait for him all night, in the hope of putting him to death as soon as he tried to pass through their gates in the morning.

But Samson was made wise by the Spirit of God, as well as strong; and he lay quiet till midnight, and then arose, and, finding the gates all fastened, he laid hold on the posts and pulled up posts and gates and all, just as a strong man might a little garden gate, and away he carried them in triumph upon his shoulders to the top of a hill near Hebron; and there he left them standing upon the top of the hill, so that all might see and know what he had done. In the engraving the artist shows Samson just before he comes to the top of the hill.

Samson had now another wife; her name was Delilah, and she was a Philistine. The Philistines wanted very much to know what made Samson so strong; so they went to Delilah, and offered her a sum of money equal to about thirty-five hundred dollars of our money, if she would find out where his strength was, and so rob him of it; most likely they thought he had got some kind of charm to enable him to do such wonders as he did. Delilah did not care much for Samson, and she was glad enough to accept of this offer; so she teased him constantly to tell her where his strength lay, and how he might be taken and bound. Samson did not want her to know, so he deceived her. At first he told her if he were bound with seven green withes, or willow branches, that had never been dried, he would be as weak as other men. Then Delilah told the Philistines, and they brought the withes, and she bound him with them, while several of the Philistines lay hidden close by. Then she said, "The Philistines be upon thee, Samson!" But he sprang up and broke the withes, as though they were little strings. Again Delilah asked him to tell her what made him so strong, and he told her, "If they bind me fast with new ropes, that have never been used, I shall be weak as another man." And Delilah tied Samson a second time, and cried, "The Philistines be upon

thee, Samson!" and he broke the ropes, and escaped again. A third time he made a false answer, and told her that if she would weave seven locks of his hair with a weaver's beam, and fasten it with the pin of the beam, he would become powerless. And she did so, while Samson was asleep; but when she told him the Philistines were at hand, he awoke and went away with the pin, and the beam, and the web.

Then Delilah told him that he mocked her, and that, if he loved her, he would not serve her so. And she pressed him daily with her words, and urged him, "Tell me now where thy great strength lies;" so that Samson was tired of his wife's asking him so often, and at last he opened his heart to her, and told this wicked woman the secret—that he was a Nazarite to God, and his head had never been shaved, but if she cut off his hair he would be as weak as any other man. In the picture,

"SAMSON AND DELILAH,"

we see him in the act of telling her. Delilah now knew that he had told her the truth. Then she called the lords of the Philistines, and told them all that Samson had said; the Philistines were very glad to think that they should soon have their enemy in their power; and they came directly, and brought money with them to give her. Then Delilah contrived to make Samson fall asleep on her knees, "and she called for a man, and caused him to shave off the seven locks of his head," in which his hair was, probably, plaited; and when he had finished, Delilah cried, "The Philistines are upon thee, Samson." Samson arose, but his strength was gone; God had taken it all away. He could not defend himself now; and so the Philistines sprang upon him, and took him, and put out his eyes, and bound him in chains, and carried him to Gaza, and made him grind in the prison-house there. So now he was obliged to work like a slave for the enemies who had so feared him. No doubt he often repented for his wickedness, and called upon God to help him in his trouble; and so, as his hair grew again, God imparted to him his former strength.

SAYINGS OF CHILDHOOD:—I want you to remember that your health and strength all come from God. Little Edgar's grandmother, when he was about three years old, as she was catechizing him, asked who made him? To which he replied, "God made me a little, and I growed the rest." Pretty good. And yet the philosophy of a child, or a sage either, might ask, "How could you grow the rest?" The Bible tells, "In Him we live and move and have our being." It is God who gives us every thing, and we must thank Him and serve Him with all we have.

THE DEATH OF SAMSON.

THE Philistines rejoiced greatly at the capture of Samson. They worshipped an ugly idol like a fish, named Dagon, and they believed that it was Dagon who had delivered their enemy into their hands. So they made a great sacrifice to Dagon, and praised him; and when they were very merry, playing, and laughing, and feasting, they sent for Samson to make sport for them, probably by ridiculing, and teasing and smiting him. Then the poor blind prisoner was led in; he could not see his cruel enemies, but that he might be seen by all, they set him in a public part of the building where they were, between two pillars. The house was very large, and full of people; about three thousand of them were upon the roof, looking and wondering at Samson. Samson asked the boy who led him, to let him lean upon the pillars on which the house stood, and he took hold of one with his right hand, and of the other with his left hand.

At this moment, Samson prayed to God to give him strength; and he bowed himself with all his might, and pulled down the whole house, and killed all the thousands of Philistines that it contained. Samson was killed himself. In the superb picture you see all this splendidly portrayed. There we can see the bent and straining figure of Samson, and the terror of the flying idolaters, amid the horror of the falling columns. And so it is said of him, "the dead which he slew at his death were more than they which he slew in his life." It was a sad death for Samson to die; but, you see, when he forgot the Lord, and the Lord's people, the Lord forsook Samson, or, rather, suffered him to bring upon himself his own punishment.

SAYINGS OF CHILDHOOD:—The Philistines, whom God punished so severely, were idolators. A mother was describing to her little son the idols which the heathen nations worship as gods; "I suppose, Mamma," said he, "that these heathens do not look upon the same sun, and moon, and stars, which we do." And when he was told that they were the same, he replied; "*Well then, I wonder that they do not think that there must be a better God than these idols.*" The heathen, dear children, are without excuse for their idolatry.

NAOMI AND HER DAUGHTERS-IN-LAW.

DEAR children, I hope you have all read the entire book of Ruth. It contains a very beautiful and interesting story. In the days of the judges, of whom we have been talking, there was a famine in the land of Israel. There lived a certain man in Bethlehem, the place where Christ was afterwards born, whose name was Elimelech. He had a wife named Naomi, and two sons, named Mahlon and Chilion. When the famine was very bad in Bethlehem, Elimelech and his family went to Moab to live there. They ought not to have done this, because the Moabites were wicked idolaters. God's people ought not to go to places where they may learn to sin.

There Elimelech died, and his two sons married two Moabitish women, "the name of the one was Orpah, and the name of the other was Ruth." In about ten years Mahlon and Chilion died also; so Naomi was in a strange country with neither husband nor sons. She had none to comfort her; all around her were those who did not serve God, and she wished to be in her own country again, where she might hear about God. So, having learned that there was bread enough in her own land, she set out to see it once more. Orpah and Ruth were both very loving towards Naomi, and they said they would go with her; but Naomi did not wish to take her daughters-in-law to a new country, against their will; so on the way, she advised them to go back to their own country and friends, and she kissed them to bid them good-bye, and they both wept, and said, "We will surely go with thee to Bethlehem." But Naomi said again, "Nay, my daughters, return to your homes; why will you go with me?" Then they wept again, and "Orpah kissed her mother-in-law, and went away, but Ruth clave unto her." In the engraving we have the parting scene. Orpah had just said farewell and departed weeping; but Ruth, of a nobler, more faithful nature, clings to her mother-in-law, and refuses to leave her. She threw her arms around Naomi; then Naomi said to Ruth, "Behold thy sister-in-law is gone back unto her people, and unto her gods; return thou after thy sister-in-law." Then Ruth told her that she had fully made up her mind, and it was of no use to try and persuade her to turn back. Her words, as recorded in the Bible, are beautiful words, and I wish you would learn them; "And Ruth said, Intreat me not to leave thee, or to return from following after thee; for whither thou goest, I

will go; and where thou lodgest, I will lodge; thy people shall be my people, and thy God my God; Where thou diest, will I die, and there will I be buried; the Lord do so to me, and more also, if ought but death part thee and me." Naomi was very glad to hear Ruth say this, for Naomi loved God, and she wished Ruth to love Him too.

SAYINGS OF CHILDHOOD:—A young lady asked one of the little boys in her Sunday School class how much he loved her. To which he replied: "I love you *up to the sky.*" And then to his mother, whose eye he had chanced to catch just then, he said: "I love you *way up to God.*" Dear children, I think Ruth loved Naomi clear "up to God."

BOAZ AND RUTH.

RUTH and Naomi went on together, till they reached Bethlehem, which, you remember, had been Naomi's home. Many of her old friends still lived there, and they all ran to see her. But they did not know her; she was so changed by time and sorrow, that they said, "Is this Naomi?" And she said unto them, "Call me not Naomi, call me Mara; for the Almighty hath dealt very bitterly with me. I went out full, and the Lord hath brought me home again empty." When she lived before at Bethlehem, she was happy with her husband and her sons; but God had taken them all away, and now she was a poor widow, and had come home to die in her own country. So she said, "Call me Mara," which means *bitterness,* for she was now a woman of *a sorrowful spirit.*

Well, now they had arrived at home they must have bread. So Ruth proposed to go and work in the field, and glean some corn with the poor; and Naomi answered, "Go, my daughter." Now Ruth was a stranger to all the people, but God was with her, and when she went out to glean, He so ordered it that she went into a field which belonged to Boaz, a near relation of Naomi's husband, and a very rich man. By-and-by Boaz came to the field to see the reapers, and he said to them, "The Lord be with you." And they answered, "The Lord bless thee." Boaz and his servants were true worshippers of God, and that was their Christian greeting. As soon as Boaz saw Ruth gleaning, he asked who she was. His servant said, "It is the damsel who came with Naomi from Moab." Then Boaz went to her, and said, "Stay here with my maidens, and follow

them, and glean after the reapers;" and that she might be the better supplied, he commanded the corn even to be dropped, on purpose, by the way, for her to glean it. Ruth wondered at the kindness of Boaz to her a perfect stranger, and she asked, "Why hast thou shown so much kindness to me a stranger?" Then he told her that he had heard about her, how good she was to her mother-in-law, and how sincerely she loved the true God, so as even to forsake everything to serve Him; and he said, "May He bless and reward thee." Don't you think Boaz was real good? Ruth thanked him; but, above all, she felt thankful to God who gave her kind friends in a strange country.

In the engraving Ruth is seen in the foreground gathering the scattered wheat, while Boaz standing near, is directing the young men respecting her. When it was evening, she took up her load and went home. Then Naomi asked, "Where hast thou gleaned to-day?" and Ruth told her all about the kindness of Boaz. Naomi was much pleased to hear this; and she told Ruth, that Boaz was her relation, and that she felt he would be kind to them and help them. And so Ruth continued gleaning to the end of barley-harvest.

At last, harvest time was over, and what would they now do for food? But Naomi and Ruth loved and trusted God, and He promises always to take care of His people. Now Boaz was very fond of Ruth. He loved her; because she loved God, and because she was so industrious, and dutiful to Naomi. Elimelech had had a possession in Canaan, and Boaz said, he would buy that possession, and marry Ruth according to a custom among the Israelites. So Boaz and Ruth married, and were happy together, because they both served God, and His blessing was upon them.

Dear children, the best part of this story is now to be told. Boaz and Ruth had a little son named Obed; Obed was the father of Jesse, and Jesse was the father of David, and Jesus Christ was called the Son of David, according to the flesh. So Jesus can be traced back in his history as springing from Ruth. And thus, by leaving her wicked people and not going back with Orpah, and resolving on living with Naomi among the true children of God, Ruth had the honor of being one of the line from which should spring that glorious Saviour, in whom all nations should be blessed.

SAYINGS OF CHILDHOOD:—Said a little child, "Mamma, I wish you had named me Ruth." "Why, my dear?" asked the mother. "*Because I love Jesus, and His friends.*" That child had gotten the right idea of the story about Ruth. But, dear little ones, you all may be like Ruth, though your names be different. You can all love Jesus, and do as He says.

LITTLE SAMUEL.

I AM sure you will be glad to have me talk about little Samuel. He was indeed a good and happy child. The meaning of his name is, "Asked of God." His mother, whose name was Hannah, had no children, and she prayed very earnestly to God for a son; and she promised that if she had one, she would lend him to the Lord all the days of his life. At last God granted her prayer, and gave her a little son, and she named him Samuel. Hannah sang a psalm to God in her joy; she was so thankful to her Heavenly father for her dear little boy.

And now Hannah remembered her promise to lend him to the Lord all his life; and she kept her promise. When he was only four years old, she brought Samuel to Eli, the high priest, at Shiloh, and gave him to wait upon the Lord. What! was she tired of him? No, indeed; but she wants him brought up to learn the service of God's house. He ought to begin while he was little; so she will leave him now, that this good man may teach him how to serve the Lord Jehovah. So Hannah bade good-bye to her little boy and returned home; but every year she came up to see him, for she lived a long way off from Shiloh; and she used to bring him a present of a little dress, made of linen, for, just like you, he would outgrow his clothes. This dress was similar to those worn by the priests. It had long sleeves, and came down to his feet, and was called an "ephod."

And so Samuel dwelt with Eli; he grew in favor with God and man—God loved him, and all his friends loved him too. Though very young, we are told, he "ministered before the Lord." I suppose he did some little services about the altar. He could light a candle, or hold a dish, or run on an errand, or shut a door; and, because he did this with a pious disposition of mind, it is called, *ministering to the Lord*, and great notice is taken of it.

Eli had two sons; they were not little boys, like Samuel, but grown up; and they were priests in the house of the Lord at Shiloh. God's priests ought to be very good and holy men; but Hophni and Phinehas, Eli's sons, behaved very badly; they did not love nor obey God. Eli loved his God, and in many ways served him truly; but he over indulged his own children. When they did evil in their childhood, their father was too fond of them to correct or punish them as he ought to have done; and as they grew older, they grew more and more wicked, and disobeyed the commands of God and their kind parent—they cared for nothing but good eating and drinking, and their own pleasures and amusements; and thus they went on from bad to worse, and their father talked with them, and tried to persuade them to turn from their wicked ways, but they did not give heed to his reproofs. Eli was very unhappy when he saw his sons so self-willed and disobedient. But was he right to let them stay and be priests at Shiloh? No, Eli did very wrong; he ought to have punished them, and not let them be priests; but Eli foolishly indulged his children, and did not like to punish them.

Then God told Samuel what He would do to Eli's wicked family. Eli slept in his room near the tabernacle. Near at hand the boy Samuel had his mat spread that he might be within hearing. Eli is now very old and nearly blind, and even in the night he sometimes needs to be waited on. Samuel had been chosen to this place of trust because he could be trusted. One night, when everyone was gone to bed, Samuel heard a voice calling, "Samuel, Samuel." It was God who called; but Samuel did not know this, because God had never called him before. He thought Eli must need something; he does not make believe he does not hear, and turn over and go to sleep again, but he answered quickly, "Here am I," and he jumped up and ran to Eli to know what he wanted. But Eli told him he did not call him, and to go back, and go to sleep again. And the kind little boy obeyed Eli, and went and lay down; but soon the voice called the second time, "Samuel." He ran to Eli, and said, "Here am I, for thou didst call me." And Eli answered, "I called not, my son; lie down again." Samuel obeyed; he did not ask questions, although he wondered who had called him; he went back to his bed again, and there, the third time, he heard the call, "Samuel." Was not Samuel tired of running to Eli? No, he went again to him at once; and when Eli saw him coming to him again, he began to think it was God Himself who had called Samuel, and that He had something to say to the child. So Eli told him when he heard it again, to answer, "Speak, Lord, for Thy servant heareth." So Samuel went back, and lay down; again the fourth time the voice called, "Samuel." Then the boy arose, and looked up humbly to Heaven, and said, "Speak, for Thy servant heareth;" and the Lord told him He was going to punish Eli for the wrong-doing of his two sons. Samuel did not like to tell Eli what the Lord had said to him. In the morning, he did not go near the old man, but went about his business, and began to open the doors round about the tabernacle. This was a part of his duty. But the old priest saw Samuel looking very sad; and he called him, and said, "My son, what did God tell thee last night? Do not fear to speak; I wish to know the truth; tell me all." Then Samuel remembered that it was very wrong to say what is untrue; so he told Eli all that God had said. Eli was too good a man to be angry with him, and only said, "It is the Lord; let Him do what seemeth Him good."

LITTLE SAMUEL.

Dear little ones, how would you like to have been in Samuel's place that wonderful night? Would you like to have God call you? Well He does; He knows your name, and where you live, and calls you. He does not call by His voice as He did in those days; and yet the Lord speaks oftener and plainer now than then. You need not think it must be something strange and startling, like a voice out of the sky. He speaks, perhaps, in the twilight when mamma is telling you some dear old Bible story; or in the late evening when you wake and find she is praying by your bed; or in church when the pastor says some tender, loving words about Jesus; or in the Sunday-school when the lesson just seems to fit into what you need. He calls by the little voice which whispers in your heart, and tells you that you are naughty. Do you want to be like Samuel? Then you must take great care to attend to that voice; or it will leave off, and then you shall get worse and worse, like those bad sons of poor old Eli.

Here is the story of Samuel's call in verse:

> "Hushed was the evening hymn,
>   The temple courts were dark,
> The lamp was burning dim
>   Before the sacred ark,
> When suddenly the voice divine
> Rang through the silence of the shrine.
>
> "The old man, meek and mild,
>   The priest of Israel, slept;
> His watch the temple child,
>   The little Levite, kept;
> And what from Eli's sense was sealed
> The Lord to Hannah's son revealed.
>
> "Oh, give me Samuel's ear,
>   The open ear, O Lord;
> Alive and quick to hear
>   Each whisper of Thy word:
> Like him, to answer at Thy call,
> And to obey Thee first of all.
>
> "Oh, give me Samuel's heart!
>   A lowly heart that waits
> Where in Thy house thou art,
>   Or watches at Thy gates!
> By day and night, a heart that still
> Moves at the breathing of Thy will.
>
> "Oh, give me Samuel's mind!
>   A sweet unmurmuring faith,
> Obedient and resigned
>   To Thee in life and death.
> That I may read with childlike eyes
> Truths that are hidden from the wise."

LITTLE SAMUEL.

You remember dear children, that God gave Samuel a message to Eli, warning him about his sons. It was twenty years after the message was given to Samuel before the punishment of both father and sons came to pass. In that time the sons might have repented, and still have been saved; but instead of that they grew more and more wicked. God permitted the Philistines to make war against the Israelites. Then the Israelites fancied that if they took the ark of the covenant out into the battle with them they would get the victory, as they had done when Joshua conquered the land. God had said that the ark of the Lord, which was kept in the tabernacle, must never be removed. But Hophni and Phinehas, Eli's wicked sons, did not obey God; they brought it into battle, and all the people shouted for joy when they saw it. When the Philistines heard the shout, they said that the gods of Israel were come, and that they must fight all the more bravely. And they did. God would not help His people because of their self-will, so He let them be beaten, and Hophni and Phinehas were killed and the holy ark was taken by these heathens. And when poor old Eli heard the sad news, he was so much shocked, that he fell down backwards and broke his neck and died.

But the ark of God brought great troubles to the Philistines. When they put it into the temple of one of their false gods the idol fell down and was broken, and wherever it was taken the people fell sick, till at last they said they would send the ark home, for they saw that the God of Israel was stronger than they, and they could not resist His power. So they made a new cart, and put the ark into it; two kine to draw the cart. They took the right road to go to the land of Israel; they did not stand still, but went straight on, without turning to the right or left.

It is this

"RETURN OF THE ARK,"

that the artist has illustrated in the picture. The people of Bethshemesh were busy reaping their wheat in the valley, for it was harvest time. They heard something coming, and looked up, to see what it was. And when they saw the ark of God, which they had lost so long, they rejoiced very much. The cart came close to them, and the kine stood still; and the Levites took out the ark, and put it upon a large stone. Then they cut up the cart for wood, and offered the kine in joyful sacrifice to the God who had sent them His holy ark again. The lords of the Philistines, who had followed the cart, saw all this and wondered, and returned to their own country.

SAUL AND DAVID.

SAUL was the first king of Israel. He began his reign well, but soon he became tired of doing right. His heart had not been made new by the Holy Spirit; so he did not pray for help to rule his people rightly. He was proud, and rebellious, and disobedient. He had forsaken God, and God had forsaken him. How sad it is to begin rightly like Saul, and soon to grow weary of well doing, and forget God, and love the world, and Satan, and sin, better than holy things! When God went away from Saul, Satan came to him; he made him every day more and more rebellious, and passionate, and cruel. He was often like a madman, so wild and angry. Saul's servants were sorry to see their master unhappy; and so they counselled Saul to seek some one who played well upon the harp, that, when the evil spirit troubled him, the music of it might solace him and give rest to his soul.

None could be found who played so well upon this instrument as David, who also possessed such an agreeable person, that Saul loved him greatly, and made him his armor-bearer. Every time that the evil spirit was upon Saul, David chased it away with his harp. But David's music could not change Saul's heart. God alone has power to do that.

One day, when the Israelites and Philistines were at war, the commander of the Philistines, named Goliath, came out and challenged any one of the Israelites to fight with him. This giant was nine feet nine inches high, or half as high again as any one you know; his spear was eighteen feet long so that if three of the tallest men you know stood one above another, they would only be as high as this great, bad fighter's spear was long; and he had a helmet on his head, and armor on his breast, and a man carried a shield before him. Now God put it into the heart of the young shepherd boy, David, to go forth and meet this strong giant. David, however, took only a sling, and a few stones in his hand; and, while the huge giant was threatening to kill David, and give his flesh to the fowls of the air, David put a stone into his sling, and let it fly; and the stone hit the giant on the forehead, and sank into his head, so that Goliath fell dead upon the ground. Then David cut off the head of the giant, and the terrified Philistines fled.

Now it came to pass, after the battle and the victory, when Saul and all his people were going home, the women came out to meet them; and they sang, and played, and

SAUL AND DAVID.

danced, and shouted for joy. They sang, "Saul has slain his thousands, but David his ten thousands." This made king Saul very angry. He thought they gave more honor to David than to him. Saul became very jealous of David. The next day, the evil spirit came into Saul again; and David took his harp and began to play, and tried to quiet him. But David's harp did not take away Saul's passion now. Saul had a javelin in his hand, and he cast the javelin at David, " for he said, I will smite David even to the wall with it." In the picture you see the beautiful figure of David, who, with harp in hand, is shrinking to the wall to avoid the king's javelin. See what terror there is on his youthful countenance, and what passionate rage in the king's. But God preserved David's life.

David married Michal, Saul's daughter, and she loved him; but Saul hated him more and more, and tried again to kill him, and commanded Jonathan, his son, and all his servants to put David to death. Then Jonathan proved a dear, good friend to David. He went to his father and persuaded him not to hurt David. So David was permitted to go into Saul's presence as before. Soon after this, however, there was war again, and David triumphed gloriously, and Saul was again jealous of him; his evil spirit returned, and David, as before, played his harp to amuse him; and again Saul flung his javelin furiously at him, so that it stuck in the wall, but God preserved David, and he slipped away without receiving any harm.

Saul now resolved that David should escape no more, and so he sent messengers to lie in wait for him at his own house. Michal, his wife, saw what was going on, and she advised David to escape, and as they guarded the doors, she "let David down through a window; and he went and fled and escaped." Our next picture shows

"MICHAL LETTING DAVID DOWN FROM THE WINDOW."

SAYINGS OF CHILDHOOD:—Willie Jones was often called "*Wilful Will*," because he wanted his own way so much. He was always saying, "Give me this," "I *will* have that," and, "I don't see why," and even "I ought to know best what I need." At last his mother said she would let him have his own way for a week. He thought he was going to be perfectly happy. But I cannot tell you now of all the troubles that having his own way led to; and how his mother would neither advise nor help him, telling him that it was his own way, and not hers, he wanted, and so he must have it. But long before the week was over he saw how foolish, as well as wicked, he was, and was glad to take his mother's wiser way. So, I think, dear children, Saul might be called "Wilful Saul;" but he never repented.

DAVID SPARING SAUL.

DAVID, after he had made his escape from Saul, wandered about from place to place. But while he was roaming about in fear of Saul, he was not alone. Many men came to him to help him; and he was their captain, and they obeyed him. It was a sad life, however; but David trusted in God, and was peaceful and happy. He wrote many beautiful psalms when he was wandering and hiding in those wild places.

Where was Jonathan? Did he ever see his friend David again? Yes, Jonathan had not forgotten him; and when he heard where David was, he went to see him secretly in the wood. David and Jonathan were very glad to meet again, and they had much to say to one another. Jonathan comforted David in the right way; he told him to trust in God.

But Saul and his soldiers went into the wilderness and wandered all about among the rocks, trying to find David. But God still kept David in safety. At last Saul came to a cave, and went into it to rest; for he was tired. This cave was a very large one, for there are caves in that part which, though very dark, are yet roomy enough to hold many thousand men. And here Saul laid down to rest, and was soon asleep. But who should be in this cave but David and his men, who, while they were concealed in the farthest part, could see Saul come in at the mouth, it being light there, while they at the farthest end were all in the dark. David's men were rejoiced, and advised their master at once to kill Saul; but David refused to lay his hand on "the anointed of the Lord." And so he only went quietly up to where he was stretched upon the ground; Saul had no power to kill David, but David could kill him if he liked. But did he kill Saul? No; David had no angry feelings in his heart; but he quietly cut off a piece of Saul's robe.

When Saul awoke, he arose to go away. He did not know what David had done; but David now boldly followed him and cried out, and said to him, "My lord, the king!" Saul turned round; and David bowed respectfully to him, and, holding up the fragment of the king's garment, he said to him: "My father, see, yea, see the skirt of thy robe in my hand; for in that I cut off the skirt of thy robe and killed thee not, know thou and see that there is neither evil nor transgression in mine hand, and I have not sinned against thee; yet thou huntest my soul to take it." In the picture you see Saul high

up on the cliff, while David stands in the open valley below, in full view of the army of Saul, holding up the skirt of the king's garment. Then Saul began to weep, and said, "Is it thy voice, my son David?" Why did Saul weep? Because he felt how unkind he had been to David, and how gentle and merciful David had been to him. Saul said, "Thou hast been more righteous than I. Thou hast rewarded me good, though I rewarded thee evil." Then Saul asked David to spare his family after his death; for Saul knew that God would give David the kingdom. David promised this, and Saul went home; and David's kindness made Saul kind for a little time.

SAYINGS OF CHILDHOOD:— A little girl one day went to her mother to show some fruit that had been given her. "Your friend," said the mother, "has been very kind." "Yes," said the child, "She gave me more than these; but I have given some away." The mother asked to whom she had given them; when she answered, "I gave them to a girl who pushes me off the path, and makes faces at me." On being asked why she gave them to her, she replied, "Because I thought it would make her know that I wish to be kind to her, and she will not, perhaps, be rude and unkind to me again." The Bible says, "Love your enemies." When people are unkind to us, like David, we must try to be kind and forgiving to them.

THE DEATH OF SAUL.

THE end of Saul was very sad. You remember that he wanted his own way, and would not do as God told him. Then God forsook him, and left him to grow worse and worse. Then his enemies, the Philistines, came up against him. The Philistines conquered in battle. They followed close after Saul and his sons. They killed three of Saul's sons; one of them was Jonathan, David's friend. Saul was hit by an arrow and wounded. He saw that he could not get away, and he feared that if the enemy took him they would abuse him; and so he did the saddest thing of all—he threw himself on his own sword, that they might not take him alive. In the picture you see Saul fallen from his horse, and his sword piercing his body. He did not quite kill himself; and when a young robber came by, trying to get garments and weapons from the dead bodies, the unhappy king begged for a death-blow as he lay. The robber gave him the last stroke, and then took the crown from his helmet, and his bracelets, and brought

them to David to show that he was dead. The robber thought that he should have a reward, but David put him to death for having dared to strike the king.

Was David pleased when he heard his enemy was dead? No; he wept for Saul, and for his dear friend Jonathan. David mourned very much for Jonathan, and wrote a beautiful song of lamentation for him, for he could not forget Jonathan's love and kindness.

Then, when Saul was killed, David was anointed to be king; and he was a very good man, and served God with all his heart. So God blessed him, and made him great and powerful.

SAYINGS OF CHILDHOOD:—A little friend asks me, "Was Saul saved? Did his soul go to heaven?" Dear children, I am sorry I must say *no*. He murdered himself. He died in his sin; and there was, therefore, no hope that his soul could be saved; self-murderers have no time to ask for pardon.

THE DEATH OF ABSALOM.

DAVID had many sons; and some of them were very wicked. One was named Absalom. He was greatly admired among the Israelites for his beauty. "From the sole of his foot to the crown of his head, there was no blemish in him." Especially was he distinguished for his beautiful hair, which grew so luxuriantly that when at the end of the year he was shorn, its weight was equal to two hundred shekels of silver. But he was fierce and proud, and wanted to be king. Absalom was a bad man. God did not look at his beauty; God looks at people's hearts, not at their persons. He does not care for beauty; He wants holiness, and love, and gentleness, and humility; and Absalom had none of these.

And when David was old, Absalom's ambition led him to plot against the king his father and to conspire with his enemies for his overthrow. He set himself diligently to work in various ways to win over the people to himself, affectionately embracing all who came to salute him, and saying to those who came to the king for judgment, "O that I were made judge in the land, that every man which hath any suit or cause might come to me, and I would do him justice." Thereby he won their hearts away from David to himself. When he had thus gathered around him a sufficient number, he proceeded to Hebron—first obtaining his father's permission, under the pretense that he wished to pay a vow unto the Lord—and was there proclaimed king.

THE DEATH OF ABSALOM.

When the news was brought to David by a messenger that the hearts of the men of Israel were with Absalom, he fled in haste from Jerusalem; weeping and barefoot, down the steep rocky pass he fled for fear of his wicked son; and cruel men called him names, and threw stones at him as he went, while Absalom was made to reign in his father's palace, and did all he pleased there. Afterwards he set out with a large army in pursuit of his father, following him across the Jordan. David gathered together his devoted people, and wished to lead them to battle himself; but they would not let him. So David sent forth his army under three trusted leaders, after charging them to deal gently with Absalom, whom he greatly loved. There was a great battle in the wood of Ephraim; Absalom was beaten, and fled away on a mule. But as he went through the wood, his long hair caught in the branches of an oak, and he could not get it loose; and his mule went away, and left him hanging in the tree. One of David's soldiers saw Absalom hanging, but the man did not hurt him, because he remembered David's command; but he told Joab, and Joab took three darts, and went to the tree where Absalom hung, and smote him, and killed him. So the battle was ended, and David's soldiers had the victory.

In the engraving the fate of Absalom is strikingly portrayed. From one of the branches of the wide-spreading oak we behold the wretched victim hanging; Joab and his followers, mounted on swift horses, are seen galloping towards him.

But what of David? When he heard the sad news of Absalom's death he was grieved to the heart. No words can say how sad he was to think that his son had died in his sins, and never asked his pardon. He arose directly and went to his own room, for he wished to be alone; and as he went up, he cried very, very sorrowfully, "O my son Absalom, my son, my son Absalom! would God I had died for thee, O Absalom, my son, my son!" His mourning is most strikingly pictured in the next illustration,

"DAVID MOURNING FOR ABSALOM."

SAYINGS OF CHILDHOOD:—A boy was coaxed by some others to pick some cherries from a tree which his father had forbidden him to touch. "You need not be afraid," said they; "for even if your father finds out you have taken them, he is so kind he will not hurt you." "That is the very reason why I should not touch them," replied the boy. "My disobedience would hurt my father, and that would be worse to me than anything else." O what a delight such a boy is to a father's heart! Absalom knew what was right. His father had taught him what he ought to do. But Absalom had not attended. God is angry with those children who will not attend to their parents' holy lessons.

SOLOMON.

DAVID died when he was about seventy years of age, and left his kingdom, and much good advice, to his son Solomon, who was the wisest among all the kings who reigned over Israel. Our first engraving is a picture of this patriarchal man, now in his old age. God was pleased with Solomon, because he cared for wisdom most and asked not for riches, or long life, or to put down his enemies; therefore, besides wisdom, God gave him all the rest—riches, and honor, and length of life; He promised him that he should be wiser, and greater, and richer, than any king ever was before him, or should be after him.

All this was because he had cared so much to have a wise and understanding heart to know good and evil. That was first with him, and so God gave him all the rest. So it will be with all who seek first of all to be good. Do you ask, Will God give us holy wisdom, as he did Solomon? Yes, St. James says, "If any of you lack wisdom, let him ask of God, and it shall be given him." The best wisdom is the knowledge of God and of Jesus Christ, and of the way to heaven. "The fear of the Lord, that is wisdom, and to depart from evil is understanding." This is better than all the riches of the world. It will make us happy now, and forever.

One of the wise judgments of Solomon has been recorded for our instruction. One day when he sat on his throne two women came to him: one with a live baby, the other with a dead one, both boys, and just of the same age. The women were angry, and quarreling with each other. One of them said, "O king, this woman and I dwelt in the same house, and each of us had a babe three days old. In the night, her child died; and she rose at midnight, while I was asleep, and took away my living child, and laid her dead child in my arms." And the other woman cried angrily, "The living child is

mine." So they spoke before the king. It was sad to see them so angry and passionate, but what could Solomon do? How was it to be known which was right?—for nobody out of the house knew the two little ones apart, and each of the women declared that she was the mother of the live child, not of the dead.

But Solomon's wonderful wisdom helped him to judge rightly; he knew that the real mother of the living child would not allow any harm to come to her child; so he said, "Bring me a sword," and they brought a sword. Then Solomon said, "Divide the living child in two, and give half to one woman, and half to the other." Was Solomon cruel? No; he wanted to know who was the right mother, and he knew she would cry to have it saved. And he thought rightly. For the woman to whom the child belonged cried out in grief and dread, "O my lord, give her the living child, and in nowise slay it!" But the other woman, said, "Yes, let it be divided;" for she did not care much for the baby because it was not her own child. Then Solomon saw in a moment which woman was full of mother's love, and which was full of hatred and jealousy; so he said, "Give *her* the living child, and in nowise slay it, she is the mother thereof." And so the true loving mother had her child safe and well; and all the people wondered at Solomon's wisdom. In our next picture,

"THE JUDGMENT OF SOLOMON,"

you see the scene portrayed. There stands Solomon on his throne, and the cruel executioner with the living child in one hand, and his drawn sword in the other. The appealing agony of the true mother is seen as she flings herself at the executioner's feet and begs him not to kill the child; the indifference of the other woman is seen as she stands close by.

SAYINGS OF CHILDHOOD:—I want that you shall get the *wisdom* that cometh from heaven. A noble youth once rose in a large meeting where a revival of religion was in progress, and said, "*I think the best thing I can do is to become a Christian.*" Take it in its largest and fullest sense, and that youth expressed what is the best thing for us all—how we may make the best of ourselves. Have you, dear children, this wisdom?

THE CEDARS DESTINED FOR THE TEMPLE.

HE last thing David did before he died was to charge his son, Solomon, to build the temple for the Lord God. Solomon now began to think of David's command, and prepared to build the temple.

As soon as he was fixed upon his throne, Hiram, king of Tyre, sent ambassadors to him, to congratulate him on his peace and prosperity. Solomon took the opportunity of sending a letter back by the ambassadors, to inform him that he intended to build a temple for the worship of God. There were very fine cedar trees, a most desirable wood for building, which grew on that part of Lebanon belonging to Hiram, and Solomon asked that he would have such a quantity as he needed, felled for him; and that he would furnish Sidonian workmen, who were skilled in hewing timber, to help Solomon's servants, at such wages as Hiram should appoint.

Then Hiram sent to Solomon, saying, "I will do all thy wish, and give thee cedar trees and fir trees from the forest in Lebanon. My servants shall cut them down, and bring them to the sea; and I will send them by sea to the place thou shalt choose." This was a very important point gained towards building the temple, for the Israelites were mostly employed in agriculture, and knew little about the art of fine building, or even of hewing down trees. Then Solomon began the work at once. He sent many of his servants to Lebanon, to help Hiram's servants to cut down the trees. Then all the wood was carried to the sea, and floated down to Joppa. In the picture before us, you see the groups of busy workmen engaged in the work of felling and removing these magnificent trees to their floats by the sea shore. Two immense cedars, on heavy, cumbrous wheels, are being conveyed down the mountain side, and the straining labor

and bustle and anxiety incident to their starting are fully brought out in the engraving. At Joppa, Solomon sent his people to take the wood, and bring it safely to Jerusalem. Hiram and Solomon were great friends, and they helped one another to work for God's service and glory.

Solomon paid Hiram for his trees and workmen's wages, by giving him what was needed in his country, where, though the people were skilled in growing and working timber, they did not so well understand how to grow the fruits of the earth. "And Solomon gave Hiram twenty thousand measures of wheat for food to his household, and twenty measures of pure oil; thus Solomon gave Hiram year by year." These measures are not of the same sort as ours, but have been carefully reckoned, and amount to twelve millions nine hundred and sixty thousand pounds of wheat, and twenty-one thousand six hundred pounds of oil; so that Hiram was very well paid, and this pay was given every year, as long as the temple was in building, and some think afterwards continued as long as Hiram lived.

Besides the help of Hiram's men, Solomon employed thirty thousand Israelites, ten thousand of whom worked every month in turns; so that each one was one month in a quarter of a year laboring for Solomon, and two months at home looking after his own grounds and family. Also Solomon had "threescore and ten," that is, seventy thousand men, that "bore burdens," or carried stones from the mountains out of which they were dug; and "eighty thousand hewers in the mountains," that cut the stones out of the quarries, and made them into proper shapes; and he employed three thousand three hundred officers, to overlook them, and see that none were careless or idle.

The temple which Solomon built was a very grand and beautiful building. There was one very remarkable thing in the building of it. "The house, when it was in building, was built of stone made ready before it was brought thither; so that there was neither hammer nor axe, nor any tool of iron heard in the house while it was in building." The joints were all made by the clever workmen, God blessing them particularly in this work with more than usual skill, so that each joint fitted exactly into the one for which it was made, and required nothing more than a wooden mallet, at most, to fit it in its place. This temple is mentioned in Scripture, as a type or likeness of heaven—that is, it was a place for serving God, and where God particularly blessed His people, and so is heaven; and this curious fact, about the stones all fitting without any more noise and labor, had its meaning, and may remind us that all those who are to be pillars in the temple of God above, must be first made fit for it.

THE CEDARS DESTINED FOR THE TEMPLE.

Solomon's servants were very industrious, and did the work very quickly; but seven years passed before the temple was finished. When the temple was finished, it exceeded in beauty all the buildings of the earth; and, on the day of dedication, when the ark was placed therein by the priests, the glory of the Lord filled the house. Solomon offered a very devout prayer to God, begging Him to hear the prayers that should be offered in the temple, and to keep off all evil, and to forgive all the faults of His people, and their shortcomings, when they cried to Him for pardon. Then God appeared to Solomon and told him that He had heard his prayer. He said, "I have blessed My house, and I will hear the prayers which My people make to Me there. And if thou wilt obey and serve Me, as David thy father did, then will I bless thee and keep thee forever. But if thou and thy people forget Me, and serve and worship idol gods, then I will forsake you. I will not then attend to your prayers. I will turn away from you and bless you no more." How happy Solomon and his people were, to have the promise of God's blessing when they were faithful to Him!

SAYINGS OF CHILDHOOD:—Said a boy, four years old, "Papa, why don't they keep our church *cleaner*? It is God's house, and it isn't as clean as our house is." I hope dear little ones, that boy will never lose his idea of the holiness of God's house. It is a holy place; God is there. We cannot see His bright glory, and the cloud which Israel saw in the temple; but we know that His Spirit is there, to bless and teach His people. And when we are in God's house, we should remember what a holy place it is.

THE QUEEN OF SHEBA'S VISIT TO SOLOMON.

KING SOLOMON was the greatest king in wisdom and riches who ever lived. After he had finished the temple, he built a beautiful house for himself—it was lined with cedar-wood. His ships used to go every year to distant countries, and bring back gold, and silver, and ivory, and apes, and peacocks; and it was said that gold was as common as silver generally is, and silver as common as stones! And the fame of Solomon's temple, and of his house, his riches, and his wisdom, went over all the earth. People came from the most distant lands to Jerusalem to see the king, and to hear his wisdom. The queen of Sheba traveled from her far-off country to see him, because of the fame of his greatness. And, according to a very common custom of the East, she prepared a number of difficult questions and riddles to put to Solomon, that she might find out whether he was so wise as report stated him to be.

When she was come to Solomon, he gave her a royal welcome. In the engraving we see the queen coming into the presence of the king; just behind her are servants, carrying the presents she has for the king. Then the queen asked him many questions, and he answered them all. And when she saw "all Solomon's wisdom" "and the house that he had built," she was so astonished and overcome that, for a time, she was utterly unable to speak; finally she said to the king, that all she had heard was not half so grand and glorious as what she saw. Very happy, said she, were the people who stood round him and heard the words of his wisdom. Then the queen blessed and praised Solomon's God, and Solomon gave her everything she wished, and she and her servants returned to their own country.

It gives me pain, dear children, in closing this talk, to tell you that as Solomon grew old he left off being good. He turned away from the true God, and began to worship the idols which his wicked wives worshipped. You wonder how so wise a man could do this! It was because he was, like ourselves, weak and sinful. All his strength and goodness came from God; and when Solomon forgot God, then God's Holy Spirit left him. Was he happy now? No; he went about from place to place, crying, "Vanity! vanity! all is vanity and vexation of spirit." And why was this? Because he had not God's smile to make him happy now. And Solomon died, after he had reigned forty years over Israel.

THE PROPHET OF BETHEL.

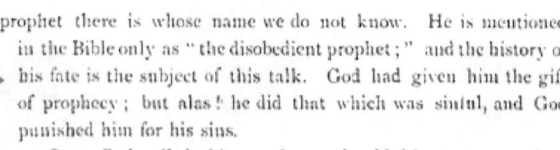

ONE prophet there is whose name we do not know. He is mentioned in the Bible only as "the disobedient prophet;" and the history of his fate is the subject of this talk. God had given him the gift of prophecy; but alas! he did that which was sinful, and God punished him for his sins.

Once God called this prophet, and told him to go to a place named Bethel, where the wicked king of Israel, Jeroboam, had set up a golden calf, and was teaching the people to pray to it. He was to tell the king of his sin, and how his idol should be overthrown and destroyed; and when he had done this, he was to come home at once, by a different way, and neither eat bread nor drink water, but come quickly back.

The prophet went to Bethel and he spoke God's word to the king boldly; then Jeroboam, in great anger, put out his hand to seize hold of the prophet, but behold, the hand of the king was withered up in an instant. God smote Jeroboam, to punish him for his wickedness in trying to hurt His servant. Jeroboam was greatly alarmed, and very penitent for his sin; and he humbly said to the prophet, "Ask God to forgive me, and to make my hand well again." So the prophet prayed and the hand of the king was restored to him again.

Then Jeroboam wanted the prophet to come to his palace with him. But the prophet said no; for God had charged him to go home at once, without eating or drinking in that wicked place. So he returned home by a different road, and thus far all was well. But before he had gone all the way he grew tired, and sat down under an oak. There met him by the way an old man who lived at Bethel, who was a prophet too, but he was not a good man. This old man told the prophet that God had told him to bring the man of God back to his house, and there to provide him with bread and water. And I am sorry to say the prophet listened, and turned back.

While he sat at the table with this stranger, there came a message from God, saying that the man who had disobeyed the Lord should not be buried in the sepulchre of his fathers. And when he went back in the evening, a lion came out of the wood and killed him. The lion did not kill the ass he rode upon, nor tear the body, but in the picture you see the lion and ass both standing by the dead prophet till the bad prophet found his body. This was the punishment of disobedience.

ELIJAH RAISES THE WIDOW'S SON.

THE Bible tells us many wonderful and beautiful stories about the prophet Elijah. He was a very holy man, one of the greatest and wisest among all the prophets of Israel. He lived in the days of Ahab, a very wicked king, who worshipped idols, and one idol in particular, called Baal; and on account of this idolatry, God sent many troubles upon Ahab and his people. One of these trials was a sore famine.

But, in the midst of this famine, God took care of Elijah. He sent him to a lonely place, by the side of a little mountain stream, where there still was water to drink. But who gave him his daily food? God sent it to him in a very wonderful way. Every morning and evening two ravens came to Elijah. One carried flesh in its beak; another carried bread. The ravens did not eat the food themselves. They brought it to Elijah; that was a wonderful miracle which God worked to feed His prophet.

After a while, the little brook dried up, and Elijah had no more water to drink. Then God told him to go to a town called Zarephath. Was there any kind friend there? Yes; God said, " Behold, I have commanded a widow woman there to sustain thee." So Elijah obeyed the voice of the Lord. And when he came to the gate of Zarephath, he saw a poor woman gathering sticks. She was pale and feeble, for she had suffered much in the famine, and she looked as if she must soon die. The good prophet knew she was the right person, and he called to her, and said, " Fetch me I pray thee, a little water in a vessel, that I may drink;" and as she was going to fetch it, he called to her and said, " Bring me, I pray thee, a morsel of bread in thine hand." And she said, "As the Lord thy God liveth, I have not a cake, but only a handful of meal in a barrel, and a little oil in a cruse; and she went on to say that she was gathering sticks to bake a cake of this for herself and her son, and when that was done they must die of hunger. But Elijah told her not to fear, but to make him a little cake first, and he said, " Thus saith the Lord God of Israel, the barrel of meal shall not waste, neither shall the cruse of oil fail, until the day that the Lord sendeth rain upon the earth." And the woman believed him and gave him a bit of her last cake. And it was as Elijah had said. There was always meal and oil enough to feed them day by day —for God fed them.

After a time, however, God sent a new sorrow into the poor woman's little family. The widow's little boy fell sick and died. She thought God had done this to punish her

for her sins, and she ran to tell the prophet of her woe. Then Elijah took the dead boy out of his mother's arms, and carried him into his own room, and there prayed earnestly to God that the child might live again. And the Lord heard the voice of Elijah, and the little child's soul came back and he was alive again. Then Elijah gave him to his mother, and said, "See, thy son liveth." The widow was happy now. In our picture you can see how happy she is as she receives her boy into her arms again. And the woman said to Elijah, "Now by this I know that thou art a man of God, and that the word of the Lord in thy mouth is truth."

SAYINGS OF CHILDHOOD:—Dear children, all this shows us how great is the power of prayer, and how infinitely greater is the power of Him who listens to it. I once knew of a homeless little girl whom a lady had taken and provided for. Hard times came, and the lady thought she must give her up. "No," said she, "God will give you something so you can keep me—I know He will." In a little while she was heard up stairs praying: "O! God, do send mother something, so she can keep me, I don't want to go away. O! good Lord, send mother something soon." She came down saying, "God will send you something; I know He will." In the evening a sack of flour was left at the door. "There," said she, "I asked Him to send something, and I knew He would." My dear children, I hope you have such faith as that! The God who sent the ravens to feed Elijah is your God!

ELIJAH CONFOUNDS THE PROPHETS OF BAAL.

AFTER Elijah had hid himself from Ahab for three years, God ordered him to go to him again. Ahab, with Obadiah, the governor of his house, was searching through the land for water and grass for their horses, when they met Elijah. Obadiah was a good man, and he was glad when he saw Elijah; but Ahab hated Elijah, and demanded of him with much bitterness, "Art thou he that troubleth Israel?" Elijah told Ahab that the cause of the troubles was because Ahab and his people were worshippers of Baal; then Elijah told the king to call all the priests of Baal to Mount Carmel, and said he, "Let us see who is the true God." So Ahab and all his wicked prophets came to Carmel—four hundred and fifty of them; Elijah was there too, and very many of the people of Israel.

Then Elijah spoke to the people, and said, "Choose now this day whom ye will

ELIJAH CONFOUNDS THE PROPHETS OF BAAL.

serve. If Baal be the true God, serve Baal; but if God be the Lord, then follow him." The people made no answer. Then Elijah said, "We will try now, and see who is the true God." He said he would build one altar, and that the four hundred prophets should build another; they should each offer a sacrifice, and each should pray to his God, and the God that sent fire to burn the sacrifice would be the true God. This was agreed to The prophets of Baal tried first. They built their altar, and put wood on it, and killed a bullock and cut it up, and they prayed to their god Baal to send fire down. But though they cried aloud, and leaped about, and cut themselves with knives, till they were all covered with blood, no answer came. Baal was no good—he could do nothing—there was no fire, no answer, no voice.

When it was evening, and they were all tired waiting, Elijah made his sacrifice And he did a very strange thing; after he had prepared an altar of stones, and placed upon it the wood and the bullock which he had cut up, he poured water all over it; he even made a trench round, and filled that with water too. Then he prayed to his God, the Lord God of Israel. And did Elijah's God hear? Yes, the fire came from heaven and burnt up the sacrifice and the wood; it was not stopped by the water! No, it dried that up in a moment; and all the people saw it and cried aloud, "The Lord, He is the God; the Lord, He is the God!"

Then Elijah commanded that all the wicked prophets should be taken; and he brought them to the brook Kishon, and he killed them there. In the engraving you see the prophets of Baal being slain. It was sad to put all these wicked men to death; but it was God's command.

ELIJAH NOURISHED BY AN ANGEL.

NOW the famine was over. Although all the people were thankful Jezebel, the wicked wife of Ahab, sought to kill Elijah. She was a heathen woman, and she would still worship Baal, and did not choose to believe in the true God; and she said, "I will kill Elijah: to-morrow he shall be dead, as my prophets of Baal are." When Elijah heard this, he arose, and escaped to Beersheba, and went alone into the wilderness, and sat down under a juniper tree; and there he was so sad, to think that all he had done was of no use, that he requested for himself that he might die, for he could do no more good with these wicked people.

Was this right? No; Elijah forgot that God could comfort him, and take care of him still. There was much for Elijah to do; it was not God's will that he should die yet; and, therefore, he was to wait patiently. Then Elijah fell asleep, for he was so tired and sorrowful; and as he slept, an angel came to him and touched him, and said, "Arise, and eat." And Elijah looked, and behold there was a cake baken on the coals, or hot stones, after the custom of the East, and a cruse of water at his head. Who had brought them? God, who before had sent the ravens to feed him. How kind was God to His prophet! And Elijah did eat and drink, and laid himself down again. Soon the angel touched him the second time, and said, "Arise, and eat," for the journey was too great for him. It was a great journey, for he was to go all the way to the mount of God, where God had spoken to Moses.

Elijah obeyed; and now he felt strong and ready for his journey. He went to Horeb, and was there forty days and forty nights. He ate nothing all that time, but he did not want food, for God kept him without it. When Moses was in the mountains, he lived forty days without food too. And there Elijah hid himself in a cave; and a voice came, and asked, "What doest thou here, Elijah? Then he told how the Israelites had forsaken their God, and killed the prophets, and "I, even I only, am left," he said; "And they seek my life to take it away." Then God showed him wonders. First there was a great wind. The wind tore the mountains and broke the rocks to pieces; but God was not in the wind. Then there was an earthquake that shook the mountain; but God was not in the earthquake. After the earthquake a fire. It burnt up all the trees and grass; but God was not in the fire. And after the fire a still small voice; it was the voice of God. Then Elijah wrapped his face in his mantle, and stood in the mouth of the cave, to hear what God would say to him. And God told him he was not alone; that he must not think he was alone, because he could not see the friends that were his; and God sent him back to return to his work among the people of Israel.

ELIJAH CAUSES FIRE FROM HEAVEN TO DESTROY THE SOLDIERS OF AHAZIAH.

AHAZIAH succeeded his father Ahab, as king over Israel, and, like his father, he was a very wicked man. He was not taught to love God when he was young.

Ahaziah did not reign many years, and the end of his life was very sad. He "fell down through a lattice in his upper chamber, that was in Samaria, and was sick." Now we may see what kind of a man he was, for, instead of asking God to cure him, or to bless the means used for his cure," he sent messengers, and said unto them, go, inquire of Baal-zebub, the God of Ekron, whether I shall recover of this disease."

While the king's messengers were going to Ekron, God sent an angel to Elijah, the prophet, to tell him to go and meet them; and to say to them, "Go, and tell Ahaziah that he shall not recover from his illness, but shall surely die." The messengers quickly returned and told their master. Then the king said, "Who is the man who sends me this message?" The servants said, "We do not know his name; he is a hairy man, and he wears a leathern girdle." Then the king said, "It is Elijah the Tishbite."

Now Ahaziah was very angry, for he hated Elijah as much as his father Ahab had done; so the king sent a captain with fifty soldiers to go and take Elijah prisoner. When they came within call of him, Elijah was sitting on the top of a hill, and they spoke in a ridiculing way to him, and sneered at him as a man of God, and said, "Thou man of God, the king hath said, come down." This was not the way to speak to one of God's messengers, especially to a prophet like Elijah. So God sent fire down from heaven, and it burnt the captain and his fifty soldiers. All died; not one escaped to tell the king. This was done, not in anger, because they had insulted *him;* but because they insulted *God*.

Then Ahaziah sent another captain, and fifty soldiers more. And Elijah called down fire again, and they were all destroyed. The wicked king was still determined to take Elijah; so he sent a third captain and fifty more soldiers. But the third captain, when he saw his comrades all lying dead around, did not dare to mock, but he fell on his knees before Elijah, and entreated for mercy. Elijah spared him, and, being ordered by an angel, went down to the king, and, as soon as he saw him, he repeated to him the word of God which he had sent before by the messengers. "So Ahaziah died according to the word of the Lord which Elijah had spoken."

ELIJAH'S ASCENT IN A CHARIOT OF FIRE.

ELIJAH'S time has now come to be taken to heaven. Very peaceful and glorious was his departure. Elijah had served God many long years; he had suffered much and done much for the honor of God, and God has said, "Them that honor Me, I will honor." But Elijah did not die as other good people do; God promised that he should go to heaven without dying.

But before he was to leave this world, Elijah went out and visited all the schools where young men and boys were being trained to sing God's praise; and Elisha, who was his scholar and friend, went with him. Elijah was going to see some of his dear friends for the last time, and to bid them farewell. As they walked along Elijah and Elisha talked together. Elijah told his faithful servant, that he was going away from him soon—he was going to heaven; and that after he was gone Elisha would have to do God's messages in his place. And all the prophets, at the different schools, knew that God was going to take Elijah from the earth; but Elisha could not bear to speak or to hear about losing his dear master, still he watched and listened to all Elijah said and did.

After visiting the schools at Bethel and Jericho, they came to the river Jordan. When they came to the banks of the river, Elijah took off his mantle, and struck the water with it, and the water divided, and left a way for Elijah and Elisha to go over on dry ground. Then Elijah said, "Ask what I shall do for thee, before I be taken from thee." And Elisha said, "I pray thee, let a double portion of thy spirit be upon me." But Elijah could not give the Holy Spirit to his servant. No; for that is the gift of God alone. He could only pray to God to bestow His grace upon him. And while he was talking to him, and giving Elisha good advice, there appeared beside them horses of fire, and a chariot of fire, and Elijah was taken away from his friend, and carried up into heaven upon a whirlwind. In the engraving you have the picture of the ascent. Elisha looked up, and he saw his dear master going to heaven in joy and triumph, and he cried, "My father, my father, the chariot of Israel, and horsemen thereof." And Elijah, as he went up, threw down his mantle; and Elisha took it up and went his way.

SAYINGS OF CHILDHOOD:—Two boys were talking about Elijah's ascent in the chariot of fire. Said one, "Would'nt you be afraid to ride in such a chariot?" "No! was the reply—"*not if God drove.*"

ELISHA AND THE FAMINE IN SAMARIA.

NOW Elisha was the prophet for Israel instead of Elijah. God gave him all the wonderful power which He had before given to Elijah. And Elisha was enabled, by God's Spirit, to work many miracles for the sons of the prophets. In this talk I want to tell you about some of them.

While he was at Jericho, the people were grieving because their land was barren, and the waters were bitter; so, when Elisha heard their complaints, he said, "Bring me a cruse of salt;" and he went to the spring of the waters and threw in the salt, and said, "Thus saith the Lord, I have healed these waters; there shall be no more dry and barren land." And this was found to be true; the people now had fertile land and good, pure water. But it was not the salt that healed them; it was not Elisha's power; it was God who did the miracle.

As God gave Elijah power to help the needy, so he had also the means of punishing the wicked. Some wicked children followed him, laughing and mocking at him, and crying, "Go up, thou bald-head!" Elisha turned and looked upon them gravely, to warn them of their sin. What was their sin? Despising God's servant. It is very wicked to laugh at and make fun of holy people, and holy things. Then Elisha cursed them in the name of the Lord. He was not angry because they were disrespectful to him, but because they tried to dishonor God. And God sent two she-bears out of the woods, and tore forty-two of them to pieces.

A poor widow of one of the prophets came to Elisha in great distress, because her husband had died in debt. The person to whom the money was due, finding that she had nothing wherewith to pay him, had threatened to take both her sons for slaves. Elisha pitied this poor woman; he said, "What hast thou in the house?" She replied that she had only a pot of oil. Elisha then told her to borrow of her neighbors a great many empty vessels; and when she had done so, he told her to go home, and shut the door, and to fill as many of these vessels as she could from the pot of oil; and when she had filled them, there was still as much oil left in the pot as before. God multiplied it. And when all the vessels were filled, Elisha told her to sell the oil, and first to pay her debts, and then there would be still money to supply the wants of the family. The widow did as she was told; and now she was happy. She owed nothing, and had no more fear that her sons would be taken away from her.

Elisha was always very grateful to those who were kind to him. A good woman at Shunem always kept a room ready for him, so that he could stop and rest there whenever he pleased. She had no child, and Elisha, wishing to show his gratitude to her, asked God to give her a son. She was very happy, and thanked God for this dear child. One day the child went out into the field with his father, and he was ill, and cried to his father. "My head, my head!" and his father said, "Carry him to his mother." But she could do him no good: he sat on her knees till noon, and then died. When the poor mother saw that her little boy was dead, she carried him into Elisha's room, and laid him upon the bed; and then she went to find the prophet and tell him her grief. As soon as the good man knew what had happened, he sent his servant, Gehazi, to go before and lay his staff upon the child's face; but the child was stiff and cold. Elisha followed with the poor mother, and he went in, and prayed to God to restore the child to life. Elisha himself had no power to raise the child to life again; Elisha knew this; but God heard his prayers, and the breath came back into the body of the dead child; and he called to the woman, and said, "Take up thy son." The mother bowed herself to the ground, and gave thanks to God and His prophet.

At another time Elisha found the sons of the prophets almost starving to death, for there was a famine in the land. He told them to make some pottage, or vegetable soup, into which, by accident, one of the men put some poisonous herb, and when they came to eat it, they cried out, "There is death in the pot!" Hungry as they were, they knew that the poison would kill them. But Elisha cast some meal into it, which made it good and wholesome, and the prophets ate it without fear. It was not Elisha, nor the meal alone, that made the soup wholesome. It was God who took away the poison. Elisha had a kind friend who sent him food during the famine—twenty loaves, and some corn to make bread. But Elisha would not keep all for himself, and he fed an hundred men with a few loaves, and when they had all satisfied their hunger, some was left for another day.

One of his greatest deeds was when he cured the leprosy of Naaman, a rich captain from the land of Syria; but he would take no reward for this, and because Gehazi, his servant, told a lie to induce Naaman to give him money and garments, he was made the instrument of punishing this Gehazi, who was covetous, false, and deceitful. Although Elisha knew God would punish Gehazi in another world if he did not repent, yet he brought a dreadful punishment upon him: Gehazi was smitten with leprosy, that he might prove an example to others.

ELISHA.

One day, the sons of the prophets came and asked Elisha to let them build a dwelling-house on the banks of the Jordan; he answered, "Yes, go." And, while they were cutting down wood, the axe, which was made of iron, slipped, and fell into the water. The man was very sorry, and ran to Elisha, saying, "Alas, master!" for it was borrowed, and he was too poor to buy another. Elisha was always ready to help the poor and unfortunate. He had no money to give him, but he cut down a stick, and threw it into the water just where the heavy iron had sunk down, and the axe head rose to the top, and swam on the water like wood. Then Elisha said, "Take it up;" and the axe was soon mended. Then the poor man went thankfully to his work again. But what made the heavy iron swim? Was it the stick? No; it was God's power that did the miracle.

Soon after this, the king of Syria, having discovered that Elisha was able to reveal all his doings and his movements to Joram, the king of Israel, whom he was trying to conquer, sent, therefore, his soldiers by night to take Elisha prisoner. When Elisha's servant saw the city surrounded with soldiers and chariots, he was frightened; but Elisha said to him, "Fear not; for they that be with us are more than they that be with them." And he prayed that the young man's eyes might be opened that he might see; and so they were. And he beheld the mountain round about full of chariots of fire and horses of fire which God had placed there to protect them; and God afterwards struck the whole army of the Syrians with blindness, and in this state led them into the heart of the city, and put them before king Joram as his prisoners. You may be sure the Syrians were much alarmed when they found themselves surrounded by their enemies; but, instead of having them put to death, as Joram desired, Elisha advised the king to give them meat and drink, and let them go home to tell the wonderful story.

But when the famine grew sore in the land, the foolish king of Israel began to fancy that Elisha was the cause of the famine, for the enemies were all round the city, headed by their king. In the picture you see the terrible results of the famine—the people dying on every hand. So the king came and threatened to put Elisha to death, but Elisha had no fear; he only told the king and his followers that food should be plentiful "by this time to-morrow." One of the king's lords laughed, and said, "If the Lord should make windows in heaven, might such a thing be?" "Thou shalt see it with thine eyes," said Elisha, "but shall not eat thereof." And the next day food was plenty; and when everybody was rushing out to get food, the lord who had laughed at Elisha was knocked down and trampled to death. So Elisha's word came true.

THE ANGEL DESTROYING THE ARMY OF SENNACHERIB.

HAVE been talking to you about many very bad kings. Now I am going to tell you about a good king. Hezekiah was his name. He was a holy man; and God was pleased with him, for "he did that which was right in the sight of the Lord." "And the Lord was with him, and he prospered whithersoever he went forth."

But there came a great danger. There was a very wicked king of Assyria, named Sennacherib, and he was very ambitious, and did not like Hezekiah to enjoy his kingdom in peace. Sennacherib brought an army into his land, and ruined all his towns and villages except Jerusalem, and shut up Hezekiah in his town, so that his people did not dare to go out. And Sennacherib wrote a letter to tell Hezekiah that it was no use to hope to escape, he was coming to take away the Jews and ruin Jerusalem. And this wicked man even said that Hezekiah need not think that God would save him, for no nation had ever yet been saved by its gods, so the God of Hezekiah could not help him.

Hezekiah's people were terribly frightened. Some wanted him to get help from the king of Egypt; but no, Hezekiah knew where to go for help. Where did he go? He went into the house of the Lord, and told all his troubles to God. He took the insulting letter from Sennacherib and spread its contents before the Lord. God knew what it contained, but this was a sign that he wished to have God's direction. God heard the good king's prayer, and sent him a promise that his enemy should not even come before Jerusalem, nor shoot one arrow at it. And Hezekiah believed in God, and trusted all to Him. And was the army of Assyria destroyed? Yes; but not by Hezekiah, nor by his soldiers, nor his people. They all waited quietly that night for God to deliver them. And, in the night, God sent His angel to destroy the army of the Assyrians. The fierce soldiers of Sennacherib were all asleep in their camp; they did not care for God; they laughed at His power, and at His people. But while they slept, the destroying angel came down from heaven, and went from tent to tent, and smote all the soldiers of that large army; one hundred and eighty-five thousand were slain, without time to repent and ask for pardon! The engraving gives a picture of the destroying angel descending into the camp, and the soldiers dying on every hand.

SAYINGS OF CHILDHOOD:—"Well, the Lord knows just how to do everything, don't He?" said a little fellow, after he had heard this talk. Yes, dear children, He does! Try to do like Hezekiah. If you are vexed, or if you are afraid, tell God all about it, and ask Him to help you.

CYRUS RETURNING THE VESSELS.

DEAR children, you have heard how kind God had been to the Israelites, and how much He had done for them; how He gave them their beautiful land, and their city of Jerusalem, and blessed them whenever they were good. But when people are wicked, sadness must always follow. The Israelites would not keep to what God told them; they would worship idols and grow worse and worse, till at last God sent a great army under the king of Babylon, and Jerusalem was given up to them. The fierce soldiers came in, and burnt the houses and robbed the temple; and the people were put to live far away in a strange land at Babylon. They spent seventy years there in captivity.

Then God moved Cyrus, king of Persia and Media, to set them all at liberty. Cyrus made a proclamation, that all the captive Jews in his kingdom should return to Jerusalem, and build a temple there to the Lord their God. It was God himself who put this good thought into the heart of Cyrus, and taught him to show kindness to the people of Judah. Many years before it had been prophesied, that after seventy years' captivity, Judah should return to their own land; and now, that the right time was come, God found a way to fulfill His promise. What God says, He always does.

How rejoiced the poor captives were to hear this proclamation! Cyrus sent back the holy vessels which had been taken from Jerusalem. There were 5400 of them, all of gold and silver; and these were given to the Jews, to carry again to Judea, for the temple they were going to build there. In the first engraving, we see Cyrus returning the vessels.

Having been restored to their land, the Jews did not long delay the rebuilding of the temple; but as the length of time it would take to rear such a building was too long to

wait for publicly worshipping God, they immediately set to work and prepared the altar, and the priests offered sacrifices upon it every morning and evening. And they kept all the feasts which God had commanded them to keep, and tried in everything to obey His laws.

In about a year, all was ready to begin the temple. They had cedar trees from Lebanon, and money enough to pay the carpenters and masons; all helped in the building, and the Levites were appointed to direct the work, and to see that everything was done rightly. Then the people assembled to see the foundation laid. It was a joyful and glorious day at Jerusalem. The priests were there in their robes, and the Levites, with instruments of music, to praise the Lord. Then "they sang together, praising and giving thanks unto the Lord, because He is good, and His mercy endureth forever to Israel. And all the people shouted with a great shout, when they praised the Lord, because the foundation of the house of the Lord was laid." In the next engraving we see the work of

"REBUILDING THE TEMPLE."

But, when the foundation of the new temple was laid, there were some people in the midst of all the joy who "wept with a loud voice." Why? Were they not glad too? Yes, they were glad; but they were the old men who had returned to Jerusalem. They were so old, that they remembered the first temple which had stood there seventy years before. They had worshipped in it, and seen its beauty; now they saw it in ruins; they could never worship in it again. They might have a new temple; but not one so beautiful, nor large, nor glorious, as the temple of Solomon was; *that* was gone forever. These thoughts made the old men weep; but they wept in thankfulness, as well as in sorrow. But there were young men, who had been born in Babylon, and had never seen the first temple, and they were so glad to have a temple at all, that they shouted for joy; so there was a mixed sound of weeping for sorrow and of crying out with joy. Then God sent His prophet Haggai to tell the old men not to be afraid, for the glory of this latter house should be greater than that of the former. He meant, the Lord was to come to this temple, and fill it with His glory; the Lord did come—first as a little babe, and afterwards as a grown man. And when He was there, the honor and glory of the temple were greater than even it was before. Now there is no one temple: but God's houses are churches, and we have them everywhere to pray to Him in, and meet Him there though we cannot see Him.

ARTAXERXES ACCORDS LIBERTY TO THE ISRAELITES.

HERE was one, among the many captives who went from Babylon to their own home in Canaan, named Ezra. He was a priest, and a scribe, or writer of God's law. Ezra was a very learned man; and what is better, he was a very good man, too; he loved and served God.

After a time, Ezra went back to Babylon, to see the king, and obtain royal assistance in carrying into complete effect all the decrees of Cyrus in favor of the Jews. To show how God approved of Ezra, He gave him the greatest success at the court of Babylon. Artaxerxes was now king; and the king wrote a letter granting him a number of favors for his people, and giving him very great power. In this letter, the king granted permission to all the Jews which yet remained at Babylon to go to Jerusalem. He also gave them rich presents, and granted them leave to collect gifts of gold and silver, and to take them to Jerusalem in aid of the temple; particularly to buy beasts for the purpose of offering them up to God according to the law. In the picture you see Artaxerxes granting permission to the Jews to go.

God took care of Ezra and his friends, and brought them all safely to Jerusalem. They had many enemies; but these good men knew who their best friend was, who could protect them from every danger, and they sought Him on their journey, and He heard their prayer, and took care of them. When we go on a journey, we may meet with many dangers; and therefore we should never set off without first asking God's blessing and protection. We should say, as Moses did, "If Thy presence go not with us, carry us not up hence."

SAYINGS OF CHILDHOOD:—I fear, dear children, we sometimes forget God when we go away from home. I read of a little girl who said to her father, with whom she was on a visit in the State of New Jersey: "Now, Pa, I won't have to say my prayers to-night, will I?" "Why so, my child?" asked the father. "Why, because I am 'way down here in Jersey, aint I?" Another, as she was closing her prayers the evening before she left for Boston, said: "Now good bye, Mr. God, I'm going to Boston in the morning, to be gone two weeks." Little ones, don't forget to take God with you in all your travels.

EZRA'S PRAYER.

WHEN Ezra came to Jerusalem, he heard much that made him very sad. Some of the pious princes went to him in great grief, and lamented that the people had acted in a very ungrateful manner towards God, and instead of serving Him more faithfully, had mingled with the idolatrous people of Canaan. Widowers had even married Canaanitish and other heathen wives, and sanctioned the same marriages among their sons; not only so, but some of the princes and rulers, who, from their higher rank, ought to have set a better example had been guilty of like offence against God's laws.

All this was very wrong. God's people were to be a holy people; they were to keep away from the heathen nations around, and to have nothing to do with them. When Ezra first heard what the people had done, he rent his clothes, tore off the hair of his head and beard, and sat down silent on the ground. These were all customs among the Jews expressive of the greatest grief. Then some of the people who truly served God, came to him, and sat down, and wept too. Dear children, it makes good people feel sad when they see others doing bad. But, though we cannot stop them, there is one thing we can do. We can pray God to pity and forgive them. And this was what Ezra did.

At the time of the evening sacrifice, Ezra rose up, fell upon his knees, and spread out his hands unto God, and prayed. The engraving shows Ezra in the act of prayer. He confessed to God how great had been the people's sin. Seeing his great grief, great numbers had now gathered around him, and while he wept they also wept—men, women, and children. As the result of Ezra's prayer, the people repented of their sins. They separated from their idolatrous friends and companions, and made a covenant with God and promised to serve Him faithfully with all their hearts. This was the right way of showing that they were truly penitent.

SAYINGS OF CHILDHOOD:—A naughty boy being told by his mother that God would not forgive him if he did something, answered: "Yes, He would too—God likes to forgive little boys; that's what He's for." Yes, children, God likes to forgive; but He will not forgive those who ask Him to forgive them, and yet mean to go on sinning. Said a little child: "It would be real mean to ask God to forgive you when you meant to do wrong again, and knew it was wrong."

NEHEMIAH AND HIS COMPANIONS VIEW THE RUINED WALLS OF JERUSALEM.

NEHEMIAH was a good Jew whom Artaxerxes, king of Persia, had made his cup-bearer. Nehemiah was in Babylon, far away from his own country, but he still loved it much. One day one of the Jews came from Jerusalem, and told him that the people there were "in great affliction and reproach," and the wall of the city was still "broken down," and the gates were "burned with fire," as the Babylonians had left them. This was sad news for Nehemiah.

At length, when he went in to wait on the king, he looked so sad, that the king asked him what was the matter. Then Nehemiah told the king that he had just heard that his dear home, where his father's tombs were, was lying waste, and that the cruel enemies were always doing harm; and he said, "If it please the king, let me be sent unto Judah, unto the city of my fathers, that I may build it." Artaxerxes asked Nehemiah how long the journey would be, and when he would return to Persia; so Nehemiah told him; and then the king gave him leave to go.

Nehemiah now set off, accompanied with a guard of honor from the king, to protect him all the way till he reached Jerusalem. When he arrived there, he found it quite as bad as he had heard. One night, Nehemiah arose, and taking a few friends with him, went out secretly to see the city. As he rode along, he saw the walls of Jerusalem lying in ruins; the gates broken down, and burnt with fire. The temple had been built; but the poor Jews had so many enemies, that they could not worship God as they wished.

In the engraving we have a picture of Nehemiah and his friends viewing the ruined city. When he had gone round the walls, he returned; but he did not sit down to weep, and do nothing for his city and people. He stirred up the Jews, and they set to work to build the walls again. Then their enemies laughed at them, and said a fox could break down all they built; and when they went on, people used to come and attack them, so that they had to work with swords ready to fight, and always on the watch to come to help if they heard a trumpet blown. But they kept on, and the wall was built, and the gates set up; and they were safe once more from enemies coming in among them. God was with His people, who trusted in Him, and He would not suffer their enemies to destroy what He had commanded to be done.

THE LAW READ BY EZRA.

HE wall of the city was now built; it was almost time for Nehemiah to return to Persia; but before he went, he counted the people, and found the number to be 42,360, besides a great many servants. So they came to dwell in their cities.

And now I am going to tell you about the first Sunday-school —a Sunday-school that was held over two thousand years ago. It was not held in a church, but out in the open air, in a square in the city of Jerusalem. The superintendent's name was Nehemiah, the pastor's name was Ezra, and they had thirteen teachers. But they had a very large school. There were thousands of people, and thousands of children there —not less, probably, than 20,000 in all. The people asked Ezra to bring out the Bible, and teach them God's word. In the picture, Ezra stands reading the law. So he brought the Bible out, and read to them out of it, from early morn till noon. Would you like to be in a Sunday-school as long as that? Well, *they* liked it, and everybody paid the very best of attention to what was read, and to what was said. As soon as Ezra opened the Bible, they all stood up. That was to show their respect for the word which God had sent them. Then Ezra thanked God for all the good which He had done to them. When he did this, all the people lifted up their hands to heaven, and said, "Amen! Amen!" And they bowed down their faces towards the ground and worshipped God. Then Ezra read the law, and the Levites, the thirteen teachers explained it, and made the people understand it. The people all wept when they heard the law. They trembled and were afraid, because they remembered how often they had disobeyed God, and how much they had displeased Him. But Nehemiah and Ezra told them not to weep, for it was a holy day unto the Lord, and a day of thankfulness and praise. They told them to go home, and eat the fat, and drink the sweet, and send food to those who had none.

DOINGS OF CHILDHOOD:—Dear children, "Search the scriptures." You have heard the story of the blind girl, who, when her fingers became callous, and she could not read her bible save with difficulty, cut her finger tips to make them more sensitive. This made them so callous she could no longer read at all. At last, after bitter weeping, she kissed her bible a farewell. To her intense joy that kiss revealed to her the fact that she could read the raised words by the *touch of her lips*. Ever after she kissed into her soul that precious truth of God's word.

QUEEN VASHTI REFUSING TO OBEY THE ORDERS OF AHASUERUS.

THERE were some Jews still living in Persia, while their brethren were building the temple at Jerusalem. The king who was then reigning in Persia, is called in the bible Ahasuerus—the same king who is elsewhere called Artaxerxes. In the third year of his reign he made a grand feast for all his nobles and princes. This feast lasted a hundred and eighty days; and, after it was over, he gave another to all the attendants in his palace, which lasted seven days. This feast was in the court of the garden of the king's palace. The place where the company met was very beautiful and splendid. The curtains were white, and green, and blue; and the pillars to which they were fastened were of fine marble. The sofas were of gold and silver; and the floor was a pavement of blue, and red, and black, and white marble. The king gave his friends everything they could wish to eat and drink; and the wine which they drank was poured into beautiful vessels of gold.

In the Eastern countries the women never mingle with the men, as they do with us; hence the queen, Vashti—or *beautiful*, which Vashti means—and the ladies, had a grand feast by themselves, at the same time also, in the royal house. After the feast had lasted seven days, Ahasuerus was talking with his nobles about the beauty of his queen; and that he might convince them how handsome she was, he sent some of his officers to fetch Vashti and show her to the company. The engraving shows the officers come to take Vashti. But she refused to obey the king's command; so the messengers returned to the king without her.

On being told that the queen would not come, the king was in a great rage, and determined to punish her; but first he asked advice of the princes and wise men, that knew the laws, and asked what he should do with Vashti. Then one of the princes said, "Vashti ought to be punished; that she had not only insulted the king, but had set a bad example to the ladies of the whole kingdom, who, if Vashti were not punished, would never mind what their husbands wished them to do; let the king send Vashti away, and choose another and a better queen." The king was pleased with this advice, and did as the princes wished. The law was made, and Vashti was sent away in disgrace.

QUEEN VASHTI REFUSING TO OBEY AHASUERUS.

Dear children, I admire Vashti's courage. The king would never have sent for her, had he not been drunk with wine; had not his wits been unseated with liquor, he never would have proposed an exhibition so disgraceful to himself and so shocking to the queen. It was against law and usage, as well as contrary to her own womanly instincts. In refusing to come before a half-drunken crowd for exhibition, Vashti did herself honor. To disobey was the best obedience to the king she could render.

THE TRIUMPH OF MORDECAI.

DEAR little folks, I know you will want to talk about queen Esther. After Vashti went away, king Ahasuerus felt very sorry for what he had done. He did not call her back again, but he determined to have a new queen; so he commanded all the beautiful maidens in his land to be brought together, that he might choose the most beautiful of them all for his queen, and the others would be kept for slaves. A great many other maidens dressed themselves up, and painted themselves to try to look beautiful, and came to the palace: but the bible tells us about only one of them. Her name was Esther. She was a Jewish girl who had been left an orphan very young, and was brought up by her kind relation Mordecai, who was one of the Jews who had not gone back to Jerusalem, but still lived in Persia. When the young women were brought before the king, he liked Esther better than any of them, and married her and put the crown upon her head and made her his queen.

But Esther was not very happy, though she was queen. How could she be? She was always shut up, and could not see her kind friend Mordecai, and she could not even go to her husband without his leave, or she would have been put to death. Mordecai used to sit by the king's gate every day, to hear news of her. While sitting there, he made himself very useful to the king. Two of the servants made a conspiracy to kill

Ahasuerus. Mordecai found it out, and went directly and told Esther; and she told the king what Mordecai had said. It was found to be true, and the two wicked men were taken and hanged upon a tree. Mordecai did right to tell the king about this conspiracy, and the account of it was written down in a book, and put away into a safe place.

Now, there was a very bad man named Haman, who used to pass by every day; and Mordecai never would bow to him, because he was one of the people whom God had forbidden the Jews to have any concern with. This made Haman so angry, that he determined not only to kill Mordecai, but all the Jews in the kingdom; for Haman hated the Jews. So he went to the king and told him a false story about the Jews, and Ahasuerus believed this and ordered that all the Jews were to be killed on one day.

When Mordecai heard of this cruel decree, he rent his clothes, and put on sackcloth and ashes, as signs of grief; and he sent secret word to Esther that she must try to save her people by telling the king that he had been deceived by Haman. Now there was a law in Persia, which made it death for any person to go in to the king without being sent for; this was to keep up his dignity, and to prevent any person from taking away his life. Esther, therefore, although queen of Persia, must run a great risk to venture into the king's presence without being sent for; still she thought it was better for her to run the risk, than to let all the Jews perish.

But, dear children, before Esther went, she took the matter to God in prayer. The Jews, and Mordecai, and Esther, all fasted and wept, and prayed before God. It was a solemn time. The queen and her maidens were fasting, and weeping, and praying in the palace, and Mordecai and the Jews in the city; none of them ate or drank for three days. But what a comfort it was for these poor people to have God for their friend now!

The three days passed, Esther dressed herself beautifully, as the king liked best to see her; and she went to his court almost fainting with fear. When Ahasuerus looked up and saw Esther standing in the court, he pitied and loved her, and held out his sceptre and called her to him. Then she knew he would not put her to death. And when he asked why she had come, and what she wanted, she said, "If it please the king, let the king and Haman come to-day to the feast I have made ready for them." So they both came to the banquet. And while Ahasuerus was drinking wine, he desired her to let him know what she wished him to do. Esther was perhaps yet timid, and she begged the king and Haman to favor her once more with their presence at another feast the next day.

Haman felt proud of his honor in being invited twice, with the king, to Esther's feast; and he went home, that day, thinking very much of himself. As he passed the king's gate, he saw Mordecai sitting there; and Mordecai did not bow to him. That made Haman very angry, and, when he got home, he told his wife. "Then Zeresh, Haman's wife, answered, 'Do not be vexed about this. Let us make a very high gallows, and to-morrow speak thou to the king, that Mordecai may be hanged upon the gallows; and then go thou in merrily to the feast.'" Then Haman was pleased, and commanded that the gallows should be made at once.

Now, on the night before the banquet, king Ahasuerus was very restless, and could not sleep. It was God who made him so wakeful all night, and we shall soon know why. So, being unable to sleep, he arose and ordered his servants to bring the chronicles or notes of what had happened in his kingdom, and to read them to him for his amusement. In those chronicles, you remember, was recorded the conspiracy which Mordecai discovered; but Ahasuerus had forgotten this long ago. Now it happened that the servant came to this story and read it; and when the king heard it, he remembered the faithfulness of Mordecai, and he asked if any reward had ever been bestowed upon Mordecai for his noble conduct in saving his life. The servants answered, "Nothing had been done for him." Then the king said, "Mordecai must be rewarded now for his services. Go into the court and see who is there; I will consult with my friends how I may best honor this good man." So the servants went into the court, and there they found Haman, who had come as soon as he could, with a secret intention to obtain the king's leave to hang Mordecai. So the king desired him to enter. As soon as he had entered, the king said to him, "What shall be done unto the man whom the king delighteth to honor?" Now Haman thought in his heart, to whom would the king delight to do honor more than to myself? he being the king's greatest favorite. So he very readily suggested honors which he thought he should enjoy. "And he said, let the royal apparel be brought which the king useth to wear, and the horse that the king rideth upon, and the crown royal which is set upon his head. And let this apparel and horse be delivered to the hands of one of the king's most noble princes, that they may array the man withal whom the king delighteth to honor, and bring him on horseback through the street of the city, and proclaim before him, 'Thus shall it be done unto the man whom the king delighteth to honor.'"

The king liked the proposal, and told Haman directly to do as he had proposed—to whom? Why to Mordecai, the Jew; to the very man whom he had come to get hanged!

THE TRIUMPH OF MORDECAI.

Do you think, children, all this was chance? No; God ordered it all for the good of His favored people, the Jews. Then Haman went out and called Mordecai, and clothed him in the royal garments, and put him upon the king's horse, and led him through the city, proclaiming before him what Ahasuerus had commanded. In our first picture we see Mordecai on the king's horse, and Haman leading him before the people. Thus Mordecai was honored. So he lost nothing by serving God; neither will you. "Verily, there is a reward for the righteous."

The next day, the king came to the feast as he promised, and brought Haman with him. While they were feasting the king again asked Esther, "What is thy petition, queen Esther? It shall be granted thee." Esther now felt that the right time was come for making her petition; so she said at once, "If it please the king, let my life be given at my petition, and my people at my request; for it is commanded, that I and my people should all be destroyed and slain. The king was startled at the news, and asked in a rage, "Who is he, and where is he that durst presume in his heart to do so?" Then Esther turned to Haman, and said, "The adversary and enemy is this wicked Haman." In the next picture, we see

"ESTHER CONFRONTING HAMAN."

There stands Esther with queenly dignity; the king has a piercing look on his face, as he turns upon Haman; and Haman is so terrified that he cannot speak.

There was no hope for Haman now. By the king's command he was hanged upon the very gallows he had meant for Mordecai. And so the Jews were saved by the good queen, who was not afraid to risk her life for her people.

JOB INFORMED OF HIS RUIN.

I KNOW you will all remember Job. He lived in the land of Uz, supposed to have been part of an Eastern country called Arabia. Job was a holy man; the bible says he "feared God and eschewed evil"—that means he avoided evil. This good man was very rich he had great possessions, of sheep, and camels, and oxen, and asses he was the greatest man in the East at that time. He had seven sons and three daughters; his children were very happy among themselves, and seemed to have loved each other, as good brothers and sisters ought with a sincere affection. At particular times of the year they had feasts, as we usually have at Christmas; and then they all met together, as many families do at least once a year with us, and the sisters were invited to meet with the brothers. And when these feasts were over, good Job, who loved their souls as well as their bodies, lost no time in offering up sacrifices for them, according to the command of God; "for Job said, it may be that my sons have sinned, and cursed God in their hearts. Thus did Job continually."

Now Satan could not behold Job's piety without desiring to tempt him. He even dared to accuse Job before God and to say, that all his goodness was false and hypocritical. But God knew all the truth about Job; and so, in order to show that the religion of Job was genuine, it pleased God to allow Satan to try Job, and to vex and afflict him. God did this for Job's own good—to make him more humble, more patient, and more believing. When Satan had leave to tempt Job, he tried him with all kinds of pains, and losses, and bereavements; but nothing could shake his faith in God. God sent thunderbolts, and slew his servants. He caused the housetop to fall in and bury all his children, his oxen and servants were carried away by the Sabeans, his sheep were

destroyed by fire; but Job still worshipped God; and when a servant came running to tell him of all these disasters, he did not repine, or rebel against God; but he bowed his head, and said meekly: "The Lord gave, and the Lord hath taken away: blessed be the name of the Lord!" How beautiful does the piety of Job here appear! In our first picture, we see Job just receiving the news of his great loss. Dear children, what would you have done? Some men, who had no God to whom they could go for relief, would have gone mad; and some would have raged furiously against God for suffering all this affliction to come upon them. But Job sinned not!

Satan, thus failing in his attempts, appeared again before God, and obtained further leave to try Job. God then suffered sore boils to smite Job, and to cover him all over from head to foot. And they were so bad that he took a piece of a broken pot to scrape himself, and he sat down in a heap of ashes. In the next picture, you see

"JOB SEATED ON THE ASH HEAP,"

and the broken pot in his hand with which to scrape himself. To add to his misery yet further, his wife, who ought to have encouraged him to trust in God, provokingly asked him if he would now be religious any longer, as he had proof enough that his religion did not save him from trouble; she told him to curse God rather than bless Him, and then die in despair. This wicked woman, however, failed in shaking the piety of Job. For he said unto her, "Thou speakest as one of the foolish women speaketh. What? shall we receive good at the hand of God, and shall we not receive evil?" "In all this did not Job sin with his lips." This was the right way to speak, and thus we should bear trouble when it pleases God to afflict us.

In the midst of his trouble three of Job's particular friends came to visit him. When they saw him in his sad condition, they were so sorrowful, that "they lifted up their voices and wept." Then they sat down with him upon the ground; and for seven days and seven nights they did not speak a word to him, for they saw that his grief was very great. Job at last broke the silence, and opened his mouth with cursing the day in which he was born. He did not indeed curse and swear—he was too good a man to do so—but he gave way to strong expressions of complaint, which is what is meant here by cursing. He was tempted to wish that he had never been born; and to murmur, and be impatient, and to find fault with God, who had so afflicted him.

His friends then spoke to him one after another. But instead of giving him any comfort, they only irritated his mind. They foolishly supposed that Job never could

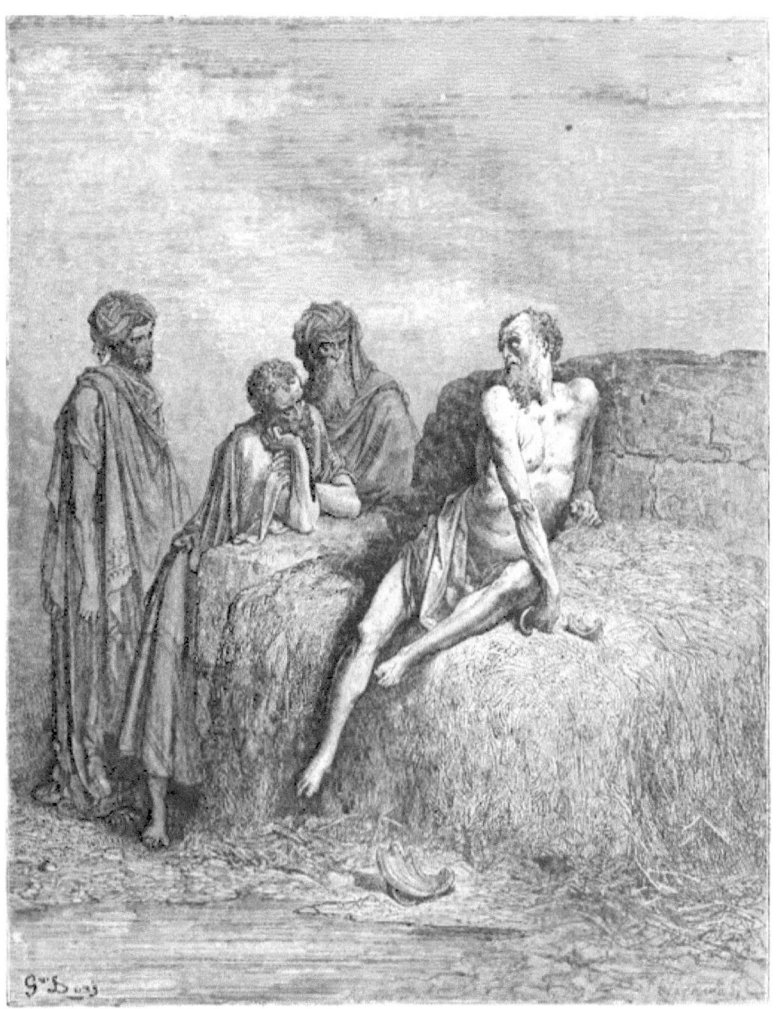

have been afflicted, if he had not done something that was very wicked. They, therefore, told him that he must have been guilty of being a hypocrite, and that all his religion was in mere show, and not in the heart. Job could not bear this, for he knew it was not true; he felt that he had been sincere, and so when they accused him, he answered, "My righteousness I hold fast, and will not let it go; my heart shall not reproach me as long as I live."

Now Job and his friends were quite right in some things that they said, but in others they were very much mistaken. Job's friends were right in advising him to humble himself before God, and ask for pardon; for afflictions are sent by God to lead His people to do this. But they were quite wrong in accusing Job of being a wicked man, and a hypocrite, because he was afflicted; for God often afflicts most those who love and serve Him best,—in love, not in anger; "Whom the Lord loveth He correcteth." And though Job was right in saying, that he had not brought his suffering on himself, by his own wickedness, yet he spoke what was wrong, too; for he almost accused God of unkindness, and injustice, in afflicting him after he had so sincerely tried to serve God.

At length Job's friends, thinking it was of no use to talk to him any longer, dropped the conversation. All this time a young man had been sitting by, and listening to the conversation. This young man's name was Elihu. He had waited till the others were through, "because they were older than he;" and the young should always give place to the old, because the old ought first to be heard, and are expected, from having more years, to have also more wisdom. But Elihu had much to say, for God had given him great wisdom. Elihu was angry with what had been said. He was displeased with Job, because he justified himself more than God; and he was displeased with his three friends, "because they had found no answer, and yet had condemned Job." After reproving all of them, he at length closed by vindicating the conduct of God in all His dealings in Providence with sinful men, and showing how impossible it is for us, His humble creatures, to search His ways even in common things. He pointed out the wonders of the thunder and lightning; the snow and the rain; the wind and the clouds; and then assured them that such a great God would not afflict without a just cause. God is perfectly holy, and perfectly wise; and therefore He will not, He cannot, do anything wrong or unjust; God can never err, never be mistaken.

Elihu having done speaking, God Himself answered Job, and spoke to him out of a whirlwind that sprung up at the time; and bade him reply to Him, if he could. Then the Lord asked Job, if he could tell how the earth was made, and if he understood the motion of the stars, or was able to rule the sea, and the light, and the darkness. And God spoke to him of some of the wonderful animals He had created; but Job could not make one of these things, nor even understand how they were made. And if Job could not understand the works of God, how could he understand God Himself? and then how could he dare to contend with Him, or to murmur at anything He did? Job felt all this. He felt humbled and ashamed; and therefore, instead of again trying to justify himself, he said, "Behold, I am vile, what shall I answer Thee? I will lay my hand upon my mouth. Once have I spoken, but I will not answer; yea, twice, but I will proceed no further."

And did God forgive Job? Yes; as soon as Job was humble and penitent, God pardoned, and accepted, and blessed him. But God was angry with Job's three friends because they had made Him out to be an unjust God. And God commanded them to offer sacrifice for their sin, and to ask Job to pray for them; and they did so, and the Lord accepted them, and received them into His favor. But did Job still remain in his affliction? No; "the Lord turned his captivity." He took away his painful disease, and made him well and strong again. The scripture tells us that the brothers and sisters of Job, and all they that had been of his acquaintance, now came and comforted him; and that "every man gave him a piece of money, and everyone an ear-ring of gold." And the "Lord gave Job twice as much as he had before"—sheep, and oxen, and camels, and asses; and he had also seven sons, and three daughters—just the same number that he had before. Why did He not double them also? Because, though the others had died, he had not really lost *them*—they were in heaven waiting for him. Job lived in comfort and prosperity for many years after, having the blessing of God to make him happy; and at last he died, "old and full of days."

SAYINGS OF CHILDHOOD:—Dear little folks, try to be patient. No matter if things don't always go as you wish. A little boy went to his mother, one morning, with a broken arrow, and begged her to mend it for him. It was a very handsome arrow, and was the pride of his heart just then; so she did not wonder to see his lip quivering, and the tears come to his eyes. "I'll *try* to fix it, darling," she said; "but I'm afraid I can't do it." He watched her anxiously for a few moments, and then said, cheerfully, "Never mind, mamma; if you can't fix it, *I'll be just as happy without it.*" That was a happy boy! Learn how to endure trouble, boys, and don't cry at everything. If a boy is not trained to endure, and to bear trouble, he will grow up a girl; and a boy that is a girl has all a girl's weakness without any of her regal qualities.

ISAIAH.

ISAIAH has justly been called "The prince of prophets." In the first picture the artist portrays him kneeling on the mountain cliff, bent in rapt and awe-struck communion with God. Of all the prophets, Isaiah speaks so clearly of Jesus Christ and His church, that he has been termed the Evangelical Prophet.

Isaiah had many wonderful visions. I want to talk with you about a few of them. One of the most remarkable was the following: While he was yet a young man, God appeared unto him in His majesty; Isaiah saw the Lord sitting upon a throne, high and lifted up, and His train filling the temple; the Lord was surrounded by seraphim, who cried, " Holy, holy, holy, is the Lord of hosts; the whole earth is full of His glory." Filled with a sense of his own unworthiness and of the divine majesty, Isaiah exclaimed, "Woe is me! for I am undone; because I am a man of unclean lips, and I dwell in the midst of a people of unclean lips; for mine eyes have seen the King, the Lord of hosts." But God was thus graciously preparing him for that complete consecration for His work which made him thenceforth the greatest of the prophets of the old dispensation. "Then flew one of the seraphim unto me, having a live coal in his hand, which he had taken with the tongs from off the altar; and he laid it upon my mouth, and said, Lo, this hath touched thy lips; and thine iniquity is taken away, and thy sin purged." Then he responded to the divine demand. "Whom shall I send, and who will go for us?" "Here am I; send me." And in the more than sixty years that followed, Isaiah was always ready to declare the whole counsel of God.

Dear children, if we would serve God acceptably we must be humble. Before we can become useful in declaring God's will to others, we must feel our own unworthiness and earnestly desire that our sin may be taken away. Those who are burdened

with the sense of their sin, and pray for its removal, shall have their prayer granted if they sincerely repent, and put their trust in Christ. He, like the live coal that touched the prophet's lips, will remove the stain of our sins.

Another of his most wonderful visions was

"ISAIAH'S DREAM OF THE DESTRUCTION OF BABYLON,"

which the artist portrays in the next picture. This vision took place two hundred years before its accomplishment. But that is what is meant by a prophecy: it tells us of things that are to come to pass a great while before they take place; and prophets are the men who tell us. After seeing in his vision the great God gathering together the armies of his wrath for the destruction of the city, he then describes the desolation of Babylon, in these words: "And Babylon, the glory of kingdoms, the beauty of the Chaldees' excellency, shall be as when God overthrew Sodom and Gomorrah. It shall never be inhabited, neither shall it be dwelt in from generation to generation: neither shall the Arabian pitch his tent there; neither shall the shepherds make their fold there. But wild beasts of the desert shall lie there; and their houses shall be full of doleful creatures; and owls shall dwell there, and satyrs shall dance there. And the wild beasts of the islands shall cry in their desolate houses, and dragons in their pleasant palaces; and her time is near to come, and her days shall not be prolonged."

All this took place just as Isaiah prophesied. After it was taken by Cyrus it began to decline, and soon ceased to be the seat of empire; then its population decreased; at length it was utterly deserted; and the desolate buildings were long the resort of every species of wild beasts and venomous reptiles, so that it was dangerous for travelers to approach them; at length, it was so utterly wasted, that no remains of it could be found; and, strange to tell, it cannot at present be exactly ascertained where this once mighty city stood! When God is pleased to destroy, nothing can withstand His power! Dear children, the fate of this proud city is a proof of the truth of the bible. It is also a warning to sinners to flee from the wrath to come, and an encouragement to believers to expect victory over every enemy of their souls, and the church of God.

I shall mention only one more of Isaiah's visions. It is his vision of

"GOD'S JUDGMENT ON LEVIATHAN,"

which the artist portrays in the next engraving. "In that day the Lord with His sore and great and strong sword shall punish leviathan the piercing serpent, even leviathan that crooked serpent; and he shall slay the dragon that is in the sea." Isaiah here

prophesies of the destruction of Satan and his kingdom, under the name of leviathan. The leviathan is the most destructive of "sea monsters;" so Satan is the great enemy of God and His church. But God will make the sword of His almighty vengeance, which is exceedingly sharp, and great, and strong, to reach unto him. Then the old serpent will be bound and cast into the bottomless pit, his power will cease, all his obstinate servants will be cut off, and the earth be overspread with truth and righteousness.

SAYINGS OF CHILDHOOD:—You remember, children, in one of the wonderful visions of Isaiah, the seraphim came to Isaiah. Do you know who the seraphim are? The cherubim are angels who excel in knowledge; the seraphim are angels who excel in loving God. When a little boy heard this, he said: "I hope, then, when I die I shall be a seraph, for I would rather *love* God, than know all things." In another vision we saw where God would destroy the great leviathan, Satan. A little boy said to his mother: "Ma, Satan must be an awful sight of trouble to God, must'nt he? I don't see how he turned out so bad, when he had no devil to put him up to it." A minister asked a little converted boy, "Does not the devil tell you that you are not a christian?" "Yes, sometimes." "Well, what do you say?" "I tell him," replied the boy, "whether I am a christian or not is none of his business." Won't you be glad, little folks, when Satan is bound? Well, if you are good and get to heaven, you will see it.

JEREMIAH DICTATING HIS PROPHECIES TO BARUCH.

JEREMIAH is called the "Sad Prophet;" sad, because of the judgments which came thick and fast upon his beloved country and nation, and because of the sorrows, trials and persecutions which his fidelity to his convictions and to the voice of God brought upon him. God called Jeremiah to be his prophet when he was only a young boy twelve years old. Like Isaiah he received a special consecration for his work from the hand of Jehovah.

In this talk I want to tell you about one of his prophecies. It was in the time of the bad, cruel king Jehoiakim. God told Jeremiah to warn the people of their sins, and of the punishments that were soon coming upon them. Jeremiah was now to write the warning in the roll of a book. So he called one of his friends, a good man named Baruch, and asked him to write upon a roll all the words which God commanded. Jeremiah spoke the words, and Baruch wrote them down in the roll. In the first picture the artist represents Jeremiah telling Baruch what to write, and Baruch is taking it down. The light coming down from above into the prophet's face shows that he received his prophecy from heaven.

When the book was finished, Jeremiah told Baruch that he could not go, but for Baruch to go and read the roll to all the people in the Lord's house. Baruch did as the prophet commanded. He went to the gate of the Lord's house, and there he read the roll to all the people. One of the men who heard the roll read was very attentive to the warning which God sent; and he went directly to the king's house, and told the princes all he had heard. Then the princes wanted to hear the roll too; so they sent for Baruch to come and read the book to them. The princes asked him, "How didst thou write all these words?" Then Baruch answered, "Jeremiah pronounced the words, and I wrote them as he commanded, with ink in the book." Then the princes said, "Go and hide, both thou and Jeremiah, and we will tell the king about the roll which we have heard. He ought to know the warning which God has sent to us."

So the princes took the roll and put it in a safe place; and Baruch returned to Jeremiah, and told him to hide himself; and then the princes went to the king Jehoiakim, and spoke to him of the fearful things they had heard. Now the king was curious to see the roll, and to know what Jeremiah had written; so he sent a messenger to bring it. The king was sitting by the fire warming himself, for it was in the winter. He listened to the reading of the roll for a little while; but when he found that it was

about his sins, and God's anger, he took out a knife and cut the whole into bits, and threw it into the fire. Some of the princes begged the king not to burn the roll; but he would not listen to them. Was he so foolish as to think that burning the prophecy would prevent it from coming to pass? If so, he made a great mistake. Then the king sent some servants to take Jeremiah and Baruch; but God Himself hid those good men, and their enemies could not find them.

Jehoiakim had burnt the roll, but he could not destroy the truth of God's word. God told Jeremiah to take a new roll, and to write on it all the words of the first roll which the king had burnt. And God sent Jeremiah with a dreadful message to Jehoiakim. This was the message: "Thus saith the Lord, of Jehoiakim, king of Judah, I will punish him and his servants for their iniquity, and I will bring upon them, and upon Judah, all the evil that I have pronounced against them." Then Jeremiah took a new roll and gave it to Baruch; and Baruch wrote in it all the words of the first roll as Jeremiah had told him. And many new words were added in this new roll. And they were dreadful words; words of anger and threatening against the wicked king, and his wicked people.

Baruch was afterwards imprisoned with Jeremiah, and was also carried with him to Egypt, where according to one tradition, he died. Another asserts that his days were ended at Babylon. In our next engraving we have a picture of

"BARUCH."

The artist has represented him reclining upon the hard prison floor, with his rolls of manuscript about him, in rapt meditation. He has an intense, but patient and sorrowful look on his face—one that would seem to convey the impression that his mind is entirely taken up in the great work to which he was called.

Dear children, how fearful it is to despise the words and warnings of God! If He says He will punish His enemies, He will surely do it. They may try to fight against Him; they may try to destroy His word and His people, but they cannot prevail. God is stronger than they; He must conquer at last, and then where will His enemies be? The bible tells us what words God Himself has pronounced against them. "Because I called and ye refused; and set at naught all my counsel, and would none of my reproof: I also will laugh at your calamity: I will mock when your fear cometh. Then shall they call upon me, but I will not answer; they shall seek me, but they shall not find me; because they hated knowledge, and did not choose the fear of the Lord."

EZEKIEL PROPHESYING.

EZEKIEL was one of the greater prophets. His name means *God will make strong*, and points to the source of his power, and accounts for his influence with his countrymen. In the first engraving we have a picture of Ezekiel prophesying. Ezekiel gives us an account of his commission in these words: "And He said unto me, son of man, stand upon thy feet, and I will speak unto thee. And the Spirit entered into me, when He spake unto me, and set me upon my feet, that I heard Him that spake unto me. And He said unto me, son of man, I send thee to the children of Israel, to a rebellious nation that hath rebelled against Me. They and their fathers have transgressed against Me, even unto this very day. For they are impudent children and stiff-hearted. I do send thee unto them, and thou shalt say unto them, Thus saith the Lord God. And they, whether they will hear or whether they will forbear (for they are a rebellious house), yet shall know that there hath been a prophet among them. And thou, son of man, be not afraid of them, neither be afraid of their words, though briars and thorns be with thee, and thou dost dwell among scorpions: be not afraid of their words, nor be dismayed at their looks, though they be a rebellious house. And thou shalt speak my words unto them, whether they will hear or whether they will forbear, for they are most rebellious. But thou, son of man, hear what I say unto thee. Be not thou rebellious like that rebellious house: open thy mouth, and eat that I give thee." The prophet, as represented in the picture, is of commanding presence. At his feet are gathered a few who are listening to him with thoughtful interest, while those beyond seem yet too timid to approach any nearer.

Among the many wonderful visions which Ezekiel had was one I will tell you about. The Lord made him have a sort of a dream, in which he was carried, under the influence of the Spirit, out into a valley that was like a vast graveyard. Over it reigned the silence of death. In the valley, on the surface of the ground, lay rank upon rank of skeletons. The valley was "full of bones"—"behold there were very many of them." Around these bones the Lord caused the prophet to pass in order that he might see how hopeless was their condition. They were "very dry"—just as bones exposed to the heat of that climate were sure soon to become. Then the Lord said to Ezekiel, "Son of man, can these bones live?" The natural answer to that question was, No. But Ezekiel knew it was not a man speaking to him; but the omnipotent One, who can do

all things; and so, very wisely, he answers, "O Lord God, Thou knowest." It is a reply that shows both modesty and faith. It implies that he believes that God can work the marvelous miracle, if He shall so choose. Again the Lord spoke unto Ezekiel and said, " Prophesy upon these bones, and say unto them : O ye dry bones, hear the word of the Lord. Thus saith the Lord God unto these bones. Behold, I will cause breath to enter into you, and ye shall live. And I will lay sinews upon you, and will bring up flesh upon you, and cover you with skin, and put breath in you, and ye shall live, and ye shall know that I am the Lord." Then Ezekiel did as he was commanded; and as he spake there was a noise, and a shaking, and the bones came together again and joined in their right places; and as he spake on, the flesh came back on them; and then the Lord bade him call to the winds of heaven, and they came and filled them with breath again, and they rose up and lived. In the next picture, the artist has shown us

"EZEKIEL'S VISION OF THE DRY BONES."

The bones are seen rising up and coming together; some are already standing on their feet; and in the distance near where Ezekiel stands, some are clothed in flesh once more.

Just so God said the kingdom of Judah was dead and scattered, but He would breathe on it, and wake it, and join it together again, like the dead bones rising to life. And, dear children, there is a lesson in this for us, too. All those who do not love God are like dry bones. A dry bone has nothing good in it; it has no power—it is worthless. You speak to it, and it cannot hear. It cannot see the beautiful things that God has made. Just so is it with one who does not listen to the Word of God. After awhile he gets so that he cannot hear. He becomes dead in sin. All the good that there was in him wastes away. Then he has no power to do right. He cannot hear his conscience speak, and he cannot see the beautiful things which God has scattered everywhere. He is worthless to himself, and to everbody else. He is like a dry bone. Satan sees that there is nothing good left upon him. Do you want to be like that? Neither did the Israelites, but they would not listen to the voice of God, and that became their condition.

"Can these bones live?" Who can make them live? God. How did He do it? By breathing upon them with His Spirit. Can He make those who are dead in sin alive again? Yes. How can He do that? In the same way. Don't you want God's Spirit to come into your heart, so that you may live, and be able to keep His law, and always do just right?

DANIEL.

MY dear children, I know you will be pleased to talk about Daniel, the boy hero. Among the Jewish captives who were carried away to Babylon there were some little boys, young princes and nob'es, who had been brought up in the palace of the house of David. They were probably about twelve years old when they were thus taken from their homes. The king of Babylon, Nebuchadnezzar, was pleased with the boys, and thought he should like to have them to wait on him. So he desired the steward of his palace to have them taken into his care, to be taught both to wait on the king, and to know all the learning of Babylon.

The bible tells us a great deal about four of these young princes. Their names were Daniel, Shadrack, Meshach, and Abednego. One of Nebuchadnezzar's servants had the care of them, whose name was Melzar. Every day he brought them meat and wine from the king's table; that grieved these boys, because they knew that all the meat there came from creatures that had been offered up to idols. Now Daniel knew that it was very wrong to eat meats that had been offered to idols. Some of the boys said they did not care, and some said they were very sorry, but they could not help it. Yes, Daniel said, they could help it if they would leave off eating meat and drinking wine, and only have beans and water. Then three more of the boys said they would stand by Daniel, and have only the beans and water, rather than break God's holy law.

So, one day, when Melzar came to see them, Daniel asked to have no more meat brought them from the king's table; but let them feed on water and pulse—that is, beans. But Melzar said he was afraid they would grow thin and pale and sickly; and then Nebuchadnezzar would be displeased with him. But Daniel said, "Only try us for just ten days." So Melzar promised to try them for ten days. They ate the pulse and drank the water given them with thankfulness, because they felt that they had God's blessing. And God so blessed the food, that at the end of ten days, Melzar examined them, and found them fairer and fatter than those who were fed from the king's table. God had kept them in health and strength, because they trusted in Him. Daniel's fidelity secured a friend in the king, and he arose, like Joseph of old, to be the second man in the kingdom. In the engraving, the artist has given us a picture of Daniel as the great prophet, with scroll in hand.

SAYINGS OF CHILDHOOD:—Daniel would not touch the king's wines. One newsboy tried to get another to just sip a little beer. "No," said the other, "I have taken a pledge not to drink strong drink." "Would you not do it for a dollar?" asked the first boy. "No, sir." "For a thousand dollars?" "No, sir." "Why not?" "*Because when the thousand dollars are all gone, and all the things I got with them are gone too, my conscience is there all the same*," answered the boy. That was a noble answer Children, dare to be like Daniel; dare to be true to God and your conscience in this Babylon of worldliness. The wine-cup is our foe. It comes pretending to make us merry and happy, but all the while it is preparing us for defeat. It will make us sorry enough by-and-by, if we drink its contents. It takes away our homes, our clothes, our food, our good characters—everything that is valuable, and leaves us nothing but rags, and poverty, and sickness, and defeat, and death.

THE THREE HEBREW CHILDREN IN THE FIERY FURNACE.

KING NEBUCHADNEZZAR, of Babylon worshipped idols. He made a great image of gold; it was set up in a plain in Babylon; and at the time of dedication he issued a proclamation, that at the sound of the various musical instruments, *every one* should fall down and worship it; and that if any should refuse, he should be cast into a burning fiery furnace. Many people, as soon as they heard the music, made haste to bow down before the golden image.

Shadrack, Meshach, and Abednego, heard the command given; and they heard, too, the dreadful punishment which was threatened to those who disobeyed; but these good men felt that they could not obey, for God had said, "Thou shalt have none other gods but Me;" and "thou shalt not make any graven images; thou shalt not bow to them, nor worship them;" so they would not bow down before the great image.

Then their enemies, who had watched to see if they would worship the golden image, or not, ran directly and told the king. Then king Nebuchadnezzar was angry, and commanded the three Jews to be brought before him. When they came, the king asked

THE THREE HEBREW CHILDREN IN THE FIERY FURNACE.

them how it was; and told them fiercely, that if they would not worship his golden image, they must be thrown into the fire. But they stood up boldly and answered, "Our God whom we serve is able to deliver us from the burning fiery furnace, and He will deliver us out of thine hand, O, king! But if not, be it known unto thee O, king, that we will not serve thy gods, nor worship the golden image which thou hast set up."

When the king heard this brave answer, he became very angry, and ordered the furnace to be heated seven times hotter than usual. Then some strong men took Shadrach, Meshach and Abednego, and bound them hand and foot, and cast them into the burning fiery furnace; and the flame was so hot, that it burnt to death the men that threw them in. But O, wonderful! When Nebuchadnezzar came to look into the furnace, he said to his governors, "Did we not cast *three* men into the fire?" "True, O, king," they said. But said Nebuchadnezzar, "Lo, I see *four* men loose, walking in the midst of the fire, and they have no harm, and the form of the fourth is like unto the Son of God." Then the king called them, and Shadrach, Meshach, and Abednego came out of the fire. Their clothes were not burnt; their hair was not singed; there was no smell of fire upon them. Then was the king *compelled* to own the truth, "There is no God who can deliver after this sort." And he sent forth a command, that no one should ever speak a word against the God of Shadrach, Meshach, and Abednego, who had saved them in the burning fiery furnace.

BELSHAZZAR'S FEAST.

ELSHAZZAR was now king of Babylon. He was a foolish, proud and rebellious young man; he did not care for anything but his own amusement. One night Belshazzar made a great feast to the principal lords of his kingdom. They all ate and drank and made merry. During this feast, the king had all the holy vessels, which had been brought from God's temple in Jerusalem, brought out; and they poured wine into them, and praised their gods of gold, and silver, and iron, and brass, and wood, and stone.

God was angry at the use thus made of the sacred vessels; He heard them

BELSHAZZAR'S FEAST.

blaspheming His holy name. All on a sudden they were terribly frightened; for just over the candlestick there were seen the fingers of a man's hand writing upon the wall. Belshazzar could not tell who was writing; he could not understand the words. Then he called all his wise men, but none of them could guess what the meaning could be. At last, the queen, the king's mother, came into the room, and told the king about Daniel. So Daniel was sent for, and he at once read the writing. There were very few words; but they were dreadful words in their meaning. What were they? "Mene, Mene, Tekel, Peres, Upharsin." Then Daniel said, "This is the interpretation: Mene, God has numbered thy kingdom, and finished it; Tekel, thou art weighed in the balances, and found wanting; Peres, Upharsin, thy kingdom is divided, and given to the Medes and Persians."

In the engraving the artist has portrayed this scene. There stands Daniel, pointing towards the fearful handwriting on the wall. Was Belshazzar frightened? No; he went on with the feast, and the company ate, and drank, and talked, and laughed, and sang, as they had done before. They thought all these dreadful things would not come to pass yet. But that very night the king was slain. "And Darius the Median took the kingdom."

DANIEL IN THE LIONS' DEN.

ABYLON had another king, whose name was Darius. King Darius greatly honored Daniel, and raised him to the highest office in the State. But Daniel had enemies in Babylon. The officers of the government were jealous of his promotion; they hated him, and tried hard to find some occasion for fault-finding; but Daniel was so good and holy a man, that even his enemies had to confess that they could not do it unless they found it "against him concerning the law of God." There was one thing of which they knew they could accuse him. That was his praying to God.

So, one day these princes went to king Darius, and begged him to make a law that for thirty days nobody should say their prayers to any god, or ask anything of any man except of Darius the king; or if they did, they should be thrown into a den of lions. Now these wicked men thought they should soon be able to accuse Daniel; for of course, they thought, Daniel would not dare keep on praying after this. But *he did*, and was not afraid to have it known. He disliked to disobey Darius; but he knew that he must obey God more than man. Then he did not try to hide and pray in some secret place where his enemies could not see him; for we read that "when Daniel knew that the writing had been signed, he went into his chamber (his windows being opened), and kneeled upon his knees three times a day, and prayed and gave thanks before his God as aforetime." Why did Daniel do this? Not to make a boast of his goodness, but to show his enemies that he was not afraid nor ashamed of praying to God. Never be afraid of doing right.

Daniel's enemies were glad, because they thought they had a sure case against him; and they ran at once to tell the king that Daniel regarded neither the decree nor himself, but went on praying three times a day. Then Darius was sorry, for he loved and honored Daniel, and he tried hard to save him; but it was useless; the law that had once been made could not be broken. So they brought Daniel to the den of lions, and cast him in. But as the men were hurrying him away, the king said, "O Daniel, thy God whom thou servest continually, He will deliver thee."

All that night Darius fasted and mourned for Daniel. He would have no music, nor singing, nor rejoicing in his palace; he could enjoy nothing; and when he lay down on his bed he could not sleep. And very early in the morning he arose and went to the den, and cried out, "O Daniel, servant of the living God, is thy God, whom thou servest continually able to deliver thee from the lions?" Let us listen to Daniel's reply: "My God hath sent His angel, and hath shut the lions' mouths, and they have not hurt me." Then Darius was glad, and he commanded that Daniel should be taken out of the den, and that the spiteful men should be put in instead: and the lions were so hungry that they broke all their bones in pieces before they ever came to the bottom of the den.

Dear little ones, let us learn from this true story how ready our God is to deliver those who really trust Him—and just as easily too. Let us never be ashamed to confess Him wherever we are, even though it comes to kneeling in prayer before those who do not believe in Him.

SAYINGS OF CHILDHOOD:—A poor widow was weeping in the room where lay the body of her husband. Their only child came in, and said, "Why do you weep so, mother?" The mother told him of their loss, and especially referred to their poverty. Looking into her face, the little fellow said, "*Is God dead, mother?*" No, dear children, God is *not* dead; He still lives; and Daniel's powerful God is your God—still able to deliver His children and to punish His enemies.

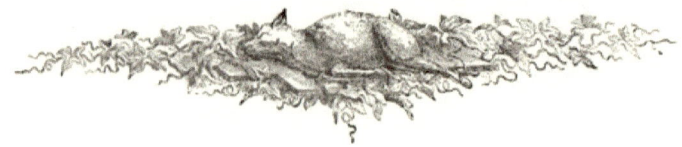

A VISION OF THE PROPHET DANIEL.

EFORE we leave Daniel, dear children, I want to talk a few moments about his wonderful vision of the four beasts which arose out of a very stormy sea. The first beast was like a lion, and had eagle's wings; the second like a bear, with three ribs in its mouth; the third like a leopard, with four wings and four heads; and the fourth a beast with ten horns. The engraving gives us a picture of this part of Daniel's vision. I suppose you know that all these were emblems or symbols. What are they symbols of? Daniel did not know at first; but God sent an angel to teach him. The angel told him that the four beasts mean four great empires, which should, one after another, have great power and dominion in the world.

But Daniel saw more in his vision; he says, "I beheld till the thrones were cast down, and the Ancient of days did sit, whose garment was white as snow, and the hair of His head like the pure wool: His throne was like the fiery flame, and His wheels as burning fire. A fiery stream issued and came forth from before Him; thousand thousands ministered unto Him, and ten thousand times ten thousand stood before Him; the judgment was set, and the books were opened." Then Daniel saw the Ancient of days destroy all the beasts; and further he says, "I saw in the night visions, and, behold, one like the Son of man came with the clouds of heaven, and came to the Ancient of days, and they brought Him near before Him. And there was given Him dominion, and glory, and a kingdom, that all people, nations, and languages, should serve Him; His dominion is an everlasting dominion, which shall not pass away, and His kingdom that which shall not be destroyed."

What was this vision for? It was to disclose the fact that all the other kingdoms, great and powerful as they were, were to perish, and to be superseded by a divine kingdom that should never be destroyed. The "Ancient of days" is the eternal God; the Son of man is Jesus. God has given to Jesus a kingdom that is to fill the whole earth. It will destroy all the other kingdoms. It will fill the earth with the song of peace on earth and good will toward men. Children, will you not belong to it now? Do you pray, "Thy kingdom come?"

THE PROPHET AMOS.

AMOS was one of the twelve minor prophets. Before he became a prophet, he was a shepherd and a dresser of sycamore trees. He foretold many of the misfortunes which should befall the kingdom of Israel; and he speaks sharply against the sins of Israel, and reproves the people for going to Bethel, Dan, Gilgal, and Beersheba, and for swearing by the gods of these places. In the engraving the artist has given us a picture of Amos, leaning upon his staff, and lost in the utter loneliness of his own thoughts.

Children, I wonder if you have noticed one thing that I have, in all the prophecies? I mean how God punishes those nations that rejoice over the afflictions of His own people. Did you ever see anybody laugh when some one else got hurt? Did you ever do it yourself? Is it right to do that way? Well, now, in the first two chapters of Amos, we read about many nations that God punished. One of them He punished for being glad because Jerusalem was destroyed. You remember a great king came up against Jerusalem, and captured it, and took many of its people away into captivity. They never saw their homes again. Was that a thing to be glad about? And yet there was a city by the name of Tyre, that was very glad that Jerusalem was overthrown. She was glad because, she said, now that Jerusalem is out of the way, we will get all the trade that has been in the habit of going to her. Wasn't that a very bad spirit to show? Do you think that God liked that? He did not like it at all, and He told that city that He would destroy it. He did destroy it.

Do you think that God likes to have you make fun of people who are unfortunate? Is it right to laugh at, or make fun of, the lame, the hunchback, the poor? What do you think God will do to you if you act in that way? He will surely punish you for it. Instead of rejoicing when others suffer, let us take this for our motto: WE WILL LOVE OUR NEIGHBORS AS OURSELVES.

JONAH CAST UP BY THE WHALE.

YOU all know, I suppose, the story of Jonah. He was a prophet in Israel, and he tells us that God commanded him to go to Nineveh and preach to the people of that city. Nineveh was a very rich and wicked city. The king and people worshipped idols, and not God. And God wanted Jonah to go and tell them how angry He was with them, and what punishment He would bring upon them if they continued in sin.

But Jonah did not want to go. Why not? He liked his own ease better than being useful. Perhaps he thought the journey would be very long and tiresome; or he was afraid the people there might be angry with his message, and try to kill him. So, instead of going to Nineveh, he arose directly and went to Joppa; and there he found a ship just going to a place called Tarshish. He paid his fare to the captain, got into the ship, and tried to sail away. He was trying to run away from God; but this was a sad piece of folly, for he forgot that God is everywhere. His eye can see us wherever we are; we can not hide from God.

On the way to Tarshish, God sent a frightful storm; the ship was blown about, and tossed upon the waves; all the sailors were terribly frightened. They threw everything overboard, to lighten the ship; still the ship was in danger; then the poor sailors began to pray to their idol gods for deliverance. But where was Jonah all this time? He was fast asleep. Then the ship-master came to Jonah, and awoke him, and said, "Why sleepest thou? Arise, and call upon thy God; and pray to Him to save us, that we perish not." Jonah arose at once, and when he saw the danger, he was frightened. He knew why the storm came, but the sailors did not; and so they said, "Let us cast lots that we may know why this storm is come upon us. Perhaps one of us has done something wrong, and this danger is sent to punish him. We will cast lots, and find who the wicked man is." This thought was doubtless suggested by God Himself, that Jonah might be detected and punished. The lot fell upon Jonah. God made it fall upon him, that Jonah might feel his sin and confess it.

Jonah then told who he was, and confessed what he had done; that he had run away from delivering God's message. The sailors were shocked, and they asked what they should do to him. He felt humble for his sin; and not wishing that they should perish with him, he desired them to cast him into the sea, and the sea would then be calm. But the sailors did not want to do this, and for a long while would not do it. They

rowed very hard, and tried to bring the ship to the land; but they could not. God had determined to punish Jonah, and He would not calm the storm while he was in the ship. Jonah told the sailors this, and asked them again to throw him into the sea. These men seeing that the God of Israel was the true God, then prayed God to forgive them for throwing Jonah overboard, for it was not their wish to commit murder. Then they cast Jonah into the sea, and it ceased raging; and thus God showed the ignorant sailors how great His power is, and they, with becoming gratitude, offered up sacrifices to God.

But what became of Jonah? Was he drowned? No; God punished him for his sin, but He did not wish him to perish. We are told that "the Lord had prepared a great fish to swallow" him up; it opened its mouth to receive him, and he went down alive into the body of the fish, and was there three days and three nights. God would not let the fish hurt Jonah. God kept him alive.

While Jonah was in the fish, he confessed his sins, and asked for pardon; he prayed for deliverance. And God ordered the fish to cast Jonah up on the dry land again. The first engraving represents Jonah just after he has been cast upon the land. How thankful he was now! He was also humbled. But God still remembered Nineveh and He called Jonah again, and said, "Arise, go to the great city of Nineveh, and preach the preaching that I shall tell thee." So Jonah went, and he cried, as he passed along in the city, "Yet forty days, and Nineveh shall be overthrown!" They believed him and did repent. A fast was proclaimed, and even the king put on sackcloth and sat in ashes. They turned from their wicked ways and God spared them.

"JONAH EXHORTING THE NINEVITES TO REPENTANCE."

In our next engraving, the effect of Jonah's appeal is shown. Some of his hearers appear awed by the majesty of his presence, and others overcome by the commanding force of his words; some gaze upon him curiously, while others have bowed their heads or fallen in humble penitence before him.

SAYINGS OF CHILDHOOD:—Several boys were playing marbles. In the midst of their sport, the rain began to fall. Freddie stopped, and said, "Boys, I must go home: mother said I must not go out in the rain."—"Your mother,—fudge! The rain won't hurt you any more than it will us," said too or three voices at once. Freddie turned upon them with a look of pity, and the courage of a hero, and replied, "*I'll not disobey my mother for any of you!*" That boy will not disobey God, either; for a boy who obeys his mother will most likely obey God.

MICAH EXHORTING ISRAEL TO REPENTANCE.

ICAH is another of the minor prophets His full name means *Who is like Jehovah*. His prophecies are directed both against Israel and Judah. He predicts the capture of both; the captivity and restoration of the Jews, and the coming and reign of the Messiah. He rebukes in severest terms the evils of idolatry which had such license in the time of Ahaz, king of Judah. The bible tells us Judah suffered much, because Ahaz "transgressed against the Lord." The idol gods of Damascus were the ruin of him and of all Israel. Sin must ruin people at last, if they do not repent, and turn away from it. But Ahaz did not repent. He grew worse and worse. He took out the holy vessels from God's house, and cut them in pieces; then he made new altars, like the idol altars of Damascus, and offered offerings upon them, and burnt incense to the gods of Assyria, and shut up the holy temple of God in Jerusalem.

Had the people no good prophets to teach them better? Yes, there were many holy men in Judah then. Hosea, and Micah, and Isaiah were living at this time. These good men tried to keep the people from wickedness, but very few would attend to them. In the engraving the artist has represented Micah exhorting the people to repent, and turn from their wicked ways.

How grieved the prophet must have felt when he looked around and saw how very wicked his country was! But God comforted him. He taught him by His Spirit that happier times were coming. He taught him to prophesy of the Lord Jesus Christ, who would come into the world to save sinners; and of that future time when His gospel should be made known to all the world.

Dear children, when we look around, and see so much wickedness, perhaps we may often feel very unhappy; but the word of God comforts us. For we read of a happy time still coming. This world will not be then as it is now. There will be no idols worshipped then; all will love, and honor, and serve the only and true God.

ZECHARIAH'S VISION OF THE FOUR CHARIOTS.

THE prophet Zechariah had nine different visions which were revealed to him by God. In one of these wonderful visions, he tells us he saw four chariots come out from between two mountains; "and the mountains were mountains of brass." "In the first chariot were red horses; and in the second chariot black horses; and in the third chariot white horses; and in the fourth chariot grisled and bay horses."

This vision, seen by Zechariah, seems to represent the ways of Divine providence in disposing of events in the world. The horses of different colors signify as follows: the first, *red*, war and bloodshed; the second, *black*, the terrible results of war, such as famine, pestilence, and desolation; the third, *white*, a return of comfort, peace and prosperity; and the fourth, *grisled and bay*, days of prosperity and days of adversity. The motion of God's providence is swift and strong, like that of chariots; and His will is as immovable as mountains of brass. History records events which happened near the time when this vision was sent to Zechariah, and to which it seems to refer. Our engraving is one of the most beautiful in the whole book.

Dear children, the designs of God's providence are always right. Whether He sends war or peace, famine or prosperity, He makes all to work together for good. They proceed from the source of perfect wisdom, justice, and truth; from One who cannot err, and whose ways are always full of mercy. Rutherford says, "The chariot of God's providence runneth not upon broken wheels." I wish the little people would all commit to memory the following beautiful stanzas from Faber.

"O God! who art my childhood's love,
My boyhood's pure delight,
A presence felt the livelong day,
A welcome fear at night.

O let me speak to Thee, dear God!
Of those old mercies past,
O'er which new mercies day by day
Such lengthening shadows cast."

SAYINGS OF CHILDHOOD:—A little boy being asked, "How many gods are there?" replied, "One." "How do you know that?" "Because" said the boy, "there is only room for one; for He fills heaven and earth." And dear children, we need not fear; this mighty God will never leave nor forsake us, if we only trust Him.

THE ANNUNCIATION.

I AM sure, little folks, that you will want to talk about the infant Jesus. But first I must tell you something about His mother. Her name was Mary; she was quite a poor woman, but most good and holy. The angel Gabriel was sent from God to visit Mary in the little town of Nazareth. His coming was evidently a day visit and not a vision. It was joyful and wonderful news which the angel brought to Mary. He said to her, "Hail, thou that art highly favored, the Lord is with thee: blessed art thou among women." This salutation greatly troubled her. So far was this above her station and sense of desert, that "she cast about in her mind what manner of salutation this should be." But the angel soon comforted her, and told her in what a wonderful way she was going to be honored by God. Gabriel said, " Thou shalt have a son, and shalt call His name Jesus. He shall be great, and shall be called the Son of the Highest; and the Lord God shall give unto Him the throne of His father David, and He shall reign over the house of Jacob forever, and of His kingdom there shall be no end." Mary wondered very much when she heard this, and she humbly said, "Behold the handmaid of the Lord; be it unto me according to thy word;" and the angel left her.

The engraving is a beautiful picture of "The Annunciation," that is, of the angel telling Mary the good news. Mary was so thankful, that, a little time after, she sang a hymn of praise. The song was this: "My soul doth magnify the Lord, and my spirit hath rejoiced in God my Saviour. For He hath regarded the low estate of His handmaiden; for, behold, from henceforth all generations shall call me

blessed. For He that is mighty hath done to me great things; and holy is His name. And His mercy is on them that fear Him from generation to generation. He hath showed strength with His arm; He hath scattered the proud in the imagination of their hearts. He hath put down the mighty from their seats, and exalted them of low degree. He hath filled the hungry with good things; and the rich He hath sent empty away. He hath holpen His servant Israel, in remembrance of His mercy; as He spake to our fathers, to Abraham, and to his seed forever."

SAYINGS OF CHILDHOOD:—Of course, children, you know why Gabriel told Mary to call her son "Jesus." Because "He shall save." That is what the name means. A little boy in Sienna, during a long illness, spoke of going to Jesus. He conceived the odd idea of giving away among his friends the several parts of his body. All seemed to be bequeathed, when the mother said that he had omitted "the dear little heart." The little sick boy replied, that "*the little heart must be kept for Jesus.*"

THE NATIVITY.

MARY, the mother of Jesus, was living at Nazareth, but it was God's will that the holy Son of God should be born at Bethlehem. The Jews were under the Roman government, and just at this time, Augustus, the Roman emperor, made a law that all his subjects should be taxed; so Mary had to go with a good man, named Joseph, a carpenter, who was to be her husband, to Bethlehem, to have their names taken down before the taxing began. The journey from Nazareth to Bethlehem was a long one; and when they came to Bethlehem in the evening, they were very weary. They had no house in Bethlehem, so they went to the inn, but were told there was no room for them. The various inns and public houses of the city were crowded, owing to the taxation; so Joseph and Mary, being strangers, wandered about from house to house till quite late, then had to go to a stable where the oxen were kept.

There God gave Mary the promised infant; the child Jesus was born. His mother, having no friend or nurse near, "wrapped Him in swaddling-clothes;" and, having no other bed for her sweet baby, she laid Him in the manger among the hay and straw. O how humble and lowly Jesus was! There isn't one of you that was born in such an humble place as that. It was "for your sakes" that He became poor. He came that way so that He might know just how poor people feel, so that no one might feel afraid to come unto Him. How we ought to love Him for that! Yes, children, Jesus was born. The great King that was so long looked for by the Israelites, the One who was to be called "Wonderful, Counselor, The Mighty God, The Everlasting Father, The Prince of Peace," came as – a babe! He came as a child, that every little child might become a child of God.

There were some persons who were expecting the Messiah to come soon. Among these were some shepherds in the fields near Bethlehem, keeping watch over their flocks; and, perhaps, they were talking about it that very night, when, all at once, an angel stood beside them, and the glory of the Lord shone round about them. How do you think they felt? How would *you* have felt? Yes, they felt afraid. But the angel told them that they need not fear – that he had brought good tidings unto them: "For unto you is born this day, in the city of David, a Saviour, which is Christ the Lord. And this shall be a sign unto you; ye shall find the babe wrapped in swaddling-clothes, lying in a manger." And while the shepherds were listening to this wonderful message, suddenly they saw, with the angel, a great multitude of other angels; and they all began to sing a song of praise to God; and the shepherds heard them. What was this song? "Glory to God in the highest, and on earth peace, good will toward men." Then the angels went away into heaven, and the shepherds saw them no more.

Do you know why the angels sang this song? Because Jesus was come. He is called the "Prince of peace," because He came to bring peace upon the earth. The religion of Jesus is a religion of peace. It does not let us fight. When you are struck, it tells you not to strike back again. When your neighbor hates you, and treats you meanly, it tells you you must love him, and not quarrel with him. Then the religion that teaches all that must be a religion of peace, because it is a religion of love. Would

252 THE NATIVITY.

you not like to see this religion everywhere? Then become a helper with Jesus, trying to bring "Peace on earth." There are two ways: First, give *yourself* to Him, and then you will be able to sing the angel-song from your heart. Second, work for Him, that is, *tell the story to others.*

As soon as the angels went away, the shepherds were so anxious to see Jesus, that they said directly, " Let us go now to Bethlehem, and see this thing which the Lord hath made known to us." So they made haste, and went to Bethlehem; and there they soon found Joseph and Mary and the babe lying in the manger, as the angel said. It is this visit of the shepherds that the artist has given us in the picture. The infant Saviour is represented lying on His mother's knees. The shepherds are bent round, adoring and worshipping their future Lord and Redeemer. The very ox and the little lambs seem drawn towards Him. When the shepherds had seen Jesus, they went and told their friends and neighbors what they had heard and seen; and afterwards returned to their flocks full of holy joy. Just what we should do. We should be, like these shepherds, anxious to see and know Jesus; and then anxious to tell our friends and neighbors the good news.

THE WISE MEN GUIDED BY THE MYSTERIOUS STAR.

THERE were other people, besides the shepherds, who came to see the blessed Jesus when He was a little babe. A long way off, in the East, in Arabia, perhaps, or some other distant country, there lived some "wise men." They were very learned and understood many things. These wise and good men had heard, in their distant country, of the promised Saviour, and they were expecting His coming. One evening, when they were gazing up into the heavens, they saw a very bright and peculiar star. Not a common star, such as they saw every night; but one quite new to them. God put it into their hearts that this star was the sign that the great King was born, and that the star would lead them to Him, so they immediately went in the direction in which it appeared. The engraving shows the grand procession of the wise men, following the mysterious star. The star went before them until it brought them near to Jerusalem, where Herod the king was living, and as they knew by inspiration that Christ was a king, they went to the palace to inquire, saying, "Where is He that is born King of the Jews? for we have seen His star in the East, and are come to worship Him." This made Herod afraid, for he thought this must be a king who would take his kingdom from him. So Herod called the priests, and the scribes, or writers of the law, and asked them where Christ must be born. How could they know? Because they had read the prophets; and there they learned that Jesus would be born in Bethlehem. So they told this to Herod. Then Herod secretly called the wise men and asked them a great many questions about the star, and the time they first saw it. They answered his questions; and then he sent them to Bethlehem, and said, "Go and search diligently for the young child; and when ye have found Him, bring me word again, that I may come and worship Him also." But Herod did not really mean to worship Him, but to kill Him.

But God Himself showed these wise men where to find our blessed Lord. When the wise men went away from Herod, the star still moved before them until it brought them to Bethlehem, and, at last, "stood over where the young child was." Then they rejoiced with very great joy; and went into the house, and "saw the young child with Mary His mother, and fell down, and worshipped Him." Though they saw a little baby, and a poor mother holding Him in her arms, they knew He was Lord and King. They offered Him the gifts they had brought—"gold, and frankincense, and myrrh." I know not

how long they remained worshipping Him, but before they returned home God warned them in a dream not to return to Herod; so they went home another way.

Ah, my children, we need not, like the wise men, travel a long way to seek the Saviour. He is always near—He can hear our softest prayer. We do not need a star to lead us to Jesus. His word and His Spirit will lead us to Him, if we ask to be led.

SAYINGS OF CHILDHOOD:—I once heard of a dear little girl who was assisting some friends to decorate a Christmas-tree; and being told the toys and ornaments were intended as presents for the different members of the family, she anxiously inquired, "What present they could make to the Lord upon His birthday?" Some of you may think that a funny question to ask; but you can give something to Jesus. What is it? *Your hearts.* I wish you would learn this beautiful verse:—

> "Jesus, take this heart of mine,
> Make it pure and wholly Thine;
> Thou hast bled and died for me,
> I will henceforth live for Thee."

Jesus would rather have that present, than all the gold, and frankincense, and myrrh which the wise men brought.

THE FLIGHT INTO EGYPT.

YOU remember in our last talk we found the wicked Herod was frightened, because he feared the little babe at Bethlehem would live to take his throne away from him; so he determined to kill Jesus, if he could. God knew that Herod meant to kill Jesus, and by a dream He sent the wise men home another way, so that Herod could not see them. When Herod heard that the wise men had gone away, without telling him what he desired, he became very angry. He was determined to kill Jesus; and as he did not know the house in which the Saviour lay, he said he would destroy all the little children in Bethlehem, hoping that Jesus would be killed among them.

But God would not let Herod do what he so wickedly wished. In another dream, the Lord appeared to Joseph, and told him to get right up that very night, and take the young child and his mother, and go to Egypt, and stay there till they should be told to come back, for Herod was seeking the child to destroy Him. You see how foolish it was

for Herod to think that he could outwit God. Before daylight, they were far on their journey, and Herod never knew anything about their going.

In the engraving the artist presents a very sweet and tender scene. The little group—Joseph, Mary, and Jesus—are seen journeying along. They have just come to the top of a little rising ground, from which Joseph looks back, to see if they are being followed; Mary's face is turned upward—she is looking to heaven for that protection she so divinely seeks; while the little Jesus sleeps, all unconscious in His mother's arms.

THE MASSACRE OF THE INNOCENTS.

WHEN Jesus was about two years of age, Herod's cruel command was given to put to death all the babies in Bethlehem, of two years old and under; he thought that by killing the children of that age he should be sure to kill the new king. Herod's hard-hearted messengers went from house to house, through the streets of Bethlehem, and slew the little innocents. The artist has presented this terrible scene in the engraving. From the cruel soldiers of Herod there is no escape. The poor mothers weep bitterly, and beg the soldiers to spare their children; and the little children cry, and cling to their mothers for safety; but nothing can save them. By the stairway, in the picture, is a mother with her three babes, awaiting, with the calmness of despair, the destruction to which they are surely doomed. Surrounded, already overtaken, she can go no farther, and, lying upon the ground, as a pitiful effort against fate, she covers them with her body as her only shield.

It is painful to dwell upon a scene of such awful horror. And yet history tells us that the wicked king Herod was so cruel that he even slew three of his own sons; no wonder he had a heart so hard as to kill the little infants in Bethlehem. But all his cruelty was vain; all this time, Jesus was safe in Egypt. Children, do you know why the little children, whom Herod killed, were called the Holy Innocents? Because they were the first who died for Jesus Christ's sake. Jesus felt for them; they were very dear to Him; and when they died they went to heaven. They have been happy ever since in heaven, and always will be.

JESUS BEFORE THE DOCTORS.

JOSEPH remained in Egypt about two years. Jesus was then four years old. At this time an angel appeared in a dream to Joseph in Egypt, and told him that Herod was dead; and the angel said, "Arise, and take the young child and His mother, and go into the land of Israel." So he went, and took up his abode in Nazareth. "And the child grew, and waxed strong in spirit, filled with wisdom; and the grace of God was upon Him." Jesus grew strong in body. God likes to see children grow that way. He wants them to be hearty, healthy, and happy. "The grace of God was upon" Jesus, and that will make any child sweet and lovable. The little boy Jesus obeyed His father and mother. He did it cheerfully—never fretted because He was asked to do anything. There is hardly anything that your parents want you to do but what Jesus did when He was a child. He drew water, carried in wood, picked up chips, and run errands. If you will follow His example, you will do as He did—grow in wisdom and in favor with God and man.

When Jesus was twelve years old, He came up with His parents to Jerusalem to keep the feast of the Passover; but when Joseph and Mary started to return home, Jesus stayed behind. But when they stopped to rest at night He was nowhere to be found; so they immediately turned back to Jerusalem to find Him. They looked for him three days all around the city, and found Him at last in the temple, among the boys who came to be taught by the learned doctors there. They saw Jesus sitting among the doctors, talking to them, and hearing, and asking questions. The picture shows this scene—the learned doctors of the law are gathered around the child Jesus. Everybody is astonished at His understanding and His answers. But when His mother Mary came to call him, He went home with her directly; and He obeyed her and Joseph in all things. He helped and worked for them, though He was really their God and King.

SAYINGS OF CHILDHOOD:—"Children, obey your parents *in the Lord.*" Do you know what those last words mean? I will illustrate it. "Say I am not at home," said a mother sending her little girl to answer the bell. "O mamma!" exclaimed the child, "won't that be a *story!* You don't want your little Fanny to tell a *story!*" Then the mother told her to say she was "engaged," which was true. Always obey your parents, when they tell you to do what is *right.*

PREACHING OF JOHN THE BAPTIST.

NOW Jesus could not always remain a boy. Since the last talk, we must think of Him as about eighteen years older. Just before it was time for Him to make Himself known as the Saviour, there was a man who commenced preaching to the people. His name was John and he was a singular looking man. He wore clothing made out of camel's hair, fastened round his loins with a leathern girdle; and his food was locusts and wild honey. In the engraving the artist has represented John standing on a high rock, preaching to the multitudes that gathered around him.

What did John say? He said, "Repent ye, for the kingdom of heaven is at hand." John told the people, that Jesus Himself was coming to show them the way to heaven and to set up His kingdom in the hearts of those who believed. But if people do not feel their sinfulness, they will not care for a Saviour; so when John was preparing the way for Christ, he said first, "Repent ye." Great numbers came out to hear him—from Jerusalem, and Judea, and round about Jordan. Some of them were really penitent; but some who came were not truly penitent. They were the Pharisees and Sadducees. They prided themselves on being "Abraham's children," because they were descended from him. But they were not a bit like that good man. John called them a "generation of vipers," they were so wicked. He told them they must "bring forth fruits meet for repentance." Do you know what that means? Suppose a little girl tells her teacher that she loves Jesus, and yet continues to bear such fruit as "Cross words," "Pride," "Selfishness?" Will her *say-so* make the fruit good? Well, that was what John meant; they must show their repentance by their fruit. A boy who has shown a great deal of bad fruit, must not only say he is "sorry." He must *show he is sorry by his actions;* that is, if he is truly sorry for disobeying mamma to-day, he will not be very likely to disobey her to-morrow, but will begin at once to show the fruit of obedience.

SAYINGS OF CHILDHOOD:—A class of scholars in a school for the deaf and dumb were asked, "What is the most precious thing in the world?" One wrote, "Going home;" another, "A mother's love." The last and youngest came to the board and wrote with trembling fingers and bowed head, ' The tear of penitence." And she was right. If we have sinned, there is no gift we can bring the Lord half so precious as repentance.

BAPTISM OF JESUS.

ONE day, as John was baptizing, Jesus came to him and desired to be baptized. All the others, who had come, were sinners needing pardon; but John knew that Jesus had never done a wrong thing in all His life, and had nothing to repent of. So, at first, John did not want to baptize Jesus, and he said, "I have need to be baptized of Thee, and comest Thou to me?" But Jesus answered, "Let it be so now, for thus it becometh us to fulfill all righteousness." Then John baptized Him. Jesus was baptized to show us that baptism is right; one of God's commands which He came to obey. In the picture the artist has represented Jesus standing in the edge of the water, and John baptizing Him.

After Jesus had been baptized, as He came up out of the water, the heavens were opened, and the Holy Spirit came down from heaven, in the shape of a dove, and rested upon the head of Jesus, and the voice of God the Father was heard from heaven, saying, "This is My beloved Son, in whom I am well pleased." Dear children, do *you* want that dove in your hearts? A man once asked a lady which of God's animals she would like to be. The lady thought that was a very funny question, but still she made a choice. Then the man said he would rather be a pure white dove than anything else, because it is the sign of the Holy Ghost. A dove is the gentlest, kindest creature God has made; but we may become more gentle and loving than a dove if we have God's Holy Spirit in our hearts; that will give our eyes a gentle look, will make our hands work to do good for others, will make our feet run to help others. Would you not like to have the Holy Spirit come into your hearts? It will be like inviting a dove to come in there. You would not be afraid of a dove—would you? I hope you know this beautiful hymn:

> "Come, Holy Spirit, heavenly dove,
>   With all Thy quickening powers,
> Kindle a flame of sacred love
>   In these *young* hearts of ours.

JESUS TEMPTED BY THE DEVIL.

SHORTLY after He had been baptized, Jesus was led by the Spirit into the wilderness. He was there forty days and forty nights, all alone; He spent the time in fasting and prayer, and communion with God. Then Satan came to tempt Him. We can't get rid of Satan anywhere. The tempter came when Jesus was the weakest—after he had fasted forty days and nights. How many times he has tempted some hungry little boy or girl to steal. He never comes that way when you have had a good dinner.

How did Satan tempt the Saviour? First, he brought stones to Jesus, and said to Him, "If thou be the Son of God, command that these stones be made bread." He knew that Jesus was hungry, and he didn't ask anything at first that seemed to be very wrong. Why should'nt Christ have turned the stones into bread? Because that would be distrusting His heavenly Father; and so Jesus told the tempter, that the Scriptures said that we do not live by bread alone, but that God takes care of us.

Then Satan tried a new temptation. He led Jesus to the top of the temple, and placed Him on the highest part of the building, and tempted Him to cast Himself down, right there where the people could see Him fall. The devil told Him that the Scriptures said that the angels would bear Him up in their hands, so that He should not be hurt one bit. If He did that, Satan said, then the people would believe immediately that He was the Saviour. But Jesus would not cast Himself down from the temple, because it was not God's will; so He said to Satan, "It is written, thou shalt not tempt the Lord thy God."

Then Satan took Jesus up into a very high mountain, and showed Him all the kingdoms of the world, and the glory of them, and said, "All these things will I give Thee, if Thou wilt fall down and worship me." The picture presents this scene. But Jesus told Satan that it was written in God's word, "Thou shalt worship the Lord thy God, and Him only shalt thou serve." So Jesus conquered again.

Then Satan left Jesus for a time, and the angels came and waited on Him.

SAYINGS OF CHILDHOOD:—A little girl gave in her testimony in a meeting not long ago, when I was present. She said: "Satan has been trying to tempt me; but I tell him he needn't waste his time, for I am on the Rock Christ Jesus." That is a good place to stand, children; Satan can't harm you there.

THE MARRIAGE IN CANA OF GALILEE.

HERE was to be a wedding at Cana, a village in the hills of Galilee, and Jesus, together with his disciples, were all invited. Mary, the Lord's mother, was there too. There Jesus is supposed to have wrought His first miracle. A great many people were at the feast; the wine was soon all drank, and they wanted more. The bridegroom was probably a poor man, and unable to buy wine to set before his guests, and Mary, the mother of Jesus, said unto Him, "They have no wine." Then Jesus told Mary not to trouble herself about this, but to wait patiently, and leave all to Him.

The servants were in the room, waiting upon the company, and Mary spoke to them, and said, "Whatsoever He saith unto you, do it." Now there were six great jars standing by, and Jesus told the servants to fill them with water. So they filled them up to the brim; and then he told them to draw out some of what they had poured in, and carry it to the governor of the feast. The servants did as Jesus commanded. In the engraving the artist has represented them carrying the jars filled with the wine.

The governor of the feast, having tasted the wine, was astonished; the wonderful power of Jesus had, in a moment, turned the water into wine; and the governor was so pleased with it, because it was so good, that he said to the bridegroom that most people began their feasts with their best wine, but that here the best had been kept for the last. And they all wondered at the great power of Jesus, and "His disciples believed on Him."

SAYINGS OF CHILDHOOD.—A boy was asked, "What is a miracle?" His answer was, "Something that nobody can do or see through but God." That was very good. Nobody but God can do a miracle. We often read of miracles in the old Testament. Moses, Elijah, and Elisha all worked miracles. But the way in which they worked them was not like the way in which Christ worked them. They wrought wonders by the *command* of God; Christ wrought them by *His own power*. He had the power Himself, *because He was God*.

JESUS AND THE WOMAN OF SAMARIA.

ONE day Jesus left Judea and went into Galilee; on the way He had to pass through Samaria; the weather was very warm, and Jesus sat down beside the well of Sychar, while his disciples were gone into the city to buy food. This well was called Jacob's well, because many years before, it had belonged to Jacob. Jesus was weary, hungry and thirsty; and as He sat there a woman came out of the city to draw water from the well. And Jesus said unto her, "Give me to drink." The woman was surprised that a Jew should ask water of a Samaritan woman, because the Jews despised the people of Samaria, on account of their having built a temple for themselves, after the Jewish captivity, when they had tried to prevent the Jews from re-building one at Jerusalem.

Jesus, however, was kind and good to the greatest sinners, and He said to the woman, "If thou knewest who it is that saith, give me to drink, thou would'st have asked of Him, and He would have given thee living water, of which whosoever drinketh thirsteth no more." By this He meant the Holy Spirit's influences, which, because they are refreshing to the thirsty soul of man, in search of peace and happiness, are often compared to water.

The woman could not understand what Jesus meant; but she thought it must be very pleasant never to thirst again, so she said to Him, "Sir, give me this water, that I thirst not, neither come hither to draw." But did Jesus give her the living water at once? No; He first told her more about it, and about Himself, for she did not yet know Him to be the Saviour. The woman wondered more and more at all Jesus said to her, and she began to think, He must be a prophet; so she asked Him some questions about the place in which God ought to be worshipped. She wished to know whether it should be Jerusalem, as the Jews said, or Mount Gerizim, as the Samaritans said. Jesus told her that God did not so much care about the *place*, as about the *spirit* in which the people worshipped Him. He said, "God is a Spirit, and those who worship Him, must worship Him in spirit and in truth; and He will accept such, in whatever place they may pray." Then the good Jesus told her that He was the Messiah, and that she must worship God in spirit and in truth. The woman was so glad to hear this that she ran at once into the city, to tell the good news to her friends, and to bring them to Jesus. She said, "Come, see a man who told me all that ever I did. Is not this the Christ?" Then the people ran out of the

city and came to Jesus. While this was taking place the disciples returned, bringing food for their Master to eat; but Jesus said, "I have meat to eat that ye know not of. My meat is to do the will of Him that sent Me, and to finish His work." Jesus was so happy, giving the water of life to the poor Samaritans, that He thought nothing of His own bodily wants.

SAYINGS OF CHILDHOOD:—"Sam do you find a spot for secret prayer?" asked a minister of a stable-boy. "Oh, yes, sir! that old coach is my closet." Children, we can find a place of worship anywhere; for we can worship wherever God is and that is *everywhere*. Be sure your worship is *sincere;* that is the only kind God accepts. But, is it sincere worship if we trifle, or play, when those about us are singing God's praise, or praying to him? No, this is mocking God, and that is a dreadful thing to do.

JESUS IN THE SYNAGOGUE.

WHILE Jesus was in Galilee, He went to Nazareth, the place where He had lived when He was a boy. Would you not think that the people there would have been glad to see Him? On the Sabbath-day He went into the synagogue there, just as He was in the habit of doing elsewhere, to teach the people. The Jews had certain parts of God's word appointed to be read every day; and the part for this day was from the prophet Isaiah. They gave Jesus the book to read, and the portion of Scripture was all about Himself, though it was written ever so many years before He was born. In the engraving the artist has represented Jesus in the act of preaching to the people.

But the people wanted something more than this. They wanted to see some wonderful thing, such as His curing the sick or raising the dead to life. And these things He could not do, because of their unbelief. He told them that God did such things only for those who believed in Him. And when He reproved them for their unbelief, they became so angry that they did not mind the fact that they were in the Lord's house, and that it was the Sabbath-day, but they rose up, and drove Him out of the city, to the top of a hill, and would have cast Him down, but He just passed through the midst of them and went on His way. That is the way He was treated by those among whom He lived when He was a little boy. How do *you* treat Him?

JESUS PREACHING BY THE SEA OF GALILEE.

GREAT crowds followed Jesus wherever he went; one day the crowd was so great that they "pressed upon Him to hear the word of God, as He stood by the lake of Gennesareth," or the sea of Galilee. Jesus saw two boats which were empty, standing at the water's edge; one of these boats belonged to Simon Peter, and Jesus got into that, and asked Simon to push it away a little from the land. He did this so that the multitude could not crowd Him any more. And then Jesus sat down and taught the people out of the boat. In the first engraving, the artist presents this beautiful scene; the Saviour sitting in the boat on the quiet peaceful lake, preaching the Gospel; and all the people standing on the shore, anxiously attending to every word He spoke.

After Jesus had finished speaking, He told Simon to let down his net, and try to catch some fish; but Simon answered, "Master, we have toiled all night and taken nothing; nevertheless, at Thy word I will let down the net." Don't you see Jesus wanted to pay Simon for being so kind as to let Him have the use of his boat. Peter had been fishing all night, and had caught nothing; and yet, because Jesus wanted him to, he let down the net again. Do you ever do anything just because Jesus wants you to do so?

Simon threw the net into the sea at once; and he caught so many fish that the net was broken by the great weight; and Simon had to call his friends in the other boat to come and help him. In the next picture we have the

"MIRACULOUS DRAUGHT OF FISHES."

They filled both the boats so full of fish that they began to sink. Christ always rewards those who do just as He tells them.

When Simon Peter saw the miracle which Jesus had done, he was so astonished that he threw himself at the feet of the Saviour and cried, "Depart from me, for I am a sinful man, O Lord!"—meaning that he was not worthy of the high honor of having Jesus on board his boat, and of continuing in His holy presence. Jesus knew what was in Peter's heart; so He encouraged the timid man, and said, "Fear not: from henceforth thou shalt catch men." What did Jesus mean by this? Peter had been a fisherman all his life; but now he was to be a preacher of the Gospel; to labor for the souls of men, and try to bring them to Jesus, that they might believe and be saved. This is what is meant by "catching men."

The two disciples, Simon and Andrew, brought their boats to land; and then they left all, and followed Jesus. They thought more of their Saviour than they did of their boats and fish. They left their friends as well. So Jesus and the two disciples walked along by the sea-side, and soon they saw two other fishermen, James and John, sitting in a boat with their father Zebedee, mending their nets. James and John loved the Lord Jesus, and Jesus knew what was in their hearts; and, as He passed, He called them to come after Him. James and John obeyed the call at once. They left everything because He wanted to make them "fishers of men." Jesus hasn't got through wanting persons to become fishers of men. Small as you are, He wants you for that purpose. He wants you to try and save others. What are you trying to do for the children that you are acquainted with? "Fishers of men"—will you be one? Do not think you are small, and not of much account.

A story is told of a king who went into his garden one morning, and found everything withered and dying. He asked an oak that stood near the gate what the trouble was. He found it was sick of life and determined to die, because it was not tall and beautiful like the pine. The pine was all out of heart, because it could not bear grapes, like the vine. The vine was going to throw its life away, because it could not stand erect and have as fine fruit as the peach tree. The geranium was fretting because it was not tall and fragrant like the lilac, and so on all through the garden. Coming to a heart's-ease, he found its bright face lifted, as cheery as ever. "Well, heart's-ease, I'm glad to find one brave little flower in this general discouragement and dying. You don't seem a bit disheartened?" "No, I am not of much account, but I thought if you had wanted an oak, or a pine, or a peach tree, or a lilac, you would have planted one; but as I knew you wanted a heart's-ease, I am determined to be the best little heart's-ease that I can." Boys and girls, if you cannot be a Paul or a Silas, if you cannot be an oak or a pine, if you cannot do great things yet for God, will you not try by doing all the good you can, by being loving and patient and gentle and obedient, to be the very best little heart's-ease that you can?

> "What though thy power, compared to some,
>   Be weak to aid and bless;
> Because the rose is queen of flowers
>   Do we love the heart's-ease less?
> Others may do a greater work,
>   But you have your part to do;
> And no one in all God's heritage
>   Can do it so well as you."

SAYINGS OF CHILDHOOD:—A little child went every day to see a little cripple; she read to her, lent her dolly, her toys, her books, carried flowers and fruits to her, and when asked once, if it was because she loved the crippled child so much, she answered: "I love her now, but I began to go, because I loved Jesus so much I wanted to do something that He would like, and you know He said: "Inasmuch as ye did it unto one of the least of these—ye did it unto Me."

JESUS PREACHING TO THE MULTITUDE.

JESUS was now very popular. In every town or village that He came to, He used to go and teach in the synagogue. A synagogue was a place where the Jews who lived too far from Jerusalem to go to the temple every Sabbath-day used to meet, and hear the Old Testament read and explained to them, and pray together. Sometimes He would withdraw Himself to a desert place; but "the people sought Him and came unto Him, and stayed Him, that He should not depart from them." In the first picture the artist has represented Jesus preaching to the multitudes who have followed Him into the wilderness.

In this talk I want to tell you about some of the wonderful cures which Jesus performed. One day Jesus was coming down the street with a multitude of people, and a poor leper, seeing Him, came and bowed before Him; he offered a very short prayer, only nine words: "Lord, if Thou wilt, Thou canst make me clean." This poor leper knew that Jesus was *able* to cure him; but he did not feel quite sure that Jesus was *willing* to cure him. But, as soon as the poor man prayed, Jesus put out His hand and touched him, and said, "I will, be thou clean;" and the leper was cleansed at once.

There was at Jerusalem a pool called the pool of Bethesda. One day Jesus saw a sick man lying beside this pool. God used to send an angel to disturb the waters at certain times, and the first person who afterwards got into the pool was healed of his disease. This poor man had been sick a very long time, and he could find no one to cure his disease. He knew the waters would cure him, and he had laid there a good while; but, being too ill and weak to get into the water, some other sufferer, who had friends to help him, would get in first, and the virtue of the water was gone. Jesus knew all this; He therefore came and asked the man, saying, "Wilt thou be made whole?" He said he would, and

then Jesus, who knew his heart, said, "Rise, take up thy bed and walk." And the man was made whole immediately, and took up his bed and walked. And as he went off with his bed, the loving Saviour warned him to leave off sinning, lest God should bring a worse punishment upon him.

Again there was a poor woman who had heard of the wonderful power of Jesus. She was sick, and nothing could help her. She found out where Jesus was, and followed the crowd that was around Him. She said within herself, "If I may but touch the hem of His garment I shall be whole." She did not say it aloud, but Jesus knew her heart's desire. She touched His garment, and, lo! she felt in her body that she was healed. Her faith *touched Jesus*, and according to her faith it was done. Jesus knew that virtue had gone out of Him, and He said, "Who touched me?" The woman who had proved the healing power came and told Him, before all the people, for what cause she had touched Him, and how she was healed. Then Jesus spoke so lovingly to her, "Daughter, thy faith hath made thee whole—go in peace and be whole of thy plague." Dear children, suppose she had refused to declare it before others, how ungrateful she would have been! Let us never be ashamed to bear testimony of His power to save.

I could tell you about many more wonderful cures which Jesus wrought. Most of them were cures to the blind, or the lame, or the sick. He made them well directly by His power and love. In the next picture you see

"JESUS HEALING THE SICK."

He is surrounded by those afflicted with terrible diseases; He is healing them. There you can see the mother, with her emaciated child in her arms; another bearing one who has the hopeless look of idiocy; a sick man prostrate on the ground; a wretched cripple trying to touch the hem of His garment; and still another, seemingly half-dead, supported by some pitying friend. The Saviour in the midst of all is seen pressing the forehead of the child, while the rest await the power of His miraculous touch.

Dear little folks, the power of Jesus is present to-day to heal. He doesn't *always* cure sick people, when asked to do so. There is an "if" that comes into all true prayer. We must say, "If it is best." Would we want what God, who knows all things, thought not best? But Jesus is *always ready* to cure the sin-sick soul. It takes no longer for Him to do that, than it did for Him to cure the body; He is no farther away, indeed, not so far; then some had to travel miles to meet Him, now we have only to whisper, and He hears. Oh! have you been to the Great Physician and been healed of your sin?

SAYINGS OF CHILDHOOD:—A Scotch girl was converted under the preaching of Whitefield. She was asked if her heart was changed, and gave this beautiful reply: "Something, I know, is changed; it may be the world, it may be my heart. There is a great change somewhere, I'm sure; for everything is different from what it once was." Sinners may come to this Jesus, every day, and be cured; none need perish, and none need wait.

SERMON ON THE MOUNT.

ONE day, Jesus sat down upon the side of a mountain, and began to preach to the people. His talk that day is called our Lord's Sermon on the Mount. In the picture we see the Saviour seated on the mountain side, beneath the large trees, expounding to His followers the solemn and sublime truths of the new dispensation.

He began His sermon by telling them who are truly blessed, who are really happy people in this world. He said, Blessed are the meek, and the humble, and the gentle; blessed are those who are sorry for sin, and that ask for pardon; blessed are those who have new hearts, and those who are willing to give up all for righteousness' sake. These are the happy people; they are happy because they are good and holy. Then Jesus told them that His disciples were not only blessed of Him, but that they bless others also. They show mercy. They help those in distress. They are peacemakers. They bring peace wherever they go. They stop all quarrelling whenever they have a chance, and, best of all, they teach people to be at peace with God. They are the salt of the earth. They keep it from going to corruption. They are the light of the world. They are like a light-house that throws its beams far out upon the waves. It is only one light, but it keeps many people from being dashed to death upon the rocks. In the same way, how much good one Christian can do! You can be a light in the home—so that you can give light unto all that are in the house. And it takes only a *little* light to do that!

Then Jesus gave His disciples some beautiful lessons about love to their fellow-creatures. He told them they must not get angry with one another. God says that whosoever *hateth* any one is a murderer. What is it that makes one man want to kill another? Isn't it just because he gets very angry? If you allow yourselves to become

SERMON ON THE MOUNT.

very angry, some time you actually may kill some one. If anger is in the heart, how will it be shown? Sometimes in blows, but oftener in unkind speech. How many times have you heard little boys call each other "fool," and names even worse than that? perhaps you have done it yourself. Is it right? Just hear what Christ says about it: "But I say unto you that whosoever shall say to his brother, thou fool, shall be in danger of hell-fire." Do you see in what danger you are when you speak in that way?

Jesus told them that they ought not to swear at all. Dear children, I hope you never do that; and *never will do it*. Remember this, that your conversation should never have an oath in it, but that your Yes should be a simple *yes*, and your No a simple *no*. People will believe you a great deal quicker.

He also told them that they ought to love not only their friends, but also their enemies. Never strike back; never say hard words when hard words have been said to you. In this way you can make friends out of your enemies, and that is a great deal better than whipping them. There is no way of winning an enemy like loving him. How shall we love him? By blessing him when he curses us—by doing good to him when he is hating us—by praying for him when he is using us very spitefully. In that way we can both overcome him and make him better.

Then Jesus spoke to His disciples about prayer. He told them not to pray like the Pharisees, in the streets, to be seen of men; but to pray in secret, in their own rooms, where only God could see them. And then he taught them how they ought to pray; He gave them that beautiful prayer which we call "The Lord's Prayer." Dear children, does it do any good to ask God for the things we want? What did Jesus say? "Ask, and it shall be given you; seek, and ye shall find; knock, and it shall be opened unto you." Did you ever ask your papa or your mamma for bread? When you asked for bread, did they ever give you a *stone?* When you asked them for fish, did they ever give you a serpent? Why not? *Because they love you.* Who do you think is the best—your parents here, or your Father which is in heaven? Jesus said, If our parents, "being evil, know how to give good gifts unto their children, how much more shall your Father which is in heaven give good things to them that ask Him?"

If God is so good to us, then how should we act towards each other? Jesus says, in this sermon, that we ought not to *judge* one another. Do you think we ought to be saying and believing hard things of each other? Why not? Because, *first*, you will be treated the same way yourself. If you think hard things of the little boys and girls with whom you play, they will always be thinking hard things of you. *Second*, as you judge them,

God will judge you. If you forgive them, He will forgive you; and if you are hard to them, He will be hard to you. Let me give you the rule Jesus laid down: "Therefore all things whatsoever ye would that men should do to you, do ye even so to them: for this is the law and the prophets."

If you act according to this verse, you will not only be little Christians, but little ladies and gentlemen.

Jesus said also, that all the people in the world are taking a long journey; but they are not all traveling on the same road, and they are not all going to the same country. There are two roads, and every person is walking in one or other of them. At the beginning of each road is a gate. One of these gates is very wide; it always stands open; and the path into which it leads is broad; it looks bright and pleasant; and many people are walking there. The other gate is straight and narrow. It is shut; but when any one knocks, it is always opened at once; and over it is written, "Knock, and it shall be opened unto you." The path to which this gate leads is very narrow; very few are seen in the narrow road, but those who are there like it very much, and wish others to walk with them. They say, "The way is a way of pleasantness, and the path is a path of peace." Jesus told His disciples of all this. Do you know what is meant by it? The broad way is the way of sin, and it leads to death. The narrow way is the way of holiness, and it leads to heaven. In which of these two roads are *you* walking?

There is one other thing Jesus said, in the sermon on the Mount, I want to talk about. Two men determined each to build himself a house. One of these men was wise, the other foolish. The wise man built his house upon a rock; when the storm came, "it fell not, for it was founded upon a rock." The foolish man built his house upon the sand; and when the storm came, "it fell, and great was the fall of it." Dear little folks, did you ever build a house? What! do you say *no?* Why you are building one every day. You are building up a *character* that is to last you for eternity. Into that house you are putting something every minute. Be careful how you listen to those people who advise you to put into that house anything that is wrong. Didn't any one ever tell you that it wouldn't do any harm, just to tell mother a little lie? Remember a lie is like a crooked brick. Didn't any one ever tell you that it was no harm to break the Sabbath? To fight? To drink a glass of beer? There are a good many that would like to have you build upon the sand. But don't do it; build your house upon the "Rock of Ages." Those who trust in Him are safe, and will be safe forever.

CHRIST STILLING THE TEMPEST.

ALL day Jesus had been working hard; and, in the evening, He went with His disciples into a ship, to cross over the sea of Galilee. Jesus was tired with preaching and walking so far, and He lay down upon a pillow to sleep—not such a pillow as you and I have, but more like a little stool. When they had gone a little way, a very heavy storm came on. God blew His breath on the sea, and that made wind and waves, such great waves that the ship was nearly filled with water; still Jesus slept. But the disciples, forgetting that Jesus was with them, and that they must be safe in His keeping, became so frightened that they went to Jesus, asleep on his pillow, and woke Him up, saying, "Lord, save us: we perish." And He said unto them, "Why are ye fearful, O ye of little faith?" Then He arose, and spoke to the winds and sea, and said, "Peace, be still;" and there was a great calm. When the storm had gone, the disciples looked at each other with fear in their faces, and said one to another, "What manner of man is this, that even the wind and the sea obey Him?" The scene, represented in the engraving, is where the disciples come to Christ and awaken Him.

Why did the winds and the sea obey Jesus? Because He is God, the God who made them. And Jesus can do something still more wonderful. He can calm and quiet our angry passions, and say to them, "Peace, be still." Once there was a storm, and all on the ship were very much frightened except one sailor; he did not seem troubled at all. When some one asked him what made him so calm, why he was not frightened, he said, "If I should drown, I would only be sinking into the hollow of my Father's hand." What a beautiful thought that is, children; *that God holds the sea in the hollow of His hand; and drowning is only sinking into God's hand.*

SAYINGS OF CHILDHOOD:—A ship was on her voyage for a southern port, when a fearful storm burst upon her, filling all hearts with fear. A sailor had his little boy on board with him. Seeing the boy's confidence, a passenger asked him, "Don't you think the boat will be lost, and all be drowned?" "Oh, no!" he answered; "I have just been out on deck; and I know we are all safe, for *father's at the wheel.*" Dear children, we need have no fear, when Jesus is with us!

THE PENITENT WOMAN.

NOW there was a Pharisee, named Simon, who, one day, asked Jesus to dine with him; the Saviour accepted the invitation, went home with the Pharisee, and sat down to meat. When reclining at the table, as was the fashion of those times, there came in with the crowd of on-lookers "a woman, in the city which was a sinner." It may have been that she had heard that gracious invitation, which Jesus gave a short time before this entertainment at the house of Simon, " Come unto Me all ye that labor and are heavy laden, and I will give you rest." Perhaps it was the memory of those tender words which had made her penitent; and when she saw Jesus go into the house, she followed Him, and came and stood behind Him, and began to weep bitterly. Some of her tears fell upon the bare feet of the Saviour, and she, noticing that, wiped them away with the hairs of her head. But that made them flow all the faster, until she literally bathed the feet of the Saviour with her tears. Then she took out a box of ointment, and poured the ointment on Jesus' feet, and anointed them, and wiped them with her hair.

The proud Pharisee was surprised that a holy prophet, as Jesus professed to be, should allow a woman of such a class to approach Him; and though he did not speak, Jesus knew what he thought. And he told him there were two debtors; and the one owed five hundred pence, and the other fifty. As they were unable to pay, their creditor kindly forgave them. Now, said Jesus to the Pharisee, which of these was likely to love the kind creditor most? "Why," said the Pharisee, "the one who had most forgiven him." "Rightly said," answered Jesus; "now thou hast not had the sense of pardon as this woman. My words touched her heart; she has sincerely repented; her many sins are forgiven her, and she therefore loves me much." And Jesus turned to the woman and said, "Thy sins are forgiven; thy faith hath saved thee; go in peace."

In the engraving the artist has presented a picture of penitence. The humble and penitent, who come to Jesus in faith and prayer, will surely be forgiven. Dear children, out of what kind of a box must we take our prayers to Jesus? *Our hearts.* The bible tells us God is best pleased with a broken heart. A heart sorry for sin is a broken heart. Jesus is always ready to forgive. A little girl wakened in the night, and cried bitterly, because she had done wrong the day before, and had not asked mamma to forgive her; and now mamma was far away, and she could not tell her. But Jesus is never far away, and can look right down into the thoughts of our hearts, and forgive them

RAISING OF THE DAUGHTER OF JAIRUS.

ONCE, when Jesus was followed by a great multitude, a man by the name of Jairus, a ruler of the synagogue, came and fell at His feet, saying, "My little daughter lieth at the point of death; come and lay Thy hands upon her, that she may be healed, and she shall live." Jesus started home with him immediately, followed by the crowd.

On the way He stopped to heal and talk with a poor woman, who had been diseased many years. While they were there, a messenger came and said to Jairus, "Thy daughter is dead; why troublest thou the Master any farther?" Jesus, hearing the remark, turned his loving face on the father, and, in tender accents, said, "Be not afraid, only believe." So they all went on, and came to the ruler's house. Then Jesus went into the room where the little girl lay. She was lying on the bed, her eyes closed in death, her hands clasped over her breast, while her parents and friends were weeping and wailing greatly. But Jesus said to them, "Weep not; the damsel is not dead, but sleepeth." And they began to laugh at Him and mock Him. Then Jesus sent them all away; only He let the father and mother stay, and Peter, and James, and John; and He went to the child, and took her by the hand, and said, "Maid, arise." And she arose and walked; she was well and strong again; and Jesus, turning to her mother, commanded her to give the child something to eat.

In the lovely picture, which the artist gives, the Master is seen standing by the side of the maiden just fallen into the sleep of death. In the background appear Peter, James and John; while the bereaved mother has thrown herself, in her anguish, at the foot of the bed whereon her daughter lies. Jesus, with hand extended, is just ready to speak the words, "Maid, arise." Oh! what wonderful power Jesus has.

SAYINGS OF CHILDHOOD:—Many little children die every day; but we don't hear that any are ever raised to life again. But, if they loved Jesus, He will come for them some day. A little boy, named Tommy, said to his pastor just before he died: "When I am buried, I want to have my little Testament put in the coffin beside me. There are a great many large people; I am only a little boy, and I am afraid when Jesus comes, He will forget me; but I will reach up my Testament, and He will know that, and will receive me." Little Tommy need not have feared; Jesus will not forget him.

THE DUMB MAN POSSESSED.

WE are filled with wonder at the miracles which Jesus performed. And yet, dear children, we must not think of them as mere exhibitions of power. Jesus did not work miracles simply to *show off*—that is to please His vanity, for He had none. He worked them because He was "moved with compassion." He healed men because of His love for them, and because their sufferings touched His heart. Such a Saviour is worthy of our deepest homage. For in Him we see, not a mere wonder-exhibitor, but one who used His divine power to benefit the distressed, and to prove that He has the authority to forgive sins.

Once the people brought to Him "a dumb man, possessed with a devil." It is thought that the wicked spirit had taken away his power of speech. "And when the devil was cast out the dumb spake; and the multitudes marvelled, saying, It was never so seen in Israel." Moses, Elijah, and Elisha were great prophets, and did wonderful things—but so many such things, and done in so wonderful a way, were never before known in Israel.

And yet the proud Pharisees would not believe Him to be the Son of God. They even said, that He cast out devils by the power of Beelzebub, or Satan, the prince of the devils, and not by His own power. This was very wicked; and more than once Jesus solemnly warned them of their great sin in rejecting Him.

In the engraving, the artist has represented the miraculous deliverance of the unhappy demoniac. His blighted soul, through the Master's divine influence, is set free to rejoice and praise; and his lips speak forth the gratitude he feels. Dear children, we are all, like this poor dumb man, under Satan's power, till Jesus Himself makes us free. We should pray God, then, to change our hearts; to give us a right mind, and a new spirit; and when we know Him ourselves, we must try to teach others to know Him also.

When an explosion had taken place in one of our cities, many lives were lost. A mother came wildly running up to find her son, and among the mangled remains she at last recognized her boy. After the first agony of grief was spent she suddenly paused, exclaiming, with great joy: "My boy was at the altar last night, and was converted." O how that helped that mother to bear her grief. He had had Satan cast out; and then Jesus came into his heart.

THE DISCIPLES PLUCKING CORN ON THE SABBATH.

JESUS was going through a corn-field, one Sabbath-day, on his way to the synagogue. His disciples were with Him, and being hungry, they plucked some of the ears of corn, as they walked along, and began to eat. There was nothing wrong in this; but there were some people there who said that it was wrong. These people were the Pharisees; and though they were wicked in their hearts, they were very particular about some outward things, wishing people to think them the most pious men in the world. So they found fault with Jesus for letting His disciples pluck the corn on the Sabbath; they said, "Why do ye that which is not lawful to do on the Sabbath day?"

Jesus, who was always full of wisdom, gave them a prompt reply, to which they could make no answer, for He reminded them how David ate the shew-bread when he was hungry, and that bread God had commanded to be given to the priests only, yet the priest gave it to David and his men. He also told them to recollect that the priests did work on the Sabbath-day, and that within the temple too, for they could not kill and sacrifice the beasts without doing work, and yet they were not doing wrong. In the picture Christ is represented as the central figure; on one side are the disciples plucking the corn; on the other the Pharisees openly rebuking Christ for breaking the laws and customs of their fathers. Christ is in the act of silencing them.

Some time after this, Jesus went into the synagogue on the Sabbath-day. There was a man there with a withered hand; it was so weak that he could not move it. The Pharisees asked Jesus if it was lawful to heal on the Sabbath-day. This they did " that they might accuse Him," for they even taught that no medicine was to be given on the Sabbath. Our Lord asked them whether it was not lawful to save a sheep on the Sabbath-day, when it had fallen into a pit; and if a sheep, why not a man, who was of so much more value than a beast? "Wherefore," said He, "it is lawful to do well on the Sabbath-day." We may not only worship God on that day, but we may relieve the poor, visit the sick, and do other works of kindness and charity. This Christ has taught us by healing the sick, for He said to the man, "Stretch forth thine hand; and he stretched it forth; and it was restored whole like as the other."

SAYINGS OF CHILDHOOD:—Henry, when six years of age, was, one Sunday, reading a little book, the leaves of which all became loose. "O, dear!" said he, "What shall I do? my book is come to pieces." "Would it be right," said his mother, "for me to get a needle and thread and stitch it again to day?" "O, no," said Henry. "Might not you pin it together till to-morrow?" said the father. The little boy looked as if he hardly thought it was quite right even to pin his book on Sunday. "Why," continued his father, "your mother pins her dress on Sunday—where then is the harm in pinning your book?" "*But you know,*" said Henry, "*she could not do without her dress on Sunday, but I could do without pinning my book till Monday.*" Dear children, there are certain necessary things we may do on Sunday; but we must be careful and not do what is unnecessary. The fourth commandment says, "Remember the Sabbath day to keep it holy." There was once a little girl who used to take Sabbath morning to clear up her doll's play-room. She was "too tired," she said, on Saturday, and it was necessary to have the room look nice for Sunday! "It only takes a few minutes," she used to say. Did she remember the commandment? A boy remembered it as a day in which he did not have to go to school and study, and was glad; but he went to walk in the fields, took off his shoes and stockings and waded in the brook, hunted a bird's nest, and built a little dam across the stream. Did he keep the command? The bible says we must keep it "holy." That means set apart to special use; and the Sabbath is set apart to serve God.

JESUS WALKING ON THE SEA.

THE disciples one dark and stormy night were trying to cross the sea of Galilee in a little ship. It was a rough night. The wind came down from the hills, and tossed the sea up in great waves; and the disciples rowed with all their might, but they made little way. They were in the greatest danger of going to the bottom; and Jesus was not there to comfort and take care of them. He had gone up into a mountain alone to pray. But He had not forgotten His disciples; He had seen them all the time. "And in the fourth watch of the night," which was between three and six in the morning, Jesus went to the disciples, "walking on the sea." In the engraving the artist

has represented this scene—the dim ship in the distance, and the wind-swept figure of Jesus walking on the boisterous sea.

When the disciples saw a figure coming toward them, walking on the waves, they did not know it was Jesus; they thought an evil spirit was coming to hurt them and cried out for fear. Then Jesus said, "It is I; be not afraid;" and they knew it was their Master, and were glad. Then Peter cried, "Lord, if it be Thou, bid me come unto Thee on the water." Jesus said, "Come;" so Peter came out of the boat, and as long as he trusted in his Master, he could walk; but the wind was very high, and the waves were very rough; and when Peter saw this, he was afraid, and began to sink, and he could only cry out, "Lord, save me." But Jesus did not let Peter sink; He caught him by the hand, and said, "O thou of little faith, wherefore didst thou doubt?" And as soon as Jesus had come into the ship the storm ceased, and they were close to the land; and the disciples worshipped Jesus, and said, "Truly Thou art the Son of God."

SAYINGS OF CHILDHOOD:—A mother, with her three children, was clinging to the wreck of the steamer "Bohemian," when the mother said she must let go and be drowned. Her little girl said, "Hold on a little longer, mother; don't let go now. Jesus walked on the water and saved Peter, and perhaps He will save us." The little girl's words so strengthened the mother, that she held on a few moments more, when a boat was sent to them, which took them safely to shore.

THE MULTITUDE FED.

REMEMBER, children, that on two occasions Jesus fed the multitude miraculously. The first was just before He walked on the sea, when He fed the five thousand; the second was afterwards, when He fed four thousand. I want to talk with you now about the second time.

Jesus was upon a mountain, near the Sea of Galilee; He was visited by "great multitudes," and He cured great numbers of all sorts of diseases. There were at this time four thousand men with Him, "besides women and children." After being on the mountain for three days, and using the

THE MULTITUDE FED.

little provision they had with them, they needed food. So Jesus called His disciples to Him, and said, "I have compassion on the multitude; I will not send them away fasting, for they might faint by the way. Give them food here to eat." The disciples answered, "We have not food enough for so many. We have only seven loaves and a few fishes." But Jesus commanded the people to sit down on the ground. Then "He took the seven loaves and the fishes," and lifted up His eyes to Heaven, and thanked God who had given them this food; and broke the bread in pieces, and divided the fishes, and gave to His disciples, and told them to feed the multitude who were sitting round.

But was not the food soon all gone? No; Jesus made the loaves and fishes more than enough for the multitude; they all ate, and were filled. And when they had finished, they gathered up the fragments that were left, and there were seven baskets full. This may teach us not to waste the food which God has given us. Many poor hungry people would be very thankful for the little pieces of bread and meat which we do not want, and sometimes carelessly throw away.

SAYINGS OF CHILDHOOD:—A little boy inquired one day of his mother: "Why doesn't pa do as grandpa does?" "How does grandpa do?" asked the mother. "Why, ma, he says grace at table." He made the same inquiry of his father, and seemed much concerned because pa did not do as grandpa did. One day, when he came to the table, he was very demure, looking at the food, but eating nothing. They said, "Why don't you eat?" Again they asked him, and at length he said: "I am waiting to ask a blessing; for I don't see that anybody will, if I don't." Children, in that home, pa does now as grandpa, and the blessing is asked at the table

THE TRANSFIGURATION.

ONE night, Jesus took Peter and James and John, and went up to the top of a high mountain, to pray. You remember He took the same disciples with Him when He raised the little daughter of Jairus from the dead, and when He suffered so in the garden of Gethsemane. They must have been very dear to Him.

When they reached the top of the mountain, Jesus withdrew a little from them, to engage, as usual, in prayer. The three disciples, meanwhile, wearied with their climbing, laid down and were soon asleep. After awhile they are awakened by an intense light, which penetrates even through their closed eyelids; it is not the light of the moon, though that is shining high in the bright sky; it is the face of their glorified Lord, shining more brightly than the sun, and illumining the whole atmosphere about Him. His very garments shone, so that they glittered like the sun upon the snow. It was the God-light shining through His body and His clothes.

And while the disciples were looking, two men also shining with glory, came and stood beside the Saviour, talking with Him. They were Moses and Elijah. What do you think they talked about? They talked about the death which Jesus would soon die at Jerusalem. They conversed with Him about dying for you and me. Peter thought it was a wonderful thing for Moses and Elijah to be there; and he asked if they should not build three tabernacles, or tents, so that they could stay there. But do you think that they came to *stay*? If you had been to heaven, would you like to come back here to live? No; they came back, just to talk with Jesus about His dying, and to strengthen Him for the cross; and after that they went back.

But before Peter was through speaking, a bright cloud came and hid the wonderful sight from them; and a voice from out of the cloud said: " This is my beloved Son, in

THE TRANSFIGURATION.

whom I am well pleased; hear ye Him." It was the Father's voice; and He said this to teach the disciples how great Jesus was; much, much greater even than Moses and Elijah. When the disciples heard the voice, they fell upon their faces with fear; but Jesus came and touched them, and said, "Arise, and be not afraid." Then the disciples arose, and looked up; and they found no one with them but Jesus alone, looking as usual. Jesus bade them tell no one about what they had seen, until the Son of man should be risen again from the dead.

Dear children did you ever see Raphael's picture of the Transfiguration of Jesus? If not, I hope you will some day. Raphael always loved to paint scenes from the Saviour's life: and his last work, on which he spent years of study, was upon the story of this talk. It was scarcely finished when he died. While he was sick, he had the picture hung in his sight, that his constant thoughts might be upon his glorified Saviour. When he was dead, the picture was hung above his lifeless body, where for days crowds came to honor his wonderful genius, as they looked with reverence at the dead artist and his wonderful picture of the Transfiguration.

THE LUNATIC HEALED.

AS Jesus and His three disciples came down from the mountain in the morning, they saw the nine disciples who had been left behind, and a great many people standing around them, talking to them. As soon as the people saw Jesus, they all ran to Him; and one of them said, "Lord, I have brought my son to Thee to be cured; for he is a lunatic, and sore vexed; ofttimes he falleth into the fire, and oft into the water. And I brought him to Thy disciples, and they could not cure him." Then Jesus said, "Bring the child to Me." So they brought him. But as the poor boy was coming to Jesus, the evil spirit tore him; "and he fell on the ground, and wallowed foaming." Then Jesus asked the father, "How long has he been troubled in this way?" The father answered, "From a little child; if Thou canst do anything, have compassion on us, and help us." Jesus said unto him, "If thou canst believe, all things are possible to him that believeth." Then the father's heart was so full of feeling for his poor child, that straightway he cried out, and said with tears, "Lord, I believe; help Thou mine unbelief." Jesus was willing to heal the child; He only wanted the father to believe; and now He spoke to the evil spirit, and said, "Thou dumb and deaf spirit, I charge thee, come out of him, and enter no more into him." And the spirit obeyed the command, and came out; but the child was left so weak, and ill, that many said, "He is dead." But Jesus took him by the hand, and lifted him up, and he arose.

All children have, by nature, an evil spirit within them. Satan fills them with angry passions and sinful tempers, and tries to destroy their souls, as this deaf and dumb spirit tried to destroy the body of the poor boy.

SAYINGS OF CHILDHOOD:—Little Kitty said one day to her mother: "Papa calls me good, Aunty calls me good, and everybody calls me good. But I am not good." "I am very sorry," said the mother. "And so am I, but I have got a naughty think." "What? A naughty what?" "My *think* is naughty, inside of me." Her mother asked what she meant. "Why," said she, "when I could not ride yesterday, I did not cry nor anything, but when you was gone, I wished the carriage would turn over and the horses would run away—and everything bad. I thought all kinds of naughty things. Nobody knew it; but God knew it, and He cannot call me good. Tell me, mamma, how can I be good inside of me?" Dear children, Kitty had an evil spirit within, like the poor lunatic. Only Jesus can cast out that evil spirit.

THE GOOD SAMARITAN.

I THINK the parable of the Good Samaritan is one of the most beautiful Jesus ever told. You must remember, children, that the Jews did not like the Samaritans; they considered themselves much better and holier; but Jesus wished to show them that their doings did not always agree with their profession. So one day, when the Jews were troubling Jesus with questions, hoping to make Him say something contrary to their law, a lawyer asked Him, saying, "Master, what shall I do to inherit eternal life?" Jesus asked him what was written in the law; and the lawyer said, that he found there, that he was to love God with all his heart, and his neighbor as himself. Jesus answered, "Thou hast said right; do this, and thou shalt live." "Who is my neighbor?" questioned the wily lawyer. Then Jesus told him this parable of the Good Samaritan.

A certain man went from Jerusalem to Jericho; he fell among thieves and was stripped, robbed, wounded, and left half dead. I must tell you that the road from Jerusalem to Jericho, was, and still is, very dreary, and always has been a hiding-place for robbers, so that it was called the "bloody way." As the poor wounded man lay in the road, covered with blood, a priest came along; but instead of showing kindness to the poor man, he passed by on the other side. Soon after, a Levite came to the place; he looked at the wounded man, but did not stay to help him; he, also, passed by on the other side.

Then a Samaritan came near where he was lying. The Samaritan did not know him; the Jews and Samaritans hated each other greatly; but this Samaritan was so kind, that, when he saw the poor man lying half dead, he ran to him at once. He "had compassion on him." The fact that he was of the hated race of Jews made no difference. He ministered to him. He did it in such a way that he showed he knew just what to do. He made no bungling work. He cleansed the wounds with wine; and poured oil into them to keep down inflammation. Then he bound them up—tearing the strips, probably, from his own garments. Next he lifted him on his own beast—going on foot himself, and tenderly supporting the sufferer.

In the first picture the artist has portrayed this scene—the Samaritan walking beside and guiding the steed, and keeping poised in the saddle the wounded and nearly exhausted man. See what suffering is depicted on the face of the poor man; and what pity and tenderness are seen in the expression of the Samaritan, who was indeed a

"neighbor" in time of trouble. In this way he brought him to an inn; and in the next picture we have the

"ARRIVAL OF THE SAMARITAN AT THE INN."

The poor man is now so prostrated that he cannot help himself at all; but the good Samaritan helps him off his beast at the inn door, while the landlord and the mistress, perhaps, of the house, receive him with a sympathizing welcome. Instead of leaving him then to the attention of the servants, as he might have done, he "took care of him" himself until the morning. He helped him through the worst, and did not leave him till he was out of danger. Nor did he stop there; but before he went away, the Samaritan called the innkeeper, and gave him two pence—worth about seventeen cents each—and said, "Take care of this poor man; and whatsoever thou spendest more, when I come again I will repay thee." Had he been a brother instead of a despised Samaritan, he could not have done more.

When Jesus had finished this parable, He turned to the lawyer, and said, "Which of these three, thinkest thou, was neighbor to the man who fell among thieves?" The lawyer answered, "He who showed mercy on him." Then said Jesus, "Go, and do thou likewise." Dear children, this parable should teach *us* a lesson, as well as the lawyer. It should teach us to be kind to all; not only our friends and relatives, but *all*, even our enemies. It is not what others are, but what we do for them, which makes them our neighbors. If we want to find who is our neighbor, we must look within our own heart. If that is full of love, we shall find them in plenty. "Better is a neighbor that is near than a brother far off."

SAYINGS OF CHILDHOOD:—A mother who was in the habit of calling her children around her at the close of the day to find what they had been doing for Jesus, was told by her little daughter, "As I went to school to-day I met little Mary ——. She had not been to school for two or three days, and I asked her why she had been absent. She told me her little brother had died, and she cried about it. We went into school together and she laid her face down on her book and cried as if her heart would break I was sorry to see Mary cry, and I laid my face down on the other page of the book and cried too. Then Mary put her arm around me and kissed me and told me I had done her good. But, mamma, I don't know how I did her good." You see, dear little folks, it was by her sympathy that this child did Mary good.

CHRIST'S VISIT TO MARY AND MARTHA.

JESUS paid a visit to Martha and Mary, two good sisters who lived in a little village called Bethany, about two miles from Jerusalem, and in this talk I want to tell you about it. Martha was a good woman and loved Jesus; and she was very much pleased when He came to see her. She made a great feast, and waited herself upon the company. Martha had a sister named Mary. Mary loved Jesus, too, and she showed her love by sitting at His feet, and listening attentively to every word He said. When Martha saw that Mary did not come to help her in providing for the entertainment of Christ and His followers, she came to Jesus and said, " Lord, dost Thou not care that my sister hath left me to serve alone? bid her, therefore, that she help me." Then Jesus turned and said, " Martha, Martha, thou art careful and troubled about many things; but one thing is needful; and Mary hath chosen that good part which shall not be taken away from her."

Why did Jesus say this? Was not Martha right to be kind and hospitable to her friends? Yes; but Jesus wanted to teach her that an over-anxiety about the things of this life is dangerous, and has a tendency to lead to the neglect of the more important things of the future. Martha, though a true believer and a good woman, was on this occasion blamable, for she was too much troubled about making a display, and the Saviour gently chided her for the fault. She was so busy about worldly things that she had no time to sit down and listen to the holy words which Jesus was saying; this was wrong.

What was the " good part" which Mary chose? To sit at Jesus' feet and hear the words of salvation. This is the good part that shall not be taken away from us, and that at death will bring us to heaven. All that we get on earth, all the worldly riches honor and fame, that some people prize so dearly, must in the end be parted from; they will serve for nothing in the life to come. Let us all, then, choose Mary's good part and, like her, by faith, sit at Jesus' feet and learn of Him!

> " Sitting at the feet of Jesus,
> O what words I hear Him say!
> Happy place! so near, so precious!
> May it find me there each day:
> Sitting at the feet of Jesus,
> I would look upon the past;
> For His love has been so gracious.
> It has won my heart at last."

LOOKING FOR THE RETURN OF THE PRODIGAL SON.

HE parable of the prodigal son is called "the pearl and crown of all parables." It is the most precious of them all because it reveals God as a tender Father.

A certain man had two sons; and the younger said to his father, "Father, give me my portion of thy possessions." I want you to notice, dear children, that it was the "younger" son that made this demand. As a rule one becomes a prodigal while he is young. In almost every boy's life there is a period of danger. It is when he begins to think he knows more than father or mother. He wants to "see the world." He is impatient of home restraints, and thinks that his parents are unnecessarily strict, and old fogyish. He is in a hurry to be his own master. So felt the younger son in this parable.

So the father divided all he had between the two sons. A few days after, the younger son gathered all his money together, and went away from father and home, and took a journey into a far country. He wanted to get far away from the restraint of his father's presence. When he thought that he was beyond his oversight, then he began to have what he thought was a "good time." He lavishly scattered his fortune. He delighted in making a display. He liked to be known as "open-handed." And so he made himself the easy prey of those who are on the watch for just such victims; and there he wasted his all in folly and wickedness.

When he had spent all, there arose a great famine in that land, and he began to be in want. When he "began to be in want," he should have gone right home. But, no, he was not quite ready yet. Pride barred the way. He felt that it would be humiliating to go back. So he went and joined himself to a citizen in that country; that "citizen"

proved to be a poor prop. He sent the boy, who once never had a want that was not satisfied, into the field to feed his swine. There he was so hungry that he was glad to eat the food that was given to the pigs. He did try to, but could not; the prodigal said, "I perish with hunger." And yet he only has himself to blame for it. He who will not be a son must become a servant; he who will not feed upon the bread of life must feed upon husks.

At length he determined to go back to his kind father. He "came to himself;" hitherto he had been "beside himself." He said, "I will arise, and go to my father." But how? What shall he say to him? His spirit of pride is all gone now. He does not think of *demanding* to be taken back. Instead, he thinks over a little speech in which he acknowledges that he has no further right as a son to any favor from his father, and entreats him to make him as one of his hired servants. He resolves to confess his sinfulness, and take any place that his father may offer him, however low it may be. The fact that he was willing to confess that he was no more worthy to be called a son, shows that he did not return merely for bread alone, but that he was more hungry for his father's forgiveness than for the food upon his table. So he arose, and went to his father.

But what about the father all this time? Was he willing to receive him? Yes, that kind father had been waiting and longing for his return. The first picture shows the family all in sorrow, anxiously troubled about the boy. And when the prodigal returned, and "was yet a great way off," "his father saw him, and had compassion." That his father saw him, while he was so far distant, not only shows that since he went away, he had been in the habit of daily looking for his return down the road; but, also, that he expected him to come back in a woeful plight—or he never would have recognized him in the ragged looking tramp that was coming along the highway! When the father saw him, the love which all the while he had felt for him gushed forth, and he ran to meet him: and, all unmindful of his filth and rags, he threw his arms about him, and kissed him. Our next picture presents

"THE FATHER EMBRACING THE RETURNING PRODIGAL."

The father raises his face to heaven with an earnest, almost painful look of thanksgiving. The servants, and even the dogs, are hurrying forward to welcome the returning son. Then the prodigal began to confess his sin. His heart is broken now; such treatment as he had received from his father could not but melt the heart of any son.

He went through his confession brokenly, I imagine; nevertheless, he went through it—all except that about taking the place of a hired servant. With his father's arms about his neck, and his kiss warm upon his cheek, he could not talk of being given a servant's place in his household. He had no need to ask to be received as a servant; for already he was received as a son. But the father hardly waited to hear his son's confession; he forgave all, and called the servants, and said, " Bring here the best robe, and put it on him; and put a ring on his hand; and shoes on his feet; and bring the fatted calf, and kill it, and let us eat and be merry; for this my son was dead, and is alive again; he was lost, and is found." So they began to be merry.

And, when the elder brother murmured at the joyous welcome that was given to the wanderer, and turned away because he was too jealous to join in the merriment, his kind father came and begged him to go in, saying, "Thou art always with me, and all that I have is thine; but we must now make merry and rejoice over this thy brother, who was lost, and is found." How glad should we be when any poor sinner is brought back to the fold of God, for we know that the angels rejoice in heaven over penitent sinners!

Dear children, what does this parable mean? The father is God; the younger son stands for all who have done wrong. The name of the far country into which they have wandered is *sin*. I wonder how many of my little people are in that far country? Jesus knows. The Heavenly Father is waiting for you to come back. He sees that little boy who thinks he can take care of himself, and that little girl who don't want to obey. He is looking for them, He wishes they would come to Him. How you could make the golden harps in heaven ring to-day! Who will do it?

LAZARUS AND THE RICH MAN.

JESUS told the people another parable. There was a certain rich man who lived in a fine house, he was clothed in purple and fine linen, both materials being very rich and costly; the linen was brought from Egypt, and, it is said, was often worth twice its weight in gold. He "fared sumptuously every day." He set a fine table, and had upon it all the dainties of the season, and all this, not on rare and festive occasions alone, but every day. At the gate of this rich man's house lay a beggar, named Lazarus. His friends laid him there. This poor man had no home to live in, no bed to lie on; all the food he had to eat was the broken pieces which the servants did not care to eat, for he was too sick to work or help himself. It was the custom for the rich to eat only the crusts of the loaves, and to use the soft part within as a napkin upon which to wipe the fingers. The portions thus used, and thrown away, were the "crumbs" the beggar hoped for. Lazarus was sick, as well as poor. He was covered with sores and no one tried to heal him, and make him well; only the dogs took pity upon him—they came and licked his sores, and tried to comfort him. But in all his pain he was happier than the rich man, for he loved God; and, as he lay at the rich man's gate, in hunger and pain, he used to think of his home in heaven, and of those good things which God has promised to those who love Him.

In the picture we have the rich man's banqueting hall finely portrayed; on the bottom steps sits Lazarus, looking up with pleading, pitiful face; close by are the dogs —the beggar's only friends; and just above, the servant, warning him away.

At last, the beggar died; and doubtless the servants of the rich man saw that his body did not long stay within his portal, and hustled it off to some hastily made and shallow grave. But what of that beyond? Suddenly the scene changes. A flood of heavenly light breaks in upon it, and the once despised beggar is borne aloft, with songs of angelic joy and triumph, by the holy angels sent to carry his happy soul to heaven.

Soon after, the rich man died also. He could only enjoy his riches and his good things as long as God gave him breath. He had a grand funeral; his body was wrapped in costly burial clothes, embalmed with spices; there was a long train of mourners, a magnificent tomb—and that was all there was of that. But where was his soul? No angels were sent to carry it to heaven; but "in hell he lifted up his eyes, being in torments." Then he looked toward heaven, and there he saw Lazarus, peaceful and happy, in Abraham's bosom. In vain the rich man cried to Abraham for a drop of water to cool his burning tongue; he had carried no water to Lazarus in his suffering; he had only cared for himself; and now Abraham tells him that Lazarus, having suffered evils in his life with patience and submission, is rewarded; but that he, who had only cared for the riches, pleasures and honors of the world, must now suffer for the bad use he had made of them.

Then the rich man wanted Abraham to let Lazarus go and warn his five brethren not to come to that place of torment. But Abraham told him no; they have their warning. "If they will not hear Moses and the prophets, they will not repent even if one went to them from the dead."

The parable ends here. The rich man's prayers could not be heard either for himself or his brethren. Prayer is not heard in hell. Dear children, let us learn from this parable not to look for all our good things upon this earth, or we will miss them in heaven. Better be poor here than poor there. "Lay up for yourselves treasures in heaven."

THE PHARISEE AND THE PUBLICAN.

I WANT to talk with you about one of Jesus' parables, in which He taught the people how they must pray. He often spoke to them on the duty of prayer. He said, Two men went up into the temple to pray. One was a Pharisee; the other was a publican. The Pharisee stood and prayed thus: "God, I thank Thee that I am not as other men are, extortioners, unjust, adulterers, or even as this publican. I fast twice in the week, I give tithes of all that I possess." The Pharisee felt much pleased with himself. His prayer was full of boastfulness. He told God how good and how perfect he was. In his own estimation he was *the* saint. He took pride in stating to the Lord that he did more than the law required of him. He actually made out God to be his debtor.

And how did the publican feel, and how did *he* pray? He stood afar off; he did not dare to lift up his eyes to heaven; he was sorry for his sin; he smote upon his breast, and said, "God be merciful to me a sinner." That was all he said. It was a very short prayer; not so long as the Pharisee's. But which prayer did God like best? I hear you say the *publican's*. And why? Because the Pharisee was proud and self-righteous; but the publican was humble and penitent. In the picture the artist has shown the humility of the one in contrast with the pride of the other.

May God keep us all from offering the prayer of the Pharisee, and help us to pray with the spirit of the publican. God always hears prayer, but He doesn't always answer as we ask. Charlie, when three years old, wanted a knife, coaxed for it; mamma knew he would only cut himself, but she treasured the "prayer," and just as soon as in her wisdom the little fingers were ready to get comfort and not pain out of the gift, she answered the prayer. God often does thus with His children; He is wise, He makes no mistakes.

LITTLE CHILDREN BROUGHT TO JESUS.

DEAR children, what is the sweetest verse in all the bible? This is the one that I should think would be just the very best; "Suffer little children to come unto Me, and forbid them not for of such is the kingdom of heaven."

Jesus had been in Galilee, and was on His way to Jerusalem to be crucified. Great multitudes followed Him as He went, preaching, healing the sick, performing miracles, and patiently answering the impertinent questions of His enemies. At the time this beautiful little incident occurred, He was in Judea, near the river Jordan; the mothers came crowding around Him, forcing their way through the crowd, with their babies in their arms, some leading theirs, some handing others over the heads of the people to friends, in order to get near Him. This is what the artist has portrayed in the picture. The mothers are crowding forward with their little ones. Christ has His hand on the shoulders of one little boy, and is reaching out the other hand to receive the little tot just before Him. Several little ones are clinging around His feet; and others are trying to get to Him, especially one little boy, just by the steps at the right of the picture.

Don't you think these mothers must have loved Jesus? Yes, they did; and they wished the children to learn to love Him too. They knew that the blessing of Jesus would make their little ones happier than anything the world can give. But the disciples were angry; they thought the children would be troublesome to Jesus; so they reproved those who brought them, and wished to send them away. They had an idea that nobody but grown people should come to Jesus. He was talking to the grown folks, and they thought He ought not to be interrupted just for the sake of little children. But, do you think Jesus liked it, when the disciples would not let the little ones come to Him? No; He was "much displeased." He stopped talking with the big people, and then he said: "Suffer little children to come unto Me, and forbid them not." The parents wanted Him to put His hands upon them. But what *did* He do? Why He took them right up in His arms, and put His hands on them, and blessed them. I can imagine I see the little ones leaping with a crow of delight into the arms of Jesus. Some put up their little mouths, ready for a kiss; some run their fingers through His hair and beard; others cling lovingly to His neck, and cry only when taken away,

My little friends, would'nt you like to have been there too? Don't you think that your mothers would like to have Christ bless you to-day? Well He can do it. What, right now? Most certainly, He can do it, right here and now. In your hearts just ask Him to do it, and He will. If you love and serve Him, His arms are about you all the time, and His hands are still laid in felt blessings on your heads, even though you are not able to see them.

I have seen a great many children, some very young, who have learned to know Jesus as their Saviour, and their happy faces told the joy that was in their hearts. Bishop Wm. Taylor tells of a little girl nine years old, who at a meeting, longed to find Jesus. The Good Spirit had spoken to her heart; and as the big tears were streaming down her face, she put her little hands together, and said, " O Lord, for Christ's sake, have mercy on me a sinner. For Christ's sake, give me a new heart " She prayed very earnestly for some time, and then as she saw that Jesus had died for her, her face brightened up, and she said. " Oh, praise the Lord ! I've found Jesus. He is my Saviour." She was so glad, that she kept on praising the Lord aloud, when a minister said to her, " Little girl, what are you praising the Lord for ?" " Because I love Him." said she. " Why do you love Him ? " " Because He first loved me, and He has pardoned my sins." The next day her brother said to her, rather tauntingly, " Ah, Virginia, I think your goodness will not last long ! " " Well, James," said she meekly, " your *think* will not remove it." Virginia grew up in the fear of the Lord, and is now a christian mother in California.

I wish you would be like the little child in the hymn I am going to repeat to you now.

"Dear Jesus! ever at my side ;
How loving Thou must be
To leave Thy home in heaven, to save
A little child like me.

"Thy beautiful and shining face
I see not, though so near ;
The sweetness of Thy soft, low voice
I am too deaf to hear.

"But I have felt Thee in my thoughts,
Fighting with sin for me ;
And when my heart loves God, I know
The sweetness is from Thee.

" Yes ; when I pray Thou prayest too ;
Thy prayer is all for me ;
But when I sleep Thou sleepest not,
But watchest patiently."

LITTLE CHILDREN BROUGHT TO JESUS.

SAYINGS OF CHILDHOOD:—A christian mother was once showing her little girl, about five years old, the picture representing Jesus receiving children, while the mothers were pushing their little ones towards Him. "There Carrie," said her mother, "That's what I would have done with you if I had been there." "I would'nt wait *to be pushed* to Jesus," said little Carrie, with beautiful and touching earnestness, "*I'd go to Him without pushing.*" That was right. That is the way we ought to go to Jesus. How kind He is! How tender! How ready to help and bless us! My dear children, won't you go to Jesus at once? Oh! go "without pushing." Will you not do so, even while I am talking with you?

RESURRECTION OF LAZARUS.

AT Bethany, there lived a family whom Jesus tenderly loved; the family consisted of two sisters, Mary and Martha, and their brother Lazarus. Lazarus seems to have been a very good man, for Jesus loved him; and he and his two sisters loved and served God together.

But one day, sorrow came into this peaceful family; for sorrow must come sometime into every family in the world. Lazarus was taken very ill; and his sisters sent to tell Jesus, saying, "Lord, he whom Thou lovest is sick." But Jesus delayed going to see him till he was dead. This He did that He might try the faith of the sisters, and show them His great power. When Jesus arrived at Bethany, Lazarus had lain in the grave four days; and there were many Jews at the house of his friends, comforting the bereaved sisters. As soon as Martha heard that Jesus was coming, she ran out to meet Him, and said, "Lord, if Thou hadst been here, my brother would not have died." Jesus answered, "Thy brother shall rise again." Martha said, "Yes, I know he will rise again at the last day. All will rise then." But Jesus meant to call Lazarus out of his grave very soon, without waiting till the last day; Martha did not understand this at first, but she trusted in Jesus, and said, "Lord, I believe that Thou art the Christ, the Son of God;" and then she went to Mary, and told her to come to Jesus.

As soon as Mary came to Jesus, she fell down at His feet, and said, as Martha had, "Lord, if Thou hadst been here, my brother would not have died." And then she began to weep very bitterly. When Jesus saw her weeping, and the Jews also weeping, which came with her, He groaned in the spirit, and was troubled, and said, "Where have you laid him?" They said unto Him, "Lord, come and see." So they led Jesus to the grave. Then the blessed Jesus, who had all the feelings of our nature, was tenderly touched, and going to the tomb, "Jesus wept." Oh, the kindness of His heart! Dear children, who could but love Him? The people were astonished to see Jesus weeping for Lazarus, and said, "Behold, how He loved him!"

At last they came to the grave. It was a cave, and a stone lay upon it. Jesus ordered them to take away the stone from the mouth of the cave; and, after praying to His Heavenly Father, He cried with a loud voice, "Lazarus, come forth!" And he that was dead came forth, bound hand and foot with grave-clothes. Jesus then said to the persons at the grave, "Loose him, and let him go." In the picture the artist has drawn the figure of Christ, standing in the mouth of the cave; by His almighty power over

life and death, the shrouded form of Lazarus has come forth from the portals of the tomb. How happy were the two sisters to see their dear brother again; and how they must have loved and praised the gracious Saviour, who, they now felt, had done all things well.

Little friends, did you ever hear the *legend of the first grave?* I will tell it to you. Abel, you remember, was the first to die. Adam and Eve sat beside his dead body, and wept, not knowing what to do. But a raven, whose bird-friend had died, said, "I will go and teach Adam what he must do with his son." The raven dug a grave, and laid the dead raven in it. When Adam saw this, he said to Eve, "Let us do the same with our child!" The Lord rewarded the raven; and no one is therefore allowed to harm their young. They have food in abundance, and their cry for rain is always heard.

Now, that is only a legend. But, whatever way the first grave was made, we all bury our dead now in the ground. But they will not always stay there. The same power that raised Lazarus will say, "Come forth;" and the "dead shall hear the voice of the Son of God, and they that hear shall live again."

CHRIST'S ENTRY INTO JERUSALEM.

NOW the time grew near when Jesus was to die, to be offered up as a sinless sacrifice for the sins of mankind, so He began His journey towards Jerusalem where He was to suffer. When He came to the mount of Olives, He called two of his disciples and told them to go into the village, and they would find an ass tied and a colt by her, and that they should loose them and bring them to Him. And He told them "If any one say to you, 'Why do you take them away?' you must answer, 'Because the Lord hath need of them;' and then the men will send them willingly." So the disciples went to the village, and found the ass and colt, as Jesus said; and as they were untying them their owner asked why they did so, and the disciples said, "The Lord hath need of them;" and the man let them go.

So they brought the ass to Jesus, and they spread their garments over it, and then set Jesus upon it, to ride into Jerusalem. And when the people saw Him coming they spread branches of trees, and possibly flowers, before Him; and those who had fine

garments spread them in the way, for the ass to walk over; and they all cried and shouted for joy, saying, "Hosanna in the highest: Blessed is He that cometh in the name of the Lord!" In the picture the artist has portrayed this scene—the rejoicing thousands, with branches of palm and acclamations of joy and praise, honoring Christ as He enters the city.

And when He came into Jerusalem, and went into the temple, there were many little children who joined in the cry, "Hosanna in the highest;" and Jesus was pleased to hear the little ones sing His praises. But the chief priests and scribes were displeased, and they said unto him, "Hearest Thou what these say?" And Jesus said unto them, "Yea; have ye never read, Out of the mouth of babes and sucklings thou hast perfected praise?"

Dear little folks, Jesus is pleased with the sincere worship of little children. I hope you love to sing His praises.

SAYINGS OF CHILDHOOD:—Two children were very ill in the same room: the older of the two was heard trying to teach the younger one to pronounce the word "Hallelujah!" but without success. The little one died before he could repeat it. When his brother was told of his death, he was silent for a moment, and then, looking up at his mother, said, "Johnny can say 'Hallelujah' now, mother!" Not long after the two brothers were united in Heaven, singing "Hallelujah" together. Dear children, many of your brothers and sisters died before they were old enough to sing the praises of their Redeemer here on earth; but they have been taught the music of the upper temple now, and they sing among the heavenly choristers.

CHRIST CLEANSING THE TEMPLE.

ESUS went into the temple; He found the outer court of it, or the court of the Gentiles, turned into a market for animals and things that the Jews used in their sacrifices; it was also partly occupied by the money-changers. Noise, confusion, wrangling, bitter words, reckless oaths, and dishonest practices filled the sacred courts where the Gentiles should have been taught the holy worship, and the commandments of God. When Jesus saw it, He was much displeased. He had driven them out before; and now he sent them away again; He cast out the buyers and sellers, and overthrew the

CHRIST CLEANSING THE TEMPLE.

tables of the money changers, and the seats of those who sold doves; and He said to them, " It is written, My house shall be a house of prayer; but ye have made it a den of thieves."

Dear children, Jesus will not suffer the temple of His Father to be dishonored. It is an awfully wicked thing to profane God's temple by wicked thoughts or acts, by trifling behavior, by disorderly conduct, by inattention. The heart is the temple of God; the heart-temple should be cleansed from all sin. Jesus drove out the men who were selling oxen, sheep, doves, and the money-changers. What would he have you drive out of your heart-temple? *Selfishness, covetousness, pride, blasphemy, boasting, lying, ingratitude, envy;* "Take these things hence," says Jesus.

A wounded soldier-boy was dying in a hospital. The lady who watched by his bedside said to him, " My dear boy, if this should be death that is coming upon you, are you ready to meet your God?" He answered, " I am ready dear lady; for this has long been his temple;" and as he spoke he placed his hand upon his heart. "Do you mean," questioned the lady gently, "that God rules and reigns in your heart?" "Yes," he answered; but his voice sounded far off, sweet and low, as if it came from a soul already well on its way through the "dark valley and shadow of death."

THE WIDOW'S MITE

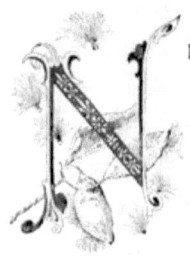

NEAR the door of the temple, Jesus sat down one day to look at the people as they stopped to put their money into the treasury. A great many people passed; and, as they passed, they cast money into the treasury; this money was to pay for the things wanted in the service of the temple. Some persons put in very much money—gold and silver; they were very rich. But as Jesus sat watching, a poor widow came and dropped in two mites, which make a farthing. It was a very little money, but it was all she had; and she felt that she must give something to show her love and gratitude. Jesus was watching the poor widow. Do you believe He thought what a mean woman she was, not to put in more, when so many were putting in piles of gold and silver?

THE WIDOW'S MITE.

No, He did not; He looked into the widow's heart, and read there that the two mites were all the money she had. No rich man gave all he had. The two mites were more than the gold when Jesus counted them; they counted more in what? *They counted more in love.* Jesus turned to His disciples and said, "Verily, I say unto you, that this poor widow hath cast more in than all they which have cast into the treasury. For all they did cast in of their abundance: but she of her want, did cast in all that she had, even all her living."

In the picture the artist has portrayed this incident. The figure of the humble, shrinking and self-sacrificing woman is seen standing by the treasury casting in her two mites; back of her stand the ostentatious and proud Pharisees; and still beyond, the blessed Christ teaching His disciples.

We should all try to be like this poor widow. There are treasuries now, where money is cast for God's service. There are Missionary societies, Bible societies, Sunday-School societies, and many more. All the money collected for these purposes is given to God. We ought all to give what we can. The rich ought to give much; the poor ought to give something. Two pennies are somewhat like two mites, because they do not make much if we count them so: *one, two*. That is the way we count; but will Jesus count them as we do if they are given with love? No; He will count them so that they will make a great deal, if we give as the poor widow did. He looks at the heart more than at the money. I will tell you of two mites you can give to God:

> "Two small mites have I to give,
> My small body in which I live;
> And my soul that ought to pray,
> And live for Jesus every day."

That is the gift that will please Him best: then all you have will be His.

SAYINGS OF CHILDHOOD:—A little girl six years old, who was very desirous of putting her pennies into the missionary-box with others, when saying her evening prayers at her father's knee, hesitated a moment, and then added, "Lord bless my two pennies, for Jesus' sake, Amen!" She prayed thus every night after giving her pennies for the missionary-box. Dear children, don't forget to ask God to bless what you give; God's blessing is better than all the riches of the world.

THE LAST SUPPER.

WHEN our blessed Lord came into the world to save sinners, He knew what He had to suffer. He was to die that we might live. And now the time of His death began rapidly to approach. One of His disciples, Judas, the wretched man! went to the chief priests and agreed to deliver up Christ to them for thirty pieces of silver—the paltry price paid for a purchased servant—about eighteen dollars and fifty cents? They dare not take Christ publicly for fear of the people, but Judas offered to take them to one of His private retreats, and there to deliver Him up: and with the greatest care, he watched for the most favorable opportunity.

The passover was kept at this time. That feast was typical of the death of Christ, the Lamb of God; and Jesus wanted to eat of it with His disciples once more, before He died. So he called two of His disciples, and told them, to go into the city, where they would find a man bearing a pitcher of water, whom they should follow, and, entering into the same house, inquire of the good-man of the house, saying, "The master saith, where is the guest chamber, where I shall eat the passover with my disciples?" and he would show them a room in which to prepare the feast. And the disciples went and found everything as Jesus had said, and when the passover was ready, Jesus came in the evening with His disciples to eat it.

And while they were eating the passover, Jesus was very sorrowful, for He knew all that was going to happen to Him; and He said to His disciples, "Verily, I say unto you, that one of you shall betray Me." Most of the disciples wondered what the Master meant, and questioned, saying, "Lord, is it I?" The Saviour answered that one who dipped his hand in the same dish with Him should betray Him. Judas alone understood the Saviour's meaning, but he also pretended to wonder, saying, "Master, is it I?" Jesus answered, "Thou hast said."

Then Satan came into the heart of Judas, and tempted him to do now the wicked thing he had been thinking of so long. Jesus knew what was in the heart of Judas, and He looked at him, and said, "What thou doest, do quickly." Then Judas arose, and went out. Where did he go? To the priests and captains, to lead them to Jesus that very night. But the other disciples thought that Jesus had sent him upon some business.

While Jesus was sitting at the table with His disciples He took bread and blessed it, and brake it, and gave a piece to each of them, and said, "Take, eat; this is My body, which is given for you: this do in remembrance of Me." Afterwards, He took the cup, in which was the juice of the grape, and gave it to them, saying, "Drink ye all of it; for this is My blood of the new testament, which is shed for many for the remission of sins: this do, as oft as ye drink it, in remembrance of Me." That was the beginning of what we call the holy sacrament of the Lord's supper. The artist has finely portrayed this scene in the picture.

"This is the feast of heavenly wine,
And God invites to sup,
The juices of the living vine
Were *pressed* to fill the cup.

O bless the Saviour, ye that eat,
With royal dainties fed;
Not heaven affords a costlier feast,
For Jesus is the bread."

CHRIST'S PRAYER IN THE GARDEN OF OLIVES.

SUPPER being over, Jesus and His disciples sang a hymn together. Then they left the upper chamber, passed through the narrow streets of Jerusalem, to the eastern gate which led to the Mount of Olives. On the way, Jesus told them again that they would soon all be afraid, and leave Him; but Peter could not think so, and said boldly that if everybody fell from Him, he never would. But Jesus answered, "Verily, verily, I say unto thee, that this night, before the cock crow, thou shalt deny Me thrice." But Peter again answered, "Though I should die with Thee, yet will I not deny Thee." And so said all the disciples.

And now Jesus and his disciples had come to the brook Cedron. They crossed the brook and came into a garden called Gethsemane. Then He said to His disciples, "Sit ye here, while I go and pray yonder;" but He called Peter, and James, and John, to come with Him a little farther. Turning to them with every feature indicating His agony of spirit, He said, "My soul is exceeding sorrowful, even unto death; tarry ye here, and watch with Me." So He left the three disciples there, and "went a little farther, and fell on His face, and prayed, saying, O My Father, if it be possible, let this cup pass from Me; nevertheless not as I will, but as Thou wilt." After this earnest prayer, He rose and came to the three disciples and found them sleeping, and said unto Peter, "Simon, sleepest thou? Couldst not thou watch with Me one hour? Watch and pray, that ye enter not into temptation; the spirit indeed is willing, but the flesh is weak." In the first picture we see Jesus in the act of prayer, and the three disciples asleep. "He went away again the second time, and prayed, saying, O My Father, if this cup may not pass away from Me, except I drink it, Thy will be done." It was needful for Jesus to suffer all this. The cup of sorrow could not be taken away; but

His Heavenly Father sent an angel from heaven, to strengthen and comfort Him. "And being in an agony, He prayed more earnestly; and His sweat was as it were great drops of blood, falling down to the ground."

Amid all this agony, He came again to His disciples, and again found them asleep; and when they were roused, they were still so dazed and heavy with sleep, that they did not know what to answer Him. A third time He went to His chosen place of prayer, perhaps under the shadow of one of the old and spreading olive trees, and asked that God's will might be done, at whatever cost of suffering to Him. After this, He came once more to His sleeping disciples, and said, "Sleep on now, and take your rest; behold, the hour is at hand, and the Son of Man is betrayed into the hands of sinners. Rise, let us be going; behold, he is at hand that doth betray Me." There was no time to watch and pray now; for Judas was coming, and a multitude with him. The disciples had wasted their time in sleep, while their Master was praying; and now the hour of temptation was come, and they had not sought strength to resist it.

In the second picture the artist has portrayed

"THE AGONY IN THE GARDEN,"

just at that point, when it was greatest, and when an angel came to strengthen Jesus. It is with tender awe that we behold this agonizing scene in our Saviour's life.

What made this fearful anguish? I think, dear children, it was because He was thinking of all He must suffer if He would save sinners like you and me, that caused that bloody sweat to stand upon His brow in the garden of Gethsemane. He saw how a world of sinners—little children as well—had wandered off into the by and forbidden paths of sin, and how they had followed on from one temptation to another, till all were lost; so that, unless One "MIGHTY TO SAVE" should stretch forth His strong arm, they must forever perish. The Sinless One, to whom all sin was so loathsome and hateful, was to take upon Himself the burden of the sins of the whole world; He, the guiltless and Holy One, was to bear the guilt and impurity of the sinners of all ages. All that He suffered for *you*. Will you give Him your heart for what He has thus done?

SAYINGS OF CHILDHOOD:—There was a great philosopher who had a child that was dying. The weeping father took the child by the hand, and asked, "Do you love me, darling?" "Yes," replied the child; "but I *love Jesus more*." Dear little ones, how can we ever love Him enough for all He suffered for us!

THE BETRAYAL.

SCARCELY had Jesus wakened his three disciples for the last time, and finished speaking, when there came a tread of soldiers, and lanterns gleaming through the olive trees. Jesus looked up, and saw Judas coming with a band of men, with swords and staves, to take Him. Judas Iscariot, the traitor, knew that the Master was apt to go to the olive garden to pray at night; and before he brought the priests and soldiers into the garden to take Jesus, he said to them, "I will give you a sign, that you may know whom you must seize. Whomsoever I shall kiss, that same is he: hold him fast."

Now, when Jesus saw His enemies coming towards Him, He did not try to hide or escape from them. He went to meet them, and asked, "Whom seek ye?" They answered, "Jesus of Nazareth." Jesus said, "I am He." And when He said this, His enemies went back, and fell on the ground. Why? Because they saw in Jesus something very different from other men; they felt the power of Jesus as God, and they were afraid, and overcome by it. Then Judas went up first to Jesus, and said, "Hail, Master," and kissed Him. All our Lord said was, "Judas, betrayest thou the Son of man with a kiss?" Jesus knew the deceit of Judas! He knew why he kissed Him. The picture presents most vividly this scene. In the background, you see the clamorous crowd, with lighted torches, led on by the cruel soldiery; in the foreground are the chief figures, Christ and Judas. What more striking than the contrast between the serene and sacred beauty of the countenance of Jesus and the wicked and leering face of His betrayer!

Then the multitude laid hands on Jesus, to take Him away. When the disciples saw that their Master was so cruelly seized by His enemies, they rushed forward to defend Him. Peter drew a sword, and cut off the ear of the high priest's servant. The servant's name was Malchus. The kind and gentle Saviour reproved Peter for his rashness, and bade him put the sword back into the sheath; and then, in His great love, our blessed Lord touched the ear, and cured it in an instant; and begged that all the disciples might be allowed to go their way. But the disciples were so alarmed at the savage multitude that they all ran away and left Jesus, except John and Peter, who both followed to see what would be done with Him.

SAYINGS OF CHILDHOOD:—Said a little boy, "Mamma, didn't the devil get Judas? I don't see how he could ever stand it to live with Jesus in heaven." I don't, either,

THE BETRAYAL.

children! I suppose you have all read Bunyan's Pilgrim's Progress. Do you recollect, they came to a place, in a bottom, where there was a door in the side of a hill? They opened the door, and they heard a rumbling noise as of fire, and a cry of some tormented. Christian asked, "What means this?" Then the shepherd told them, "This is a by-way to hell, a way that hypocrites go in at;" and among the hypocrites he named Judas, and such as sell their Master as he did. Let us be careful that we never betray our blessed Lord

PETER'S DENIAL.

OUR blessed Lord was dragged by the soldiers to the house of Caiaphas, the high priest, where His enemies tried to make out some charge to bring against Him; but as He was good and holy, and had no sin at all, they could accuse Him of nothing.

All this time, Peter was in the high priest's palace, warming himself by the fire. Both John and Peter, anxious to see what would be done with their Master, had followed on at a safe distance, and John first, and Peter later, had entered the palace-hall. Peter tried to hide himself in the crowd; he told no one that he was a disciple of Jesus, for he was afraid of being known among so many enemies.

But as he warmed himself, one of the maids there looked at him, and asked if he did not belong to Jesus of Nazareth. Peter was afraid, and said, "I know not what thou sayest." Then he went out into the porch; and the cock crew. The cock crowing ought to have reminded Peter of the warning Jesus had given him. Then another maid saw Peter, and said, "This fellow was also with Jesus of Nazareth." Peter grew more afraid, and went on declaring, he did not know such a person. Not long after, some more of the people came to him, and said, "Surely thou art one of the friends of Jesus; for thou art a Galilean, and speakest as they do." Then Peter began to curse and swear, and said, "I know not this man of whom you speak." Just then the cock crew again. Jesus was not far off. He could see and hear Peter. When the cock crew, Jesus

turned round and looked upon Peter. He did not speak a word, but Peter understood the look. It went to his heart. It made him think of the warning which Jesus had given him when Peter said, "I will never deny Thee." Peter thought how he had forgotten that warning, and denied his kind Master. He could not bear the sad thought; "he went out and wept bitterly."

Dear children this is a very sad history. Peter told lies, he denied his Master, he cursed and swore, and took God's holy name in vain. And why was this? Because he trusted in himself. We should learn from this, not to trust in ourselves, but to pray for grace to enable us to resist temptation. Jesus afterwards forgave Peter. Peter repented and prayed for pardon; and Jesus saw his tears, and heard his prayers, and forgave him.

SAYINGS OF CHILDHOOD:—One of my little friends says, "I think it was just too good in Jesus to forgive Peter. I'm afraid I couldn't forgive anybody that would do so to me." Yes, children, it was *good* in Jesus. He tells us, that, when we have done wrong, if we will come to Him, He will forgive. Jesus is willing to pardon even when we sin like Peter, if we will truly repent and turn to Him.

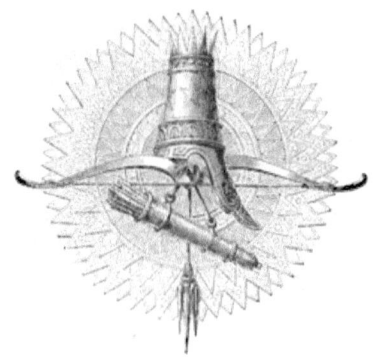

JESUS SCOURGED

YOU remember, dear children, that the cruel soldiers had taken Jesus to the palace of Caiaphas, the high priest. The priests and enemies of Jesus now tried to accuse Him of some wickedness, that they might condemn Him to death. But no one could prove that He had broken the law; and whenever a story was brought against Him, it turned out not to be true. All this time Jesus held His peace, and said not a word. At last the high priest stood up and commanded Him to say whether He were the Christ or not. Then Jesus answered, "I am; and hereafter you shall see the Son of Man sitting on the right hand of power, and coming in the clouds of heaven." But the high priest would not believe Him; he cried out, "This is blasphemy. You have heard it. What think ye?" They all answered, "He is guilty of death." And then they began to spit in His face, and to smite Him, and mock Him. And all the time He stood gentle and patient, and said not one word of complaint or anger.

Then the people brought Jesus to Pontius Pilate the governor, and began to accuse Him. But Pilate could find no fault in Him, and wished to set Him free; but he was afraid of offending the rich Jews, so he sent Him to Herod, who was staying at Jerusalem at that time. Herod and his soldiers cruelly mocked and railed at Jesus, and sent Him back to Pilate.

Pilate felt in his heart that Jesus was innocent; so he thought he had found a way of saving Him without offending the Romans. It was the custom that at the feasts of the passover he should set some prisoner free, whomsoever the Jews asked for. He thought they would certainly ask for Jesus. But when Pilate proposed to let Jesus go, the people cried, "No, no; we do not wish Him to be set free. Let Him be crucified, and release unto us Barabbas." Barabbas was a wicked murderer, who was a prisoner at this time. Pilate said again, "Why, what evil has He done?" But the people cried again, "Crucify Him, crucify Him." Then Pilate let them have their way; he knew what was just, but he was afraid, and cared for himself more than for his duty. But first he took water, and washed his hands before the people, and said, "I am innocent of the blood of this just man: see ye to it." The people cried, "His blood be upon us, and upon our children." Then Pilate, who feared man more than he feared God, gave the innocent Jesus into the hands of His enemies, and released Barabbas. But God did not free Pilate from blame, for we hear and read every day that Jesus was crucified, and suffered under Pontius Pilate. And the Jews have suffered many sorrows for their sins.

Then the soldiers took Jesus to scourge Him. This is the scene which the artist has portrayed in the picture. They tore off His clothes; they scourged Him. The scourge was a whip composed of ox nerves, extremely sharp, interwoven with sheep bones, so as to cut the flesh. With this they whipped Jesus. He who had never lifted up His hand but to do good, was made to suffer this most degrading punishment. Not only were the hands of men raised to inflict torture upon the Saviour, but their tongues also were actively employed in reviling Him; thus adding insult to injury. And when they had beaten the blessed Jesus till He was bleeding all over, they took one of their old red soldiers' cloaks and threw it over Him.

And why was all this? Why was the scourge made to descend on the innocent? Why was Jesus thus to suffer? It was to save us from our sins; it was that the whole world might be reconciled to God.

THE CROWN OF THORNS.

THAT many might see the insults that Jesus suffered, the soldiers, after they had scourged Him, led Jesus into the governor's hall, and called together the whole band of soldiers. There were about six hundred men in this band; and they are now called in to witness the degradation of the victim. Then the soldiers put on Him a purple robe; this was done in derision—for that was the color proper to the robes of kings. And to make the mockery more complete, they plaited a crown of thorns, and put it about His head. The next picture shows the cruel soldiers forcing it upon His head. When they pressed the crown down, the thorns pierced into His head, and the blood trickled down His brow. Oh! what pain Jesus suffered then!

My dear children, I cannot tell you my feelings, as I talk with you about this cruel treatment of our Saviour. A lady, while on a visit to the Exposition at Paris, died. During her last moments, speech had left her; but she managed to speak the word "Bring." Her friends in ignorance of her meaning offered her food; but she shook her head, and again repeated the word "Bring." They then offered her grapes, which she also declined, and for a third time uttered the word "Bring." Thinking she desired to to see some absent friends, they brought them to her; but again she shook her head; and then, by a great effort, she succeeded in finishing the sentence,—

"Bring forth the royal diadem,
And crown Him Lord of all;"

and then passed away to be with Jesus.

SAYINGS OF CHILDHOOD:—A teacher described to her Sunday-school class the crown of thorns that was put on the brow of Jesus. Shortly after, one of the class was discovered twining a wreath of rare flowers. Being asked what he was doing, he replied, "Long ago, Jesus wore a crown of thorns, and even died for me; and now I am making Him a wreath, to show how much I love Him."

CHRIST INSULTED.

AFTER the soldiers had dressed Jesus in mockery in a purple robe, like a pretended king, and had put the crown of thorns upon His head, then they gave him a reed, to hold in His right hand as a sham sceptre. All this the Saviour submitted to with the greatest meekness. Then, to finish their mockery, the Jews bowed their knees to Him, pretending to honor Him as a king; and said, "Hail, king of the Jews!" This is what the artist has represented in the next picture. They are bowing down pretending to do Him honor. Then they spit on Him, and smote Him on the head with the reed. And after they had mocked Him, they took off the purple robe, and put His own raiment on Him.

O, think of it, my dear children, think of the cruel insult Jesus suffered, and all to save us. If He had been only a man, though He might have been a very good man, His sufferings would not have done us any good. But He was God as well as man; He is the One "mighty to save." Yes my little friends, He is able to save every one of you. But though it is such an easy thing to come to Christ and be saved, it was not an easy thing for Jesus to suffer in our stead. I can never, never tell you how much He suffered for us. And yet He loved us so much that He did not shrink from the suffering which He must endure. When the heavy lashes were being laid upon His bleeding back in Pilate's hall, when He was crowned with thorns and spit upon, when He was insulted by the crowd that pretended to do Him honor, He might in a moment have destroyed His cruel tormentors, and gone away to heaven. But if He had done that He could never take us to heaven with Him when He comes again to receive His own. He knew what He would have to endure for us, yet He gave himself up willingly to be "led as a lamb to the slaughter and, as a sheep before her shearers is dumb, so He opened not His mouth."

CHRIST PRESENTED BY PILATE TO THE PEOPLE.

OUR Jesus never spoke one word of anger all this time; and when Pilate saw His meek, brave, patient face, pale and faint with pain, and streaming with blood, he thought the people would pity Him; so Pilate went forth once more, and said unto the people, "Behold, I bring Him forth to you, that ye may know that I find no fault in Him." Then Jesus came forth to the top of the steps of the judgment-hall, wearing the crown of thorns, and the purple robe. And Pilate said unto them, "Behold the Man!" This is the scene portrayed in the engraving.

But the people were too mad to have any pity or feeling, and they only cried louder and louder still. "Crucify Him! Crucify Him!" Pilate was not brave enough to go against them all, even to save an innocent man; so he said, "Take ye Him, and crucify Him; for I find no fault in Him." The Jews answered him, "We have a law, and by our law He ought to die, because He made Himself the Son of God." As much as to say, If you, as a Roman, do not feel it lawful and just, we have plenty of law.

When Pilate therefore heard that saying, he was the more afraid; and went again into the judgment-hall, and said unto Jesus, "Whence art Thou?" But Jesus gave him no answer. Then said Pilate unto Him, "Speakest Thou not unto me? Knowest Thou not, that I have power to crucify Thee, and have power to release Thee?" Jesus answered, "Thou could'st have no power at all against Me, except it be given thee from above; therefore he that delivered Me unto thee hath the greater sin." After that Pilate tried to release Him; but the Jews cried out, "If thou let this man go, thou art not Cæsar's friend. Whosoever maketh himself a king, speaketh against Cæsar." When Pilate heard that, he brought Jesus forth, and sat down in the judgment-seat. "And it was the preparation of the passover, and about the sixth hour: and he said unto the Jews, Behold your King!" But they cried out, "Away with Him, away with Him, crucify Him." Pilate said unto them, "Shall I crucify your King?" The chief priests answered, "We have no king but Cæsar." Then Pilate delivered Jesus up to be crucified.

SAYINGS OF CHILDHOOD:—My little neighbor friend says, "I think Pilate was a great big coward. *I would die before letting Jesus go!*" Yes, children, he was a coward; he knew in his heart that Jesus did not deserve to die, and yet he let Him be crucified.

CHRIST FAINTING UNDER THE CROSS.

PILATE gave up our Lord to the four soldiers who were to crucify Him. His cross, a heavy beam of wood, with another fastened across it, was laid on His shoulders; and He was told to take up the heavy cross and carry it to Mount Calvary—the place where He was to suffer outside the walls of Jerusalem. He was so weak and worn out after the long night, and the bleeding from the cuts where they had beaten Him with leather whips, that He could hardly walk under the cross; He sometimes almost fainted by the way. It was very hard for Jesus to carry the cross, but He knew what it meant; and that made Him willing to bear it and suffer. After a while they met a man named Simon, and the soldiers made him carry it after Jesus. The artist has given us this scene in the picture; Christ is crushed to the earth—too weak to carry the cross farther; and the sturdy Simon, "a Cyrenian," is seen bearing the cruel weight of the cross.

As Jesus passed along, many of His friends came out, and followed Him, weeping very bitterly. Some of them were the women, and other people, to whom the Saviour had shown kindness; and Jesus turned to them, and said, "Daughters of Jerusalem, weep not for Me, but weep for yourselves, and for your children. Weep for your country, and for all the sorrow which is coming upon it." Jesus could feel for His friends and His country in all His sufferings. He cared more for their sorrow than for His own.

Dear children, Jesus bore the cross for us; and He says, "he that taketh not his cross, and followeth after Me, is not worthy of Me. If we would belong to Jesus, we must not be ashamed to bear the cross for Him. We are bid to *take*, not to make, our cross. God provides it. We are bid to *take it up*. Some writer has said, "The cross is easier to him who takes it up, than to him who drags it."

CHRIST'S ARRIVAL AT MOUNT CALVARY.

AT last, they came to a spot outside the gate of Jerusalem, called Golgotha or Calvary. The word means "a skull." Why it was so called is not known. It may possibly have been so called from a supposed resemblance of the ground to a human skull. Nothing is known, at the present time, respecting its site. All that we know of Golgotha, perhaps all that God willed to be known, is that it was without the city gate.

In the first picture the artist has portrayed the arrival at the hill Calvary. So utterly broken down is Christ's physical strength that He sinks to the ground. It was usual to give to the condemned, immediately before crucifixion, some wine mixed with some powerful opiate, to quiet their pain, and help them to bear it. It had been the custom of wealthy ladies in Jerusalem to provide this spiced wine at their own expense, and they did so quite irrespectively of their sympathy for any individual criminal. In this case it was probably offered to Jesus by the pitiful women who followed Him to the place of crucifixion, weeping as they went, and to whom He spoke the tender words by the way. When Jesus had tasted the wine mingled with bitter gall, He would not drink. Jesus did not wish His pain to be lessened. He was willing to endure the pangs which He had left heaven to bear for the sake of a sinful world. And thus an old prophecy of the Messiah was literally fulfilled: "They gave Me also gall for My meat; and in My thirst they gave Me vinegar to drink."

And all this Jesus suffered without the least impatience or anger. Dear children, let us especially consider this conduct of our Saviour as our pattern. Let us remember, that we are called to *do good*, and *suffer evil*, in this present world; let us keep a guard over our spirits and at the door of our lips, when we are injured, insulted, and afflicted; and let us consider how "light our afflictions" are, and how mixed with consolations, when compared with those of our divine Saviour.

The soldiers next proceeded to crucify Jesus. This was done in the following manner: He was stripped almost naked of His clothes; then the soldiers made Him lie down on the beam of wood, and they stretched His arms out on the cross-beam, and drove a large nail through each of the palms of His hands into the wood; and the feet, possibly placed one over the other, were fastened to the upright part of the cross, by another huge nail. In the next picture,

"THE CRUCIFIXION,"

they have laid hold of Him, thrust Him down upon the cross, and with blow after blow they drive the cruel nails through His hands and His feet. O think of it, my dear children, think of having nails driven right through your hands and feet. Do you suppose, if you could save the life of some little friend of yours, that you would be willing to have nails driven through your hands and feet, and to be fastened to a cross, and left there to die? Suppose some one had suffered such a death as that for you, that he might save you from temporal death, do you not think you would love the very name of that friend? I am sure you would. It seems to me you could not help it. Well, that is just what Jesus did—only He died to save you from *eternal* death. Ah, how can you help loving this dear Jesus? I should think you would hate all the sins that you have ever committed, when you remember that it was your sin that helped to nail the loving Jesus to the cross.

A little girl in a mission-school sat on the front seat; and, when the superintendent was telling about how they nailed Jesus on the cross, the tears came to her eyes, and she had to get up and go out. In the afternoon, she came back, smiling, and the superintendent asked her, "Mary, where did you go this morning?" And she said, "O, teacher! I could not stand it when you spoke to us about Jesus being nailed on the cross; for I felt just as if I helped to pound the nails in; and I went off a little piece from the school, and got down on my knees, and told Jesus that my sins helped to hang Him on the cross; and I asked Him to please forgive me for helping to kill Him; that I was so sorry! but now I feel so happy!"

The bible says: "Ye were not redeemed with corruptible things, as silver and gold, but with the precious blood of Christ." You know that when the great nails were driven through His hands and feet, the blood oozed out, and trickled down upon the ground. So that when the bible says, "Ye are redeemed with the precious blood of Christ," it means, that when we had broken God's good laws, and deserved to be punished, Christ gave Himself up to suffer in our place. He gave Himself a *ransom* for us. What a great heart of love He must have had to be willing to die! Have you ever thanked Him for this wonderful love? Do you love Him for it?

When the soldiers had finished nailing Jesus to the cross, then the cross was slowly lifted up by strong men, and the foot of it sunk into a hole, with a violent jerk, producing the most agonizing torture. The third picture portrays

"THE LIFTING UP OF THE CROSS."

The shame of the cross was made greater by our Saviour being crucified between two

robbers—as though He were the worst of the three. But all this was a fulfilment of those words of Isaiah : " And He was numbered with the transgressors." The spite of men had all been foreseen and foretold. The soldiers took the garments of Jesus and divided them among them, except the inner garment or tunic, which St. John tells us was without seam, and for this they gambled or cast lots, fulfilling the prophecy of David, saying, " They part my garments among them, and cast lots upon my vesture." Then they sat down and watched Him, while many wicked men jeered Him, saying, " He saved others, Himself He cannot save." But all this time the gentle Saviour only pitied them, and said, " Father, forgive them, for they know not what they do." That was the patient way He bore the pain to save us.

Over the head of the blessed Lord on the cross was a tablet, with the words, " JESUS OF NAZARETH THE KING OF THE JEWS." Pilate wrote it in mockery ; and those who read it only laughed, and reviled Jesus the more. Yet the writing was true. Jesus *was* king of the Jews. The Jews indeed would not receive Him as their king ; but a time is coming when they will receive Him. There Jesus hung patiently, while the chief priests and Pharisees passed by, mocking and laughing at His pain. Even the robbers at first joined in the cry ; but by-and-by one of them began to feel that He who was so patient and so great in all that agony must truly be the Son of God, and so he rebuked his fellow, and said to Jesus, " Lord remember me when Thou comest into Thy kingdom !" And the Lord answered, " To-day shalt thou be with Me in paradise !"

The mother of Jesus had come to stand by the foot of His cross, and with her, her sister and some other women, and His beloved disciple John. When Jesus saw His mother and John standing near Him, He spoke to them, and comforted them. His own pain did not make Him forgetful of those He loved. He spoke first to His mother and said, " Woman behold thy son !" and He looked at John, and said, " Behold thy mother !" He meant that John should take care of her, and be like a son to her, when her own Son was gone. And John understood what his dear Master meant, and took Mary home with him, and was always like a son to her afterwards.

SAYINGS OF CHILDHOOD :—What a lesson of forgiveness, little people, there is in all this for us. In a school in Ireland, one boy struck another ; and, when he was about to be punished, the injured boy begged for his pardon. The master asked, " Why do you wish to keep him from being flogged ? " The boy replied, " I have read in the New Testament that our Lord Jesus Christ forgave His enemies when He hung upon the cross ; and therefore I forgive him, and beg he may not be punished for my sake."

THE DEATH OF CHRIST.

IT was noon. And now a dreadful darkness came over all the land. It lasted from noon until three o'clock. The mockery of the Jews was interrupted by three hours of gloom and consternation. It would seem as if nature was unable to behold the agony of her Creator, and also sought to hide it from the gaze of men. Jesus was still alive; but He did not speak all that time. He was suffering more than we can understand; more than any mere man could ever suffer. His body was in great pain. The wounds caused by the scourge, and by the nails, festered and became inflamed, and were attacked by great swarms of flies; the head throbbed; burning fever set in; the joints ached, and every movement for their relief only increased the pain; there was dizziness, intense thirst, and heaviness of the heart.

But, great as were His bodily sufferings, these were nothing compared with those of His soul. Jesus was dying; dying for sinners. He had promised His Father to do this; and His Father was now putting upon Him the punishment due to the sins of the world. And at "the ninth hour," or three o'clock in the afternoon, Jesus cried with a loud voice, saying, "My God, My God, why hast Thou forsaken Me?" Why should Jesus make that cry? Because He was on the cross in the sinner's place. God hates sin. And for a time He felt as sinners feel when God withdraws His presence from them forever. He took the sinner's place, and experienced his despair in order that the sinner might experience the joy of the beloved Son. God had not forgotten His beloved Son; He had not ceased to love Him; but He did not smile upon Him, nor comfort Him now; this was His worst suffering. For God to forsake Him at that moment, how awful! Well may we adore the blessed Jesus for such a display of love. But, if He cried out beneath the weight of man's guilt, what must those sinners endure, who will not believe in Him and be saved, and so doom themselves to bear the weight of their own guilt forever.

Some of them that stood there, when they heard Jesus cry out with anguish, said, "This man calleth for Elias." Then one of the soldiers ran and filled a sponge with vinegar, and lifted it up to the Saviour's lips. This was done in response to His cry: "I thirst." No doubt that it was given by some one who was touched by that appeal. But his more brutal companions said, "Let be, let us see whether Elias will come to

save Him." When Jesus had received the vinegar, He said, "It is finished;" and then He cried with a loud voice, "Father, into Thy hands I commend My spirit;" and He bowed His head, and gave up the ghost.

Jesus was dead. This is what the artist has portrayed in the first picture. "It is finished." The work of grace was done. The work which His Father had given Him to do was now performed. The Father's will was done. Jesus would have hung on the cross for two or three days before dying, but when He thought of all the wicked people in the world, He thought of you and me; then His heart broke, and He died after He had been on the cross only six hours. He died of a broken heart!

Then the veil, which hung before the Holy of Holies in the temple, was torn in two; and the earth shook with a great earthquake; and the rocks rent; and the graves opened, and the bodies of many of the saints which slept arose. The artist, in the next picture,

"THE DARKNESS WHICH ACCOMPANIED THE DEATH OF OUR LORD," tries to give us some idea of this thrilling event in nature. And why was all this? Why did nature thus feel this great event? Because Jesus was God. Everything felt His power; and everything trembled with fear and horror, when wicked men put to death the Lord of life and glory. The soldiers who watched Jesus, and the centurion who commanded them, felt this, and cried, "Truly this was the Son of God." He acted just as the Son of God would act.

Now, my dear little friends, does not this wonderful story of the death of Jesus make you feel that you ought to be Christians? Try and offer this little prayer from the heart: "O God, show me that Jesus, the Saviour, is very near me now, and that He is willing to love me; and teach me how He suffered that I might be forgiven my many sins, and be found at last in His fold. Holy Spirit, help me to see Jesus as *my* Saviour; and O, dear Jesus, forgive me that I have not loved Thee; give me a new heart, that I may love Thee now; take me as I am, and make me Thine forever, for Thine own sake. Amen."

SAYINGS OF CHILDHOOD:—A minister was once speaking about sin finding us out. He said, "If you do not find out your sin, and bring it to Calvary, to get it pardoned, and washed away through the blood of Jesus, your sin will find you out, and bring you to judgment to be condemned, and sent away by Jesus Christ to everlasting punishment." Oh!" thought a little girl who had told her mother a lie—"Oh, that lie! I must either find it, and bring it to Calvary, or it will cause me to be punished forever." She rested not till she knew what it was to have sin forgiven.

CHRIST TAKEN DOWN FROM THE CROSS.

OUR Saviour was crucified on Friday. The next day was the Jewish Sabbath. And the Sabbath after the crucifixion happened to be a great day among the Jews—because it was the feast of the passover. So some of them went to Pilate, and asked him to let them take the bodies down from the crosses, that the Sabbath might not be dishonored, and that the law of Moses might not be broken. Then Pilate sent the soldiers to see if those who were crucified were yet dead, and to kill them if they were not. This was done by striking the legs of the sufferers with a heavy mallet, which generally caused instant death.

The soldiers broke the legs of the two thieves first; and then, coming to Jesus, they saw that He was dead already, and so did not break His legs. But one of them with a spear pierced His side, and there came out blood and water. These things, too, had been foretold by the prophets.

And now two of Christ's secret friends and lovers come to the light. Nicodemus, who, at first, came to Him by night, was one; and Joseph of Arimathea, who had been some time a disciple of Jesus, but secretly, for fear of the Jews, was the other. Joseph went boldly to Pilate, and begged the body of Jesus that he might give it burial. Nicodemus brought a mixture of myrrh and aloes, about a hundred pounds weight, for the purpose of embalming it. In the depth and sincerity of their love they did this; and now, when Jesus and His disciples had so many enemies, Joseph and Nicodemus, instead of being afraid, felt strong and courageous.

Pilate was astonished when Joseph told him that Jesus was dead. A death so soon after crucifixion was a thing so unusual that he called to him the centurion, in order to make sure of the fact. When he was certain, he gave the body to Joseph. Joseph went

370   CHRIST TAKEN DOWN FROM THE CROSS.

to the cross, and took down the body of Jesus. In the picture the artist has shown us these good men carefully lifting Jesus from the cross.

When the body was taken down, Joseph and Nicodemus carried it to Joseph's garden near the place of crucifixion, where there was a cave in which Joseph meant to be buried, but where no one had yet been laid. They carried our Lord's body there; and the good women who followed, Mary Magdalene and the rest, wrapped it up in clean linen and sweet spices. They wanted to do more for it; but it was getting late on Friday evening, and the Sabbath or seventh day was counted from sunset, and then they could do no manner of work. So they had to wait till the Sabbath should be over.

In our next picture

"THE BURIAL OF JESUS,"

we see Joseph and Nicodemus bearing to the tomb the silent form of Him who only lived for others, and who died to win them eternal life. As became royalty, the body was placed in a new tomb, hewn out of the rock, "wherein never man before was laid." And thus was fulfilled that scripture, which in the same breath implied both shame and honor, "He made His grave with the wicked, and with the rich in His death."

When they had laid the body in the tomb, Joseph rolled a great stone close up to the rock; and they went away in their grief. The day following, the chief priests and Pharisees went to Pilate, and told him that they were afraid that Christ's disciples would go to the tomb secretly, by night, and steal the body away; and then they will pretend that He is risen from the dead, and persuade the people to believe in Him; so they begged Pilate that they might have the tomb guarded. Pilate said, "Go your way; set a watch at the sepulchre, and make it as sure as you can." So they went away, and made all as sure as they could, and sealed the stone that nobody might remove it, and set a watch or guard of soldiers to prevent any one approaching. These foolish men thought that they could thus keep the body of Jesus in the tomb. We shall soon see how vain all their hopes were.

THE ANGEL AND THE WOMEN AT THE SEPULCHRE.

HOW sad a Sabbath was the day after the burial! The disciples were all despondent. They felt that all hope was gone. Although Christ had told them that He should rise again, yet they were not looking for His resurrection, for who ever had come back again from the dead?

As soon as the Sabbath was past, Mary Magdalene and the other women, who loved Jesus so much, came, with the sweet spices they had prepared, to the tomb to anoint His body. It was very early in the morning when they set off;—just beginning to be light. So little were *they* thinking of a resurrection, that as they went along they were troubled with the thought, "who shall roll us away the stone from the door of the sepulchre?" for it was very heavy. But when they came nearer, they saw that it was taken away; and the door was open.

How was this? Who had rolled away the stone? The angel of the Lord sent down from heaven. The stone, and the seal, and the soldiers who watched by the tomb, had no power to keep Jesus within the tomb. "And, behold, there was a great earthquake: for the angel of the Lord descended from heaven, and came and rolled back the stone from the door, and sat upon it. His countenance was like lightning, and his raiment white as snow: and for fear of him the keepers did shake, and became as dead men." These keepers were Roman soldiers, the most courageous men in the world; but they were frightened at the scene. Jesus had risen, as He said; the grave had given up its dead, and Christ was alive again.

Mary Magdalene was so astonished at what she saw, that she ran back, and told the disciples. But Salome and the other Mary stayed and went into the sepulchre; and there they saw a young man clothed in a long white garment: and they were afraid; But he said to them. "Be not afraid; ye seek Jesus of Nazareth, which was crucified; He has risen; He is not here: behold the place where they laid Him. But go your way, tell His disciples and Peter, that He goeth before you into Galilee: there shall ye see Him, as He said unto you." In the picture we have this striking scene portrayed. Then the women went away quickly from the sepulchre; but they were so much frightened at all they had seen, that they could not speak to any one they met on the road.

Mary Magdalene had gone to tell Peter and John. As soon as she saw them, she

THE ANGEL AND THE WOMEN AT THE SEPULCHRE.

said, "They have taken away the Lord out of the sepulchre, and we know not where they have laid Him." You see Peter's sin had been forgiven, because he had repented ; and when he heard from Mary Magdalene that Jesus was not in the tomb, both he and John ran to the sepulchre ; John ran faster than Peter, and came there first, and saw the linen clothes lying ; but he did not go in. Soon after, Peter came, and went in, and he too saw the linen clothes lying ; and the napkin that had been about Jesus' head, folded together in a place by itself. By-and-by John also went into the sepulchre ; and then they believed that Jesus had risen, so they went away.

But Mary Magdalene still stayed outside the sepulchre, weeping. At last she stooped down and looked in ; and she saw two angels clothed in white sitting there, and they said to Mary, " Why weepest thou ? " She answered, " Because they have taken away my Lord, and I know not where they have laid Him." As she said this, she turned round and saw some one standing near her. He asked her the same question, " Why weepest thou ? " Mary did not know that it was Jesus when she saw Him ; she thought it was the gardener who spoke to her ; so she said, " Sir, if thou hast borne Him hence, tell me where thou hast laid Him, and I will take Him away." Jesus said unto her, " Mary! " She who so loved her Saviour knew His voice at once, and in tones of joy she answered, " Master." Mary was so glad, she would have embraced His feet, but Jesus forbade her, and desired her to go and tell His brethren, saying, " I ascend to My Father, and to your Father ; to My God, and to your God."

Then Mary went to tell the disciples. As she was going, she met Salome and the other Mary ; and while they were all together, Jesus Himself came to them, and said, " All hail ! " Then they fell down and worshipped Him. Jesus said to them. " Be not afraid ; go and tell My brethren to go into Galilee, and there they shall see Me." So they went, and did as Jesus said.

But what did the Roman soldiers do ? They were set to guard the body of Jesus, and yet He had escaped. How could they escape punishment for this ? They went into the city and told the simple story how it happened, and how terrified they were. " They showed unto the priests all the things that were done." The priests were very much surprised to hear this. But they would not believe in Jesus even now ; and they determined to prevent the people too from believing on Him, if they could. So it was settled that a story should be made up ; they called the soldiers, and gave them a large sum of money, and said, " Say ye, His disciples came by night, and stole Him away while we slept : " and they told the soldiers, they need not be afraid, for they would speak to the

THE ANGEL AND THE WOMEN AT THE SEPULCHRE.

governor, and take care that they were not punished. So the soldiers took the money, and promised to do as they were told; and then they went away and told this wicked falsehood to all the people.

Dear children, a very little thought will show the weakness of this story. In the first place, if the soldiers had been asleep, they could not have known what had passed during that time. Secondly, if any of them had been awake, they would naturally have awakened their comrades, and have prevented the act they were to assert as having taken place. And, thirdly, if they had been asleep, they would not have dared to own it; the priests and elders would themselves have demanded their punishment.

Yes; it is a blessed truth—*Jesus rose from the dead!* And if we sleep in Jesus, God will bring us with Him; because He lives, we shall live also. As surely as the sepulchre of Christ became an empty sepulchre, so surely the sepulchres of His people shall become empty also; as surely as He got up, and sung a jubilee of life and immortality, so surely shall His people come out of the grave and sing forever.

SAYINGS OF CHILDHOOD:—Little Mary said, "They took little brother and laid him in the ground where the trees grow." "The *cold* ground," said Kate, shuddering "No, the *warm* ground," replied Mary, where ugly seeds are turned into beautiful flowers, and where good people turn into angels, and fly away to heaven." Yes, dear little ones, the ground has been "*warm*," since our Saviour laid in it.

THE WALK TO EMMAUS.

THE same day that Christ rose from the dead, two of his disciples were walking to Emmaus, a little village near Jerusalem. They were talking "of all the things which had happened." The question which they were talking over evidently was, "Was Jesus the Messiah?" The particular thing which troubled them was, "Could he be the Christ and suffer the shameful death that He did?" "Was it possible for His enemies so to triumph over the true Messiah?"

As they talked in this way, Jesus came up behind them, and joined them as though He were a common traveler going their way. He made the promise, "For where two or three are gathered together in My name, there am I in the midst of them," and was already fulfilling it. That promise He still fulfills. If we were to look for the reason why he appeared unto Mary Magdalene and to these two disciples first, before He appeared unto any of His apostles, perhaps we should find it in this—that they were in the most need of comfort. Mary was weeping at the sepulchre, and these two men were walking along talking about their Lord, lonely and sad. The Lord dried Mary's tears, and changed their sadness into joy. He had a design in comforting them. And how soon they carried it out by trying to comfort others! Are we as zealous as were they?

When Jesus came near them, He asked, "What are you talking about?" They replied, "Have you not heard what has happened yonder in Jerusalem?" "What things," said He. Then they told Him it was of Jesus of Nazareth, who had been a great prophet, and they had hoped would have redeemed Israel; but now He had been put to death the day before yesterday, yet that some of the women said that they had seen a vision of angels which said that He was alive.

And then this wonderful Stranger began to explain to them, in all the scriptures, the things which were written of Christ. As He talked to them, they felt that they had never before understood the scripture so clearly; and they began to be quite sure that Jesus was indeed the true Messiah. It is this meeting that the artist has so touchingly portrayed in the picture. At last they came to Emmaus, and went into a house; and the Stranger made as if He would have gone farther, but they pressed Him to come in. He sat down with them, and took bread and blessed and brake it; then their eyes were opened—*it was Jesus!* and they knew Him. And as soon as they knew Him, He vanished out of their sight. Then they said, "Did not our hearts burn within us as

THE WALK TO EMMAUS.

He talked with us by the way?" They returned to Jerusalem that same hour, and found the other disciples, and said to them, "The Lord is risen indeed;" and while they were telling them the things that had just happened, though the door was not opened, Jesus Himself stood in the midst of them, and said, "Peace be unto you." They were afraid at first; but again He said, "Why are ye troubled? and why do thoughts arise in your hearts? Behold My hands and My feet, that it is I, Myself, handle Me, and see; for a spirit hath not flesh and bones, as ye see Me have." Then He showed them that there were the marks of the nails in His hands and feet, and the spear-wound in His side; so that it was His own real body that had come again from the dead.

The disciples could hardly believe for joy; but Jesus asked them, "Have ye here any meat?" And they gave Him a piece of broiled fish and a honey-comb; and He took it, and ate with them, to make them quite sure that it was Himself. Then He said, "These are the words which I spake unto you, while I was yet with you, that all things must be fulfilled which were written in the law of Moses, and in the prophets, and in the psalms, concerning me." Then He explained all to them, and showed them how He really is the Christ the Son of God; and He said, "Now go, and teach all nations what I have done to save sinners. Begin at Jerusalem; for the Jews must first have the gospel preached to them; and then go to the Gentiles. Tell them to repent of their sins, and believe in Me, that they may be saved. Baptize them in the name of the Father, and of the Son, and of the Holy Ghost." Thomas was not with the other disciples when Jesus appeared to them; but when they next saw him, they told him the good news. They said, "We have seen the Lord." But Thomas said he should never believe that it was the Lord Himself, unless he could put his finger into the print of the nails, and his hand into the wound in His side.

The next Sunday evening, Thomas and the other ten were all in the upper room together, when Jesus came and stood in the midst, and said, "Peace be unto you." There was no need for Jesus to open the door, to come into the room. He had power to come and go as He pleased, in a wonderful way which we cannot understand; and He came now, that Thomas might see for himself, and be quite sure that Jesus was risen from the dead. So Jesus called Thomas, and said, "Reach hither thy finger, and behold My hands; and reach hither thy hand, and thrust it into My side; and be not faithless, but believing." Then Thomas knew that it was really Jesus, and he cried out in faith and joy, "My Lord and my God!" And Jesus answered, "Thomas, because thou hast seen Me, thou hast believed; blessed are they that have not seen, and yet have believed." And this is the blessing for all who have lived since our blessed Lord was on earth. We do not see Him, as Thomas did; but we may look upon Him by faith, and believe in Him in our hearts; and all will be truly "blessed," really happy, who thus believe in Jesus.

Our Lord told His apostles to go into Galilee; and there, one night, seven of them went out fishing on the lake, as they used to do; but they fished all night, and caught nothing. In the morning, Jesus came and stood upon the shore; but the disciples did not know that it was Jesus. So he called to them, and said, "Children, have you any meat?" They said, "No." Then He said, "Cast the net on the right side of the ship." And directly the net was full of fishes, all large and good, and it did not break! When John saw this, he turned to Peter, and said, "It is the Lord." And Peter was so glad, that he sprang right out of the boat, and came hurrying through the water to his Master's feet. And the other disciples came in the ship, dragging the net full of fishes; as soon as they were all come to land, they saw a fire of coals there, and fish laid on it, and bread. The disciples did not know how and whence all this food came; it was the kind care of Jesus that prepared it for them. And Jesus said, "Come and dine." So they sat down to meat.

When they had eaten, Jesus called Peter, and said to him, "Simon, son of Jonas, lovest thou Me more than these?" Peter answered, "Yea, Lord, Thou knowest that I love Thee." "Feed My sheep," Jesus said. Soon after, Jesus asked again, "Simon, son of Jonas, lovest thou Me?" "Yea, Lord, Thou knowest that I love Thee," said Peter. "Feed My lambs," Jesus said. Jesus asked the third time, "Simon, son of Jonas, lovest thou Me?" Peter now began to feel grieved; and he said, "Lord, Thou knowest all things; Thou knowest that I love Thee." And once more Jesus said, "Feed My sheep."

What did this mean? Christ is the Good Shepherd, and He calls His people His sheep. Peter was to give spiritual food to those sheep. He was to go and preach the gospel to them.

SAYINGS OF CHILDHOOD:—In a certain christian family, a little boy, on asking his father to allow him to be baptized, was told that he was too young—that he might fall back if he made a profession when he was only a little boy. To this he made reply: '*Jesus has promised to carry the lambs in His arms. I am only a little boy—it will be easier for Jesus to carry me.*" This logic was too much for the father. He took him with him, and the child was ere long baptized.

THE ASCENSION.

FOR forty days our Lord came in ways like what I have told you, to see and teach His disciples. At last, the time came for Jesus to be taken from them, and to go up to heaven. So He led them out once more to the village of Bethany. Then Jesus lifted up His hands and blessed His disciples; and it came to pass, that while He was blessing them, and talking with them, He was parted from them, and ascended up into heaven, going higher and higher, till "a cloud received Him out of their sight."

This is the scene portrayed so beautifully in the engraving; the ascending figure of our Saviour, rising above the group of His joyful yet sorrowing worshippers, is powerfully expressed by the artist. The disciples kept looking towards heaven, as he went up; they watched the bright cloud which hid Him finally from their eyes. At last Jesus was gone. He had gone into heaven, to set down on the right hand of His Father's throne.

While they still looked after Him, two angels appeared and said, "Ye men of Galilee, why stand ye gazing up into heaven? this same Jesus, which is taken up from you into heaven shall so come in like manner as ye have seen Him go into heaven." Then the disciples were comforted; and they returned to Jerusalem with great joy, there to wait for the promise of the Holy Ghost, as Jesus commanded them.

Dear children, Where is Jesus now? In the heavens. Though He has gone up from the earth and ascended into His glory, He will not forget His children for a moment that are left behind Him. Do you know what He is doing there? He is watching over us, **and** laying our prayers before His Father, and getting ready our home there. Another thing He is doing: He is *interceding* for us. Do you know what that big word means? It means that He is pleading for you and me, that our sins may be forgiven and that we may not do wrong any more. Won't you try to do all that you can to keep from doing wrong.

SAYINGS OF CHILDHOOD:—The question was asked in a Sunday school, "What is meant by intercession?" One little fellow replied, "Speaking a word to God for us, sir." Wasn't that a good answer? Jesus *ever* lives to intercede—that is, "speak a word to God for us."

DAY OF PENTECOST.

CHRIST had told His apostles, that though He was going to heaven He would send them another comforter, who would be with them forever. The time was now come when that promise must be fulfilled. Ten days after the ascension, was the feast of pentecost—one of the great feasts of the Jews. On that day the disciples of Jesus were all met together "in one place" at Jerusalem; and while they were so met, suddenly a singular sound filled the house, as though a wind were rushing through it, and flames, like fire, appeared on each of them, having the shape of tongues, cloven, or divided; and they were all filled with the Holy Ghost, and wonderful knowledge came to all of them—so that they could speak all sorts of different languages, without ever having learned them.

Now, you know, it takes some time and labor to learn different languages, but these disciples spoke several languages at once; and the reason of this was, that they might at once tell the people of different countries who came to Jerusalem, about all the great things that Jesus had done, and what had happened to Him; that sinners of mankind, in every country, might be saved. These wonders were to show them that God the Holy Ghost had come down from heaven.

In the first picture we have portrayed the wonderful descent of the fire upon their heads. All the Jews who had visited Jerusalem, when they heard of the wonderful event which had taken place, ran to the house where the disciples were, and there was great astonishment when they found that these disciples could speak the languages of all the countries whence they had come. They said, "How is this? Are not these men Galileans? How is it they can speak to us in our own tongues?" But some of the people of Jerusalem, who hated Christ and His disciples, mocked, and said, "These men

are full of new wine;" that is, they charged them with being drunk. But, children, I think they were more like drunken men themselves, who could suppose that men could speak other languages merely because they were tipsy; and, if they had not been full of prejudice and hatred against Christ and His disciples, they would never have suggested such a reason for this miraculous gift.

Then Peter thought it best to preach to the multitude. In the next picture we have

"THE APOSTLES PREACHING THE GOSPEL."

Peter, being the oldest, and perhaps the most thoroughly instructed in His Master's will and purposes, took the lead of the apostolic band. He stood up in the midst, and said, " Ye men of Judea, and all ye that dwell at Jerusalem, these wonderful things, which you now hear and see, are only the fulfillment of what God's prophet Joel foretold many years ago. He said that God would, in the last days, pour out His Spirit upon His servants, and teach them to prophesy. And so it is. And now hear these words. Jesus of Nazareth came among you, and worked miracles, as you know. He was taken by wicked men, and crucified, and slain. But God raised Him up; and we are witnesses of His resurrection, and say to you, that He is the Son of God, the true Messiah. And now He is ascended up to heaven; and it is He who has sent the Holy Ghost upon us, and given us this wonderful power of speaking which you have heard to-day."

When the people heard this, " they were pricked in their heart;" that is they felt as you have perhaps felt when you have been detected in doing something you ought not to have done, and something perhaps very bad indeed; for shame and guilt pierce and wound the soul, as a sword cuts and pains the body. And they said unto Peter and to the rest of the apostles, " Men and brethren, what shall we do?" Peter told them, " Repent, and be baptized, everyone of you, in the name of Jesus Christ, for the remission of sins; and ye shall receive the gift of the Holy Ghost." They must " repent "— that is seek forgiveness from Christ for the wickedness they had done; and they must be " baptized "—that is, as a proof that they had embraced the religion of Jesus; and then the Holy Ghost would work in their hearts, and make them both holy and happy.

During that one day, children, about " three thousand " repented and believed, through the preaching of Peter, and were baptized.

PETER AND JOHN HEALING THE LAME MAN.

WE have talked, dear children, about many wonderful miracles which Jesus did. But I am going to tell you now about a miracle wrought by the apostles Peter and John. We are told that they went up one day into the temple to pray. At the entrance-gate, which was called "Beautiful" on account of its being more handsome than the other gates, they saw a poor man who was born lame. Every day he was carried to the gate, and there he lay, asking money from those who went into the temple. As Peter and John entered, he asked them also to give him something. These disciples were themselves poor, but they had something better than money to give. So Peter said to the poor cripple, "Look on us;" the poor man did so at once, hoping to receive some money from them. But Peter said, "Silver and gold have I none; but such as I have give I thee: in the name of Jesus Christ of Nazareth, rise up and walk." And Peter took him by the hand, and lifted him up; and instantly his feet became strong; he stood up, and walked, and entered the temple, leaping, and walking, and praising God.

In the engraving the artist has represented the scene just as Peter lifts the lame man to his feet. His crutches drop; and his hands are lifted in praise. The cure of this man drew together a great many people, all wondering at what they saw. Peter said to them, "Why do you wonder?" Then he explained to them that not by their own power or holiness had they given the lame man ability to walk, but that God had done this miracle by His own power and mercy; and he preached to them of Christ crucified, and touched their hearts; so that about five thousand more were added to the church.

The Sadducees, and the high priest and others, being grieved because the apostles taught the people, had Peter and John brought before them. They asked them by what power they had cured the man, whether by the help of the devil, as they thought, or by the help of God. At this moment the Holy Ghost filled Peter's heart with the greatest courage, and he again preached, having the rulers and priests to hear him. These were not converted, but nevertheless they were struck with wonder at the boldness of Peter and John.

From this, let us learn the duty of holy boldness for the sake of Christ. One of the reformers being told, "All the world are against you," replied, "Then I am against all the world." The record on the tomb of John Knox is, "Here lies the man who never feared the face of clay."

MARTYRDOM OF ST. STEPHEN.

DEAR children, how many of you can tell me what the word *martyr* means? It means a person who dies in defence of his religion; and many of the first followers of the Lord were martyred, or put to death, for loving Jesus, and teaching in His name. In those days the disciples had chosen, from among the many newly converted Christians, seven holy and wise men, who were called deacons, to assist them in visiting the sick, and giving alms to the needy. Among those thus chosen was a man named Stephen. He was a man very "full of faith," and he "did great wonders and miracles among the people." But the powerful enemies of Christ rose up against Stephen, and dragged him before the council, and as there was no crime committed by him to condemn him, false witnesses, for the sake of a reward, made up a story against him, and accused him of preaching things contrary to their law.

All this time Stephen stood calmly before his enemies. He looked so holy and gentle, that "all that sat in the council, looking steadfastly on him, saw his face, as it had been the face of an angel." At last the high priest spoke to Stephen, and asked, "Are these things so?" Then the good man made a noble defence, and boldly told them of their wickedness, and of that of their fathers before them. He charged them with being "the betrayers and murderers" of Christ, and cut them so to the heart with what he said, that in their rage they, like a pack of dogs, "gnashed on him with their teeth." But Stephen was still calm and gentle; and being full of the Holy Ghost, he looked up into heaven, and saw Jesus standing on the right hand of God. Then Stephen said, "I see the heavens opened, and the Son of man standing on the right hand of God." But his enemies would not attend to what he said. They cried out with a loud voice,

MARTYRDOM OF ST. STEPHEN.

and stopped their ears, and ran upon him, and cast him out of the city, and stoned him.

In the engraving, Stephen lies against the wall, with lifted face, bearing the pitiless storm of stones hurled by his foes, who surround him on every hand. Then Stephen called upon God, and said, "Lord Jesus, receive my spirit." And even in his sufferings, he prayed for his murderers, following the example of our blessed Saviour; he kneeled down and cried with a loud voice, "Lord, lay not this sin to their charge." And when he had said this, "he fell asleep."

So Stephen died; but the Bible does not say he "died;" it only says he "fell asleep." Just think of it, children, Stephen was in the midst of a shower of stones, and yet he fell asleep! How peaceful his death was! So peaceful and happy, that it was not like death; it was like calm and quiet sleep. What do you suppose made Stephen so forget all his pain? It was the bright and glorious sight of his Saviour standing at God's right hand, to take him up to heaven.

All God's saints, when they die, fall asleep. When we sleep we rest; and death to them is no punishment, but only a rest.

SAYINGS OF CHILDHOOD :—A little boy in an infant class, one day said to his teacher, "Our little baby's dead!" After speaking about it for a few minutes, the teacher asked the scholar, "Would you like to die?" He replied, "Not yet." The child, when asked what he meant by saying, "Not yet," said, "Not till I get a new heart." Dear children, Stephen had a new heart; and if you want to be peaceful and calm when you come to die, like him, you must have a *new heart*.

SAUL'S CONVERSION ON THE WAY TO DAMASCUS.

NOW in this talk I want to tell you the history of the most wonderful man among all the apostles. There was a rich young man, whose name was Saul; he was born at Tarsus, and studied law at Jerusalem, under Gamaliel; he became very learned, and was very strict in keeping the laws of Moses, and thought himself very righteous. Saul thought himself too good to need a Saviour, for he did not know the sinfulness of his own heart then.

So when Saul first heard of Jesus and His followers, he despised, and rejected, and hated Him; and he persecuted every one who loved and believed in the Saviour. He even thought it was his duty to do this, and to try to prevent them from believing in the Lord Jesus. He made havoc of the church in Jerusalem, falling on them like a wild beast on its prey, "entering into every house," and dragging out men and women, and putting them in prison. After doing all he could to persecute the Christians in Jerusalem, Saul went to the high-priest, and begged him to give him authority to go to Damascus, that he might there search out for the Christians, and bring all that he could find bound to Jerusalem.

Then the high-priest gave him permission, and Saul set off to Damascus. But God in His mercy had other work for Saul; so God met him on his journey. As he came near to Damascus, suddenly a great light from heaven shone round about him and he fell to the ground, and heard a voice saying to him, "Saul, Saul, why persecutest thou Me?" In the picture the artist has portrayed this moment in the conversion of Saul—when the vivid light from heaven and the mysterious voice strike the fiery persecutor to the earth, and scatter dismay and terror among his trembling attendants.

Then Saul cried, "Who art thou Lord?" And the voice again said, "I am Jesus, whom thou persecutest." Saul's spirit was at once subdued; he was humbled and astonished; and he who had made others tremble now trembled himself, and said, "Lord, what wilt Thou have me to do?" And the Lord said unto him, "Arise and go into the city, and it shall be told thee what thou must do. Then Saul arose; but he was not able to see; the great light which had flashed upon him had blinded his eyes, so that those who were with him had to lead him by the hand; and they brought him to Damascus.

Saul was three days at Damascus, without eating or drinking; and he was blind too, all that time. Yet all was sent in mercy to Saul, to bring him to repentance. As he sat alone, blind and unhappy, he thought of his past life; and he felt, for the first time, that he was a sinner before God; and then he began to pray for pardon. And did God hear his prayer? Yes; God had been looking upon Saul all this time; and as soon as Saul began really to pray, God heard and answered him.

Then a certain good man, named Ananias, to whom the Lord appeared in a vision, and told him what to do, came in search of Saul. Ananias went into the room where Saul was, and, putting his hands upon him, said, "Brother Saul, the Lord, even Jesus, that appeared to thee in the way as thou camest, hath sent me that thou mightest receive thy sight, and be filled with the Holy Ghost." And Saul received his sight instantly, and arose, and was baptized. Then he ate some food; and he stayed some days with the disciples at Damascus, where he boldly preached Christ in their synagogues.

ST. PETER AT THE HOUSE OF CORNELIUS.

BEFORE I tell you anything more about Saul, afterwards called Paul, I will tell you something about Peter. There was a man living, at this time, in Cesarea, whose name was Cornelius, and he was a centurion, that is, an officer commanding a hundred men. Cornelius was very pious and charitable, and particularly fond of praying to God. He did not yet know very much of holy things; but he wished to know more, and prayed daily to be taught. One day, while he was devoutly engaged in prayer, an angel of God spoke to him in a vision; that is, he saw the angel, not in a dream by night, but in broad day; and the angel called him, and said, "Cornelius." Cornelius looked upon the angel, and asked, "What is it, Lord?" And the angel said to him, "Thy prayers and thine alms are come up for a memorial before God;" meaning, that the prayers which he had put up in faith, for himself and family, and the charitable deeds he had done from a feeling of love, were like sacrifices upon the altar, which ascended to God with acceptance. Then the angel told Cornelius, "Send men to Joppa, and call for one Simon, whose surname is Peter; he lodgeth with one Simon a tanner, whose house is by the sea-side; he shall tell thee what thou oughtest to do." So Cornelius sent two of his servants, and a pious soldier, to Joppa to fetch Peter.

Now, it so happened, that the very day that the messengers set off on their journey, Peter, who was now at Joppa, went on the house-top to pray; and while he was praying he fell into a trance—a kind of vision or dream. That is, he lost all sense of what was doing here, and felt as if he were a happy spirit, departed from the body; and he saw heaven opened, and a large sheet let down to earth and spread out before him as a table cloth, in which were wild beasts and creeping things, as well as tame beasts and fowls;

and a voice said, "Arise, Peter, kill and eat." But Peter answered, "Not so, Lord; for I have never eaten anything common or unclean." The voice then said, "What God hath cleansed, that call thou not common." This was done three times, to impress his mind the more strongly; and then the sheet was taken up again into heaven; and Peter awoke.

Peter, on coming to himself, could not think what all this could mean; but while he was thinking upon it, the messengers from Cornelius arrived at his door; and just at that moment the Spirit said to Peter, "These men are seeking thee; go with them, and fear not; for I have sent them." So Peter went down, and met them at the gate, and said, "I am the man you seek. Tell me, why are you come?" They answered, "We are come from Cornelius, the centurion. He is a just man, and fears God; and he has been warned by an angel to send for thee." Then Peter called the messengers into the house, and lodged them that night; and the next day he went with them to Cesarea.

Cornelius was very anxiously waiting to see Peter. He called together his relatives and friends, and told them all to come and hear the words which Peter would have to say to them. On seeing Peter, Cornelius ran out to meet him, and fell at his feet "and worshipped him," or paid him reverence. He was not a foolish heathen, who paid him worship as if he had been a god, but he paid him very high respect as a servant of God, sent to instruct him. Peter, however, thought that he paid him more reverence than he ought, and fearing that he might rob Christ of the honor which was really due to Him, and none other, Peter said, "Stand up; I myself also am a man." Then Cornelius brought Peter into the house where all his friends were gathered together, waiting.

Now Peter saw the plain meaning of the sheet, with the unclean creatures of which he was to eat. Cornelius and his friends were all Gentiles; and Peter, as a Jew, might think it unlawful to keep company with those of other nations; but this vision was a sign to teach him, that though he was a Jew, yet he was now to unite with those who would belong to Christ of all nations; and he said to the company, "Ye know how that it is an unlawful thing for a man that is a Jew, to keep company, or come unto one of another nation; but God hath shown me that I should not call any man common or unclean." Then he asked Cornelius, "Why have you sent for me?" Cornelius now told Peter for what reason he had sent for him, and that his little company were met together to hear from him any words which God might speak through his lips.

Then Peter preached to this Gentile company the same truths which he had preached to the Jews. In the engraving you see him preaching the gospel. He encouraged them to believe in Jesus as a Saviour, assuring them, that "in every nation he that feareth" God, "and worketh righteousness, is accepted with Him;" and that whosoever believeth in Jesus shall receive the pardon of their sins, so that they shall not be brought against them in the day of judgment. While Peter was preaching, the Holy Ghost also came upon these Gentiles, as on the Jews assembled on the day of pentecost. They also were now filled with zeal for the honor of Christ, and could speak in tongues they had never learned, so as to explain to all they might meet, of any country, the great things about their salvation. Then Peter commanded them to be baptized in the name of the Lord, to show that they were the disciples of Christ. And after this, he stayed with them many days.

SAYINGS OF CHILDHOOD:—A little black girl eight years old was setting the tea-table, when a boy who was lying on the lounge said to her: "Mollie, do you ever pray?" "*Yes, sir, every night.*" "Do you think God hears you?" "*Yes, I know He does.*" "But do you think," said he, "that He hears your prayers as quickly as He does those of white children?" "*Mr. George*," said she, "*I pray into God's ear, and not to His eyes. I reckon my voice is just like any other little girl's, and if I say what I ought, God doesn't stop to think about my skin.*" Dear children, God is no respecter of persons, however men may be.

PETER DELIVERED FROM PRISON.

ALL the Herods were bad men. Herod the great slew the infants at Bethlehem; Herod Antipas beheaded John the Baptist; and Herod Agrippa "killed James, the brother of John, with the sword." And because he saw that it pleased the Jews, he determined to take Peter also. As soon as Herod heard that Peter was come to Jerusalem, he sent, and took him, and put him into prison, and commanded a number of soldiers to guard him safely. It was impossible that he could escape but by some miracle, for his hands were chained, and when he slept at night, he had two soldiers lying by him, one on each side, and the chain on each hand was fastened to a hand of each soldier.

But nothing is too great for God; and when the Christians met together to pray for Peter's deliverance, God heard their prayers, and sent an angel to set him free. The very night that this happened was to have been Peter's last night in prison. He lay sleeping in the prison, bound with two strong chains. How could Peter sleep? Was he not too anxious, too unhappy, to rest quietly? No; Peter could sleep calmly though he expected to be brought before his enemies the next morning, and perhaps put to a cruel death. And why was he so calm and happy? Because he was at peace with God; Peter was ready to die, and therefore he had no cause for fear.

While Peter was sleeping, suddenly a light shone in the prison, and the angel touched his side, and said, "Arise up quickly. Gird thyself, and follow me." Immediately Peter's chains fell off from his hands; and he rose up, and put on his garments, and followed the angel. They passed through the prison, but the soldiers did not awake; then they came to the door, but the keepers were still sleeping; so they went out, until they came to the iron gate that led into the city; and the gate opened of its own accord, and Peter and the angel passed through, and down one street, and then, in a moment,

the angel was gone. In representing this incident the artist has given us, in the engraving, a wild night scene, with the angel leading the Apostle down the rough stone steps, amid the sleeping guard.

All this was so sudden and surprising, that Peter scarcely believed it was real, and thought he must be dreaming. But as soon as he came to himself, after the angel left him, he said, "Now I know of a surety that the Lord hath sent His angel, and hath delivered me out of the hand of Herod." Then, without loss of time, he hastened to his fellow-Christians, who were just then met together for prayer at the house of "Mary, the mother of John, whose surname was Mark." Having knocked for admission, a young woman named Rhoda, went out to the gate to ask who was there; and when she heard Peter's voice answering, she was so glad, that, instead of stopping to let him in, she ran in and told those in the house that Peter was come. Though they were praying, and no doubt praying for his release, yet they could hardly believe that it had happened so soon, and they said to the young woman, "Thou art mad." But Rhoda told them she was quite sure that it was really Peter; then they said, "It is his angel." They thought it was some heavenly messenger that had assumed his form to bring them some news about him. All this time Peter stood knocking at the gate; so at last they went and opened it, and, to their great joy, they saw Peter himself, and he then told them how he had escaped. Then he bade them, "Go and tell the good news unto the brethren;" and he departed to another place, where he would be safe from his enemies.

When daylight came, Peter being missed from the prison, the soldiers were all in alarm; no one knew how he had escaped, nor where he was. Herod, on being told what had happened, was so enraged, that he cruelly put the keepers of the prison to death; but God punished Herod for his wickedness. One day he sat on the throne, dressed in his robes, and made a fine speech; but God struck him with a fearful illness, and he soon after died a very miserable death.

PAUL IN THE SYNAGOGUE AT THESSALONICA.

NOW, dear children, we will come back to Paul again. During his many travels, preaching the Gospel here and there, Paul came one day to Thessalonica, a city of Macedonia. Here there was a Jewish synagogue; and, during three successive Sabbaths, Paul went in and reasoned with the people about what the Scriptures said of the Messiah, and proved that Jesus was He. Some of the Jews believed, and so did many of the Greeks. But the Jews who did not believe were greatly enraged; they called together some wicked men, and went to the house where the apostles lodged, to seek for them. The house belonged to a good man named Jason. The wicked men could not find the apostles; so they laid hold of Jason and the other brethren, and dragged them out to the rulers of the city, and charged them with turning the world upside down, or throwing every place which they visited into confusion by their doctrines.

This troubled the rulers very much; but they did no hurt at that time to Jason and the others, but let them go. As these Christians were accused of being troublers, they only required pledges of them that they would not in future disturb the peace of the city. Then the brethren sent away Paul and Silas by night; and they came to Berea. God blessed Paul's preaching to many people at Thessalonica, and a Christian church was formed there, to which Paul afterwards wrote the two epistles to the Thessalonians.

SAYINGS OF CHILDHOOD:—Dear little ones, you cannot all be great preachers, like Paul; yet you can do something for Jesus. A little boy stood among a crowd of ladies and gentlemen who were watching the laying of the railroad track over which President Garfield, when wounded, was to be carried to his sea-side cottage at Long Branch. His little heart ached for the sick President. He longed to do something to help. Suddenly he left the crowd, and going toward a pleasant-looking man who was driving the spikes through the rails into the ties, he said: "Won't you please let me drive one of those in?" The man glanced up. He was such a little fellow who wanted to drive the spike. "I'm afraid you can't, my man," he said. "Won't you let me try?" The man saw the purpose in the boy's eyes, and putting the hammer into his hand, said: "It's a heavy job, but go ahead and try." Try he did, and worked with all his might, and the workman struck an occasional blow for him, and at last the spike was driven home, and the happy little boy went back to his father. "I did something for the President, didn't I, papa?" Yes, he had done something, and all children can do something for Christ and His cause, if they will only be contented to do a child's work, and not fret because it's little.

PAUL AT EPHESUS.

YOU remember, children, that Paul traveled a great deal, preaching, and working miracles in the name of Jesus. After visiting many different countries, he came a second time to Ephesus. There were many disciples at Ephesus; but they had not yet received the Holy Ghost in that wonderful way in which He had been given to many others. Their hearts had been changed and made new by the Spirit; but they had not yet been taught by Him to speak with tongues, and to prophesy. So Paul, after he had baptized them in the name of the Lord Jesus, laid his hands on them, and prayed; and then the Holy Ghost came upon them, and they spoke with tongues, and prophesied.

And God did special miracles by the hands of Paul, "so that from his body were brought unto the sick handkerchiefs or aprons, and the diseases departed from them and the evil spirits went out of them." At last, some "vagabond Jews," who went from place to place, gaining a livelihood by their tricks, pretended that they could do these wonders too; so they called over a man who had an evil spirit, the name of Jesus, say-

ing, "We adjure you by Jesus whom Paul preacheth." But the evil spirit answered, "Jesus I know, and Paul I know, but who are ye?" The man who had the evil spirit knew that they were not holy men and followers of Christ, so he rushed upon them and wounded them, so that they were glad to escape with their lives.

This affair was soon spread over the city of Ephesus, and produced a great change in many persons, both among the Jews and Greeks. It showed them that Paul was not a mere pretender, but that he worked miracles by the power of God. And many of those who had been magicians, or sorcerers, when they believed the gospel, and found how foolish and sinful their arts were, brought their books, and burnt them before all men. Those books were full of what was wicked, and could do no good; so the Ephesians did right to burn them. This is the scene represented in the picture. The zealous people are bringing their books to cast them into the flames; St. Paul stands exhorting and encouraging them from the steps of the temple.

But in a short time so many of the people became Christians, that the silversmiths who made little images of Diana, whom they called their goddess, had no sale for their images, because the people worshipped Jesus instead of Diana. Wherefore one of these smiths, named Demetrius, made a great uproar in the city against Paul, and a great crowd of people ran about, crying, "Great is Diana of the Ephesians!" And they tried to get hold of Paul, until the town clerk came out and addressed the people, advising them to be quiet, and to let Demetrius carry the matter to the law. At length the people dispersed, and Paul took leave of his friends, and once more went forth on his mission.

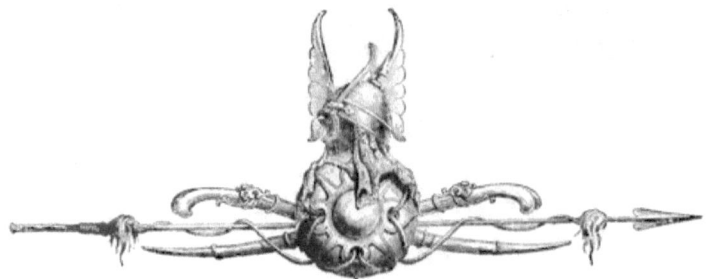

PAUL MENACED BY THE JEWS.

THE great feast of pentecost was near at hand. Paul wanted to be at Jerusalem, that he might have an opportunity of preaching the gospel to a great number of Jews, out of all countries, whom he knew would come to that feast.

While Paul was stopping with Philip, at Cesarea, a prophet came from Judea, named Agabus. This prophet had been taught, by the Holy Spirit, the things which should happen to Paul at Jerusalem. So he took Paul's girdle, and bound his own hands and feet, and said, "Thus saith the Holy Ghost, so shall the Jews at Jerusalem bind the man who owneth this girdle, and shall give him up to the Gentiles."

This made Paul's companions weep and beg him not to go to Jerusalem; but the holy servant of God was not frightened; he turned to his weeping friends, and said, "What mean ye to weep, and to break my heart! for I am ready not to be bound only, but also to die at Jerusalem for the name of the Lord Jesus." And when his friends saw how determined he was, they did not try to persuade him any more; but only said, "The will of the Lord be done."

So Paul came to Jerusalem. The Christians there received him with great joy; but very soon, the unbelieving Jews began to persecute him, as Agabus had prophesied. They accused him of speaking against the law, not understanding what it was that he really preached; and then they laid hold of him in the temple, and drew him out, and treated him so cruelly, that they would have killed him had not the Roman captain rushed in among them with some soldiers and rescued him. The captain took him, and bound him with two chains; and then he asked the people who Paul was, and what he had done. Some cried one thing and some another; and the chief captain could not understand what they meant; but he commanded Paul to be taken to the castle. As

PAUL MENANCED BY THE JEWS.

he was carried along by the soldiers, the multitude followed, crying "Away with him;" just as many had cried when Christ Himself was taken to be put to death. The engraving shows Paul on the castle stairs, borne along by the soldiers; the mob is seen in the confused mass of struggling figures below.

At length the chief captain got him safely to the castle. Then Paul asked permission to speak to the people; permission was granted, and Paul told them all his history, and of the command which God gave him, to go and preach to the Gentiles. The people heard Paul patiently till he came to this, and then they grew very angry indeed. They were jealous of the Gentiles, and could not bear that God should show them any love or favor; so they cried out, "Away with this man; it is not right that he should live."

Then the chief captain brought Paul into the castle, and commanded that he should be beaten. But when they found that he was a Roman, they began to be frightened; for it was unlawful to treat a free citizen of Rome as Paul had been treated. So the next day, the chief captain called together the chief priests and their council; and Paul being loosed from his bonds, was ordered to appear before the council, where he nobly defended himself.

PAUL'S SHIPWRECK.

AUL had now been a prisoner for more than two years. At last he appealed to Cæsar. So Paul was now given up to the care of a centurion to sail for Rome. When they had got part of the way—to a place called the Fair Haven—Paul, finding it very stormy, tried to persuade the captain to stay there for the winter; but no one would listen to Paul, and in a few days, a stormy wind arose, and the ship was tossed about upon the waves, and the sky became black with clouds, and they saw neither sun nor stars for many days.

Then they wished they had taken Paul's advice. Rash people have often to repent of not taking kind and wise advice, when it is too late. So they cast everything heavy

PAUL'S SHIPWRECK.

overboard to lighten the ship; but soon all hope was taken away; everyone was in terror, expecting that the ship would sink, and that they would be drowned. But while they were all in a state of despair, God showed Paul in a vision that he should not perish by the storm, but should yet bear witness to His truth before Cæsar at Rome. So standing in the midst of them, Paul said, "Fear not; there shall be no loss of any man's life, but only of the ship. For there stood by me this night, the angel of God, whose I am, and whom I serve, saying, 'Fear not, Paul, thou must be brought before Cæsar; and God has given thee all them that sail in the ship with thee.' Be of good comfort, then; for I believe God, that it shall be as it was told me. But we must be cast on a certain island."

All that Paul said came true; the ship was driven on the rocks at Melita, and all broken to pieces; but some of them managed to swim ashore, others on boards or broken pieces of the ship got to land. And so it came to pass, that they all got safely to land. In the engraving the figure of Paul stands out in great prominence; all around are the inmates of the ship struggling in various ways to the shore.

The island of Melita, now called Malta, was inhabited by heathens; but although ignorant, they were very kind to Paul and his shipwrecked companions, and they lighted a fire of sticks to warm them, for it was very cold, rainy weather. Paul gathered some sticks together and threw on the fire, and a viper, which had been concealed among them, sprang up, and fastened on his hand. The people knew that the bite of the viper was poisonous, and expected to see Paul fall down dead, but God did not permit him to be hurt; he shook the viper off into the fire, and felt no harm. The people thought he must be a god, when they saw this miracle; but Paul soon taught them about Jesus. Three months after this Paul left Melita, and sailed in another ship to Rome, where he was kindly received, and allowed to live in a house by himself, where many Jews were converted. Here he wrote the most of his epistles, and a few years after he was put to death for the love of his Saviour, with whom he now lives in heaven.

JOHN ON THE ISLE OF PATMOS.

MOST of the disciples suffered in the service of their Divine Master. The apostle who lived the longest was John, "the disciple whom Jesus loved," and to whose care He had given His mother, when dying on the cross.

John was not put to death, as the others were; but after being cruelly persecuted, he was banished to a solitary and rocky island in the sea, called Patmos, where he lived in a cave or grotto. The good man is never alone, for God is with him everywhere. Here God favored John with wonderful visions of what should hereafter happen to the Church and the world.

One Lord's day, the first day of the week, John was sitting alone, thinking on heavenly things. Suddenly he heard behind him a great voice, like the sound of waters; and turning round, he saw standing by him "one like unto the Son of man." It was the Lord Jesus Christ Himself, who had come to comfort His servant John; but how changed from what John had ever seen Him before! He appeared now in glory. "His head and His hairs were white like wool, as white as snow; and His eyes were as a flame of fire; and His feet like unto fine brass; and His voice as the sound of many trumpets; and His countenance was as the sun shineth in his strength." The sight was too glorious for John to bear, and he fell at His feet as dead. But Jesus laid His hand on John, and said, "Fear not; I am the first and the last: I am He that liveth and was dead; and behold I am alive for evermore. Amen; and have the keys of hell and of death." Then John was comforted.

In the engraving, the artist has portrayed John seated on a rock; in his right hand he holds a pen, and in his left a tablet; he is in the act of waiting to be told what to write. Then the Lord Jesus told him to write down the messages to the Seven Churches. Most of these churches have now passed away. They forsook God after a time; and then, at last, His blessing was taken from them, and some were destroyed altogether, and others are left in ignorance and error.

After John had heard the messages to the churches, he saw, in vision, many wonderful and glorious things. He saw heaven opened, and God Himself sitting on His throne, with a rainbow round His head; and round about the throne were the happy company of Christ's redeemed people, clothed in white raiment, with crowns of gold upon their heads. And they fell down before Him that sat on the throne, and cast their crowns before Him, saying, "Thou art worthy, O Lord, to receive glory, and honor, and power; for Thou hast created all things, and for Thy pleasure they are, and were created."

After this, John saw, in the midst of the throne "a Lamb as it had been slain"—the Lamb of God, that taketh away the sins of the world. And then John saw the happy company of heaven fall down before the Lamb; and they sang a new song, saying, "Thou wast slain, and hast redeemed us to God by Thy blood, out of every kindred and tongue, and people, and nation." And then he heard the voice of many angels round about the throne, and the number of them was ten thousand times ten thousand, and thousands of thousands; saying with a loud voice, "Worthy is the Lamb that was slain, to receive power, and riches, and wisdom, and strength, and honor, and glory, and blessing."

Dear children, how shall we take part in the new song there? By learning to sing it here. If you love Jesus, so that your heart sings to Him, you will be sure to sing in that great chorus up there. Those who praise Him *here* shall praise Him *there*.

DEATH ON THE PALE HORSE.

OHN had many wonderful visions while he was in Patmos. I will try and tell you about some of them, though I will not undertake to explain them. The book of the Revelation is at present a great mystery.

John saw four horses. The first was a *white* horse; "and he that sat on him had a bow; and a crown was given unto him; and he went forth conquering and to conquer." The second was a *red* horse; "and power was given to him that sat thereon to take peace from the earth, and that they should kill one another; and there was given unto him a great sword." The third was a *black* horse; "and he that sat on him had a pair of balances in his hand." The fourth was a *pale* horse; "and his name that sat on him was Death, and Hell followed with him. And power was given unto them over the fourth part of the earth, to kill with sword, and with hunger, and with death, and with the beasts of the earth."

This picture of Death on the Pale Horse is what our artist has portrayed in the engraving. The horse is seen galloping, with fiery nostrils and flowing mane, headlong down the fearful blackness through which it makes its resistless way; the frightful figure seated on the steed, and the long train of fiends following after—all tell of the terrible mission of Death.

BABYLON IN RUINS.

IN another vision, John saw an angel come down from heaven, having great power; and the earth was lightened with his glory. And the angel cried mightily with a strong voice, saying, "Babylon the great is fallen, is fallen, and is become the habitation of devils, and the hold of every foul spirit, and a cage of every unclean and hateful bird." Babylon had fallen totally and finally. It was become not only desolate, but a kind of hell upon earth.

Then John heard another voice from heaven, saying, "Come out of her, my people, that ye be not partakers of her sins, and that ye receive not of her plagues: for her sins have reached unto heaven, and God hath remembered her iniquities." As Lot was called forth out of Sodom, before it was destroyed by fire and brimstone, so the people of God are directed by a voice from heaven, to come out of Babylon before her fall. How terrible was her wickedness! Her crimes, her daring and presumptuous sins, resembled mountains "reaching to heaven." But God had remembered her iniquities. The persons, therefore, or nations, who had been persecuted by her, were called on to retaliate upon her; and to give her a double measure of the wine of God's wrath, from the cup of His indignation. Because she was proud and presumptuous, declaring that "she sat as a queen, was no widow, and should see no sorrow," whatever the word of God had threatened, therefore all the plagues which had been denounced against her would surely "come on her in one day," suddenly and unexpectedly; death in every dreadful form would fill the city with mourning, and dire famine would attend the other desolations; till she should *utterly* be burned with fire; and then she would know that the Lord, who had judged and condemned her, was strong, and fully able to execute the awful sentence.

The engraving is a picture of the fearful ruins of Babylon—the habitation of wild beasts, and the "cage of every unclean and hateful bird."

THE LAST JUDGMENT.

WOULD you be afraid, dear children, to go before the court, where the judge sits, and be tried for your life? Would you, if you had done nothing wrong? Would you if your own brother was the judge? Well we all will have to stand before a greater Judge than any here upon the earth. We have got to come before the judgment-seat of Christ—and He is our Elder Brother!

The Bible tells us He shall come "in His glory, and all the holy angels with Him;" He will not come as He did at first in the lowliness of the manger-cradle; but with the glory that He had with the Father before the world was. And yet, in the midst of all His glory, how kind and loving His face will be toward all of those who love Him! The Son of man will not be lost in the Son of God—the Saviour will not be unrecognizable in the King and the Judge.

Before Him shall be gathered all nations. Every one among them come to receive according to the deeds done in the body. While in Patmos, John had a vision of this great and terrible day. He says, "And I saw a great white throne, and Him that sat on it, from whose face the earth and the heaven fled away; and there was found no place for them. And I saw the dead, small and great, stand before God: and the books were open; and another book was opened, which is the book of life: and the dead were judged out of those things which were written in the books, according to their works. And the sea gave up the dead which were in it; and death and hell delivered up the dead which were in them; and they were judged every man according to their works."

Then He will separate them just as a shepherd separates his sheep from the goats. Does a shepherd have any trouble in telling the sheep from the goats? Neither will He have any trouble in telling the good from the bad. He will set the sheep on His right

hand, but the goats on the left; that is the good on the right, and the bad on the left. This separation is what the artist has represented as taking place in the engraving. To those on His right hand He will say, "Come, ye blessed of My Father, inherit the kingdom prepared for you from the foundation of the world." It is a blessed thing, you see, to belong to God—blessed even now, and much more then. There is a place in heaven prepared for you, if you are prepared for it. Jesus has gone before to make your place ready for you.

But what an awful thing it will be to be unprepared to meet Christ on that great day! The guilty one always fears to meet the judge, no matter how kind of heart that judge may be. What will the King say to the wicked? Then shall He say unto them on His left hand, "Depart from Me, ye cursed, into everlasting fire, prepared for the devil and his angels;" and these shall go away into everlasting punishment. And dear children, how terrible is that punishment! In hell, there is no hope. They have not even the hope of dying. They are forever, *forever*, FOREVER lost!

I hope you will all begin at once to prepare for that awful day! You can't begin too young.

SAYINGS OF CHILDHOOD:—A young prince, whose mind had learned in some degree to value religious truth, asked his tutor to give him suitable instruction, that he might be prepared for death. "Plenty of time for that when you are older," was the reply. "No!" said the prince, "I have been to the church-yard and measured the graves; and there are many *shorter* than I am."

THE HEAVENLY CITY.

OUR last talk will be about the heavenly home. I think the last two chapters of Revelation are the best of all. Reading them, how many have been comforted, and how many have been homesick for the rest, the peace, the joy, and the communion of that holy city!

John tells us that an angel came to him, and talked with him, saying, "Come hither, I will show thee the bride, the Lamb's wife. And he carried me away in the spirit to a great and high mountain, and showed me that great city, the holy Jerusalem, descending out of heaven from God, having the glory of God; and her light was like unto a stone most precious, even like a jasper stone, clear as crystal; and had a wall great and high, and had twelve gates, and at the gates twelve angels, and names written thereon, which are the names of the twelve tribes of the children of Israel. On the east three gates; on the north three gates; on the south three gates; and on the west three gates. And the wall of the city had twelve foundations, and in them the names of the twelve apostles of the Lamb."

In the engraving, you can see John and the angel standing on the high mountain, overlooking the holy Jerusalem. But no vision is equal to the reality. The " half hath never been told." I want to tell you some things about it:

1. *It is a place of wonderful beauty.* Its wall is of jasper—of the most crystalline clearness and flashing brilliancy. Each gate is composed of one great pearl. The city itself, its streets and its mansions, are of " pure gold, like unto clear glass "—transparent and more beautiful than any gold ever here seen. Heaven is indeed a *beautiful* place. We may think our very best about it, and when we have pictured to ourselves the loveliest place we can possibly *dream* of, it won't be half as beautiful as heaven really is.

And if even the streets are represented as laid with pure gold, and the gates as made of pearls, what must be the interior of the mansions that Christ has prepared for them that love Him!

2. *It is a great place.* It is meant for a great multitude. Here the church now seems small, but it is nothing compared with what it shall be. God has made great preparations; and the host of the redeemed will be a great company, which no man can number. "They shall come from the east, and from the west, and from the north, and from the south, and shall sit down in the kingdom of God." There will be plenty of room in heaven for all who may wish to enter.

3. *It is a place of joy.* "God shall wipe away all tears from their eyes." There shall be no more death, neither sorrow nor pain; for sin, the cause of all affliction, shall have passed away. Its inhabitants walk in the light of God and of the Lamb. They drink of the river of the water of life. They eat of the trees of life that bear twelve manner of fruits. "And there shall be no more curse." How restful that sounds! For ages the world has been troubled by the curse of sin. But sin will trouble no more. The people there serve God; and they shall see His face. Nothing there shall intervene to hide the face of the Father from any of His children. And beholding that, their souls forever shall be satisfied. "His name shall be in their foreheads." They there shall bear the impress of His approval instead of His curse. It will be evident that they are His accepted ones.

"And there shall be no night there." "No night!"—no chill, no gropings, no stumblings in the dark, no weariness, no restless tossings, no watchings, no longings for the morning! No candles—no lamps—no sun—no moon—God is the light. His servants reign forever and ever.

4. *It is a place of supreme purity.* Not all can enter there. Only those can walk in its light who are the children of light. Some are excluded, not by force, but by their very natures. "There shall in nowise enter into it anything that defileth, neither whatsoever worketh abomination, or maketh a lie." No characters that blacken those whom they touch can pass through those open portals. Men of unclean habits of thought would never try to go in. No foul-thoughted man, with filthy soul, would care to enter where there is such stainless virtue, any more than a drunkard who has just crawled out of the gutter would care to enter a parlor under the blaze of gas jets to face a refined company of ladies and gentlemen. The spotless, glittering robes of the redeemed alone would keep out those who are covered only with filthy rags.

But who shall enter there? "They which are written in the Lamb's book of life." Oh! how much depends upon our decision now, while the opportunity remains! I trust, my dear little friends, that you will see to it *now* that your names are "written in the Lamb's book of life," that at the last you may be found among the happy number, adoring Jesus, "the Lamb of God," and singing forever, "Salvation to our God, which sitteth upon the throne, and unto the Lamb!"

SAYINGS OF CHILDHOOD:—A little girl, while gazing up into the sky, was asked by her father, of what was she thinking. "*I was thinking father,*" said she "*if the outside of heaven is so beautiful what must the inside be!*" Another little child's idea of heaven was very beautiful. One day Essie said to her nurse: "In heaven, where my mother lives, every one is kind. No one ever gets angry and speaks loud there. Everybody loves everybody. Must'nt that be beautiful? Oh! how I should love to be there, and never be afraid any more." And do you want to know the way to that beautiful home? Let a little child tell you: "I know the way to heaven," said little Minnie to little Johnny, who stood by her side, looking on a picture-book that Minnie had in her hand. "You do?" said little John. "Well, won't you tell me how to get there?" "Oh, yes! I'll tell you. Just commence going up, and keep on going up all the time, and you'll get there. But Johnny, *you must not turn back.*" Dear children, *Are you ——— on your way to heaven?* Not are you going to start by-and-by, but are you really on your way now? Do you see the little line I have left in the question? I left it so that you might put in there, each one of you, your own name. I don't know your names, but Jesus does, and you know it is really Jesus who asks you the question. Are you on the way to heaven?

But I must say, farewell. We have had many pleasant talks together; and now, in conclusion, this is my earnest prayer: "The Lord bless thee, and keep thee: the Lord make His face shine upon thee, and be gracious unto thee; the Lord lift up His countenance upon thee, and give thee peace." If I should never talk with you again on earth, I hope I shall meet you in heaven.

"That unchangable home is for you and for me,
 Where Jesus of Nazareth stands;
The King of all kingdoms forever is He,
 And He holdeth our crowns in His hands.

"Oh, how sweet it will be in that beautiful land,
 So free from all sorrow and pain;
With songs on our lips and with harps in our hands
 To meet one another again."

www.ingramcontent.com/pod-product-compliance
Lightning Source LLC
Chambersburg PA
CBHW022106290426
44112CB00008B/571